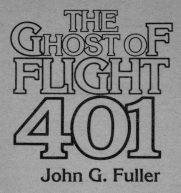

# THE GHOST OF FLIGHT 401

## John G. Fuller

A BERKLEY MEDALLION BOOK

published by

BERKLEY PUBLISHING CORPORATION

International Creative Management
40 West 57th Street
New York, N.Y. 10019

Library of Congress Catalog Card Number: 76-16205
SBN 425-03553-0

*BERKLEY MEDALLION BOOKS are published by*
*Berkley Publishing Corporation*
*200 Madison Avenue*
*New York, N. Y. 10016*

BERKLEY MEDALLION BOOK ® TM 757,375

Printed in the United States of America

Berkley Medallion Edition, JANUARY, 1978

To Elizabeth

# Note

The details of this story are factual and accurate as reported to the author by the people involved, or by many official documents and reports. In a story of this strange nature, however, some people are reluctant to talk. As a consequence, some of the material is not firsthand. Where it is, it is labeled as such, or is clearly evident in the context of the material. In the case of certain Eastern Airlines employees, some of the names have been changed at their request. The names so used are indicated by an asterisk (*) the first time they are mentioned. All other names not indicated by an asterisk are the real names.

# Foreword

I first heard of the ghost of Flight 401 on a Scandinavian Airlines flight from Stockholm to Copenhagen, in March 1974. The stewardess was friendly and congenial. She told me she had heard one of the strangest stories she ever encountered from a friend of hers, a flight attendant on British Airways. Dead members of the flight crew of an Eastern Airlines plane which had crashed in the Everglades in late 1972, were reappearing as very distinct and solid apparitions in several Eastern Airlines flights. The stories were so vivid, she continued, that they had traveled consistently among crews of most international airlines.

I asked her why the legend of the ghost hadn't been shifted from Eastern Airlines to SAS or other European airlines, where the story would have much more local appeal; most folklore changes robes with the telling of the story. As it is repeated, the details often take on the local fabric of the person telling it. Soon only the basic outline remains, to wear whatever uniform the storyteller decides to drape it with.

She was quiet a moment, then said, ''That thought is very interesting. Perhaps the story doesn't change because it actually happened on Eastern?''

We both laughed. She went on with the complexities of serving the delightful Scandinavian food that SAS offers on its flights. What intrigued me about the story was that it had traveled across the airlines such a distance, and that it maintained an identity with a specific type of plane and a specific airline like Eastern.

At that time, I was working on an extremely difficult book to research. It involved a serious accident in a nuclear power plant near Detroit and the dangerous implications of nuclear

power proliferation throughout the world. I had no time to think about a ghost story, however intriguing.

About a year later, I was riding on an Eastern jet from San Juan to New York. Half-joking and half-embarrassed, I asked the flight attendant who was serving the meal if she had ever run into the story of the apparitions. She appeared shocked.

"That's not funny," she said. "It happened to me. I had an experience in the lower galley I'll never forget."

I apologized, saying that I didn't mean to take it lightly, but that I was curious about it because the story had traveled so far. I asked her to tell me more about it.

The attendant was busy at the time, but returned later after she had finished serving the meals. "Of course there are many stories going around," she said. "But my experience happened before I knew about any of them. It was in late February 1973, about two months after the crash. I was in the lower galley. I felt this presence there. It was eerie. I know it sounds ridiculous, and it's really impossible to describe. There was definitely a presence there, even though I didn't see anyone—as some of my friends did later. The temperature of the whole galley literally became freezing. I'll never forget it."

She was visibly upset in recalling the incident. "By the way," she added. "I spoke impulsively. Please don't mention my name about this." She went on to say that soon afterward, she began hearing that flight-crew members were directly encountering full-scale apparitions of one or two members of the flight crew who had been killed in the Eastern jumbo jet that had crashed. She had felt that her experience might bring some helpful information to the Eastern authorities, vague as it was.

She went to her supervisor and explained what had happened. Instead of being interested, her supervisor told her that she knew a psychiatrist whose wife was a flight attendant, who understood all the problems the girls might develop on the job. Perhaps a visit with the psychiatrist might be helpful?

"I was never so furious in my life," the stewardess continued. "I have never experienced anything like that before

or since. Later I learned that any crew members who reported any of the incidents that followed have been referred to the company shrink. So very few will talk about the story anymore. A lot of them feel they'll be fired or laid off.''

It was many months before I finally succumbed to looking into the details of the incredible story. When I did, an intricate web of circumstances began forming, among the most baffling I have ever encountered.

The result is a ghost story. It deals with the question of life after death. It is hard to believe, even if you have an inclination to believe in ghosts. It is a ghost story that has happened not in a dark castle or a Victorian mansion, but in a most unlikely place; a modern jumbo-jet airliner.

There are two opposing forces that confront a ghost story. One of them is an attitude of total skepticism; the other is an attitude of total uncritical acceptance. Neither is healthy.

There are certain concepts that both schools of thought can accept. We are born and we die. During that space of time, we observe, we feel, we think, we communicate. We really don't know where we came from, or where we're going. It is hard even to guess. It is almost axiomatic that there is knowledge beyond our own perception; history has shown that. Our pool of knowledge has grown over the years. While the total is vast, there is still more to be learned. We are born to explore, to try to find what is around the next bend in the river.

Carl Sandburg once said that death is simply part of life. If it is, it is a legitimate area to explore, even if it is difficult. The tools for exploring it are limited and fall into the hands of theologists, philosophers, and parapsychologists. Only the last have made attempts to find hard, rational evidence to any extent. Only recently has parapsychology been admitted to the discipline of science, as demonstrated by its acceptance into the American Association for the Advancement of Science.

If death is part of life, then it is of overwhelming importance. The fragility of life and the durability of death remain a dominant theme. The story of Flight 401 symbolizes both, not in a mood of despair, but of adventure and exploration.

—J.G.F.

# THE GHOST OF FLIGHT 401

"It is impossible to meditate on Time and the mystery of the creative passage of Nature without an overwhelming emotion at the limitations of human intelligence."

—Alfred North Whitehead

# Chapter I

I have been conditioned all my life to think that there are no such things as ghosts. They are merely vestigial remnants of ancient superstition—suitable for Hamlet's father and a Halloween romp—and that was about it. When I returned to the United States in April 1974 from the European research for my book on nuclear power development, I was swamped by a massive television and radio tour on a book of mine that had just been published. The tour would take me all over the United States for interviews on a pressing schedule of one-night stands. It would be spread over a period of eight or nine weeks, right on the heels of the two-month trek on the nuclear story. During this time, I would be trying to complete as much as I could of the nuclear book research.

I had about four days' rest in Connecticut before starting out on the promotion tour. I had no time for reflection, but the four-day respite was welcome. In that brief time span, I had a chat with my neighbor Don Blinn, who was a DC-8 pilot for Seaboard Airlines. He also began telling me about the strange ghosts that were haunting the Eastern planes, the big new L-1011 superjets of Eastern known as the Tristar Whisperliner. It seemed that everyone who had anything to do with any airline in the world knew about them. The following day, I had dinner with Pete and Sharon Henning in Ridgefield. Pete is an extremely talented cameraman and filmmaker, and his wife Sharon was a flight attendant for Pan Am. An Eastern 727 pilot was at the dinner, and Eastern's ghosts dominated the conversation for the entire evening.

Sharon Henning had been deadheading on a trip and had been seated next to an FAA executive. He told her that he heard that some nonstructural components from the wrecked

plane, said to be reutilized on Plane #318 were being removed from the plane, and that Eastern was considering changing the number of 318, because of the stories circulating about it. The theory was, if there was anything to it, that the apparitions went along with the parts that were salvaged. Also at the dinner were Sharon's sister Marsha and her husband. Marsha is a flight attendant for United, and she had run into a long series of stories from various friends at Eastern. While the general public knew little about the story, it was a frequent subject of conversation among airline people.

The question that came up constantly was why the stories were so consistent. Why did they never shift from Eastern and the L-1011 to another airline or another type of plane? The events did not follow the usual pattern of rumors, which constantly shift base. No one at the dinner knew the answer, of course.

On the day following the dinner at the Hennings, Frank Umhoefer, another Seaboard Airlines flight crew officer who lived near me, stopped by my house to drop off a newsletter published by the Flight Safety Foundation. This publication was sponsored by a group of aviation insurance companies in the interest of accident prevention. Each article deals with some feature of aviation safety. In among the safety items was the following story:

RESIDENT GHOST?

Today's world (and outer world, too) frequently seems to abound with strange happenings, with what some might refer to as extraterrestrial aberrations or possibly transcendental occurrences. One such happening recently came to our attention, and it was reported to be fact enough to have been written up in the logbook of a specific trijet jumbo. FSF (Flight Safety Foundation) is passing on the "experience," hopeful of the comments of other flight or cabin crews. It may not seem to have much to do with safety . . . and yet. . . ? Anyway, here's the report.

One of the flight attendants on this particular trijet was in the lower galley of the jumbo, when, in the course of

her duties, she happened to glance into the glass window of one of the ovens or meal heating units. There, looking out at her (or was it a reflection?), was the face of the flight engineer that had lost his life in the Everglades crash of one of the airlines's trijets several months earlier. He had been below, checking the position of the jumbo's nose gear, when the big trijet slammed into the marsh. The mystified and not unstartled flight attendant "went topside" and asked another stewardess to go below. She did . . . and verified what the girl had seen. They then asked the flight engineer of their flight to go below. He did . . . and he not only saw but he talked to the vision, or ghost if you will, who said, "Watch out for fire on this airplane."

Shortly thereafter, that airplane (No. 318) was in Mexico City when a problem developed in one of its three engines. The flight crew asked for and was given permission to make a two-engine ferry flight to the airline's maintenance base for an engine change.

On takeoff from Mexico City's airport, nearly a mile and a half above sea level, a fire developed in one of the big jumbo's two remaining engines. The engine had to be shut down, and it was. Only through the flight crew's almost unbelievable expertise in handling the big jet were they able to come around and land safely on one engine, never having gotten any higher than 400 feet AGL [above ground level].

We say "*almost* unbelievable" because it did happen, but perhaps it wasn't "*only* through the flight crew's expertise." What do you think . . . and have you heard this story before? We understand it is not unknown and has been extensively discussed by many professional airline pilots. What do you think?

This was probably the most distracting piece of material I could come across at this time. But it indicated the amount of attention the subject was getting among *all* the airlines. I was

4

intrigued, yet even if I had been sure I wanted to follow up on the Eastern story, I still had no time whatever to even consider it.

I had to mix up the promotion trip with the remainder of the research left on the nuclear book which was to be published a year and a half later under the title *We Almost Lost Detroit.* The route took me to Washington; Chicago; Detroit; High Point, North Carolina; back to Washington, and then out to San Francisco and Los Angeles.

I had no time for the story, yet I found myself checking every cabin crew on nearly half a dozen different airlines about the Eastern story. This informal survey must have covered a total of some thirty different people. At least twenty-five of them not only knew about the stories, but were able to add further details. It became routine for me to canvass the crews on each flight.

When May 1974 arrived, it was necessary to set up a rigid schedule so that I could complete the writing of *We Almost Lost Detroit.* I had seven large cartons full of research, five or six major textbooks on nuclear physics, and over two dozen ninety-minute tape-recorded interviews. Just sorting out the research was a major job.

I was lucky enough to find an opening at the MacDowell Colony, in southern New Hampshire, where some thirty writers, artists, and composers can live and work in secluded studios in lovely pine woods, without disturbance. It is an endowed foundation, and a writer can be spoiled rotten by it.

I had written two other books at MacDowell and I found the atmosphere conducive to getting work done. Thornton Wilder did much of his work there, and drew on the town of Peterboro and neighboring villages as prototypes for *Our Town.* Elinor Wylie wrote many of her poems there. Leonard Bernstein composed there, as did Aaron Copland. Edward Arlington Robinson was a regular guest and joined many colonists over the years in claiming there was something about the place that generously spurred the creative muse.

Each colonist scratches his name on a wooden plaque above the fireplace, in ink, as he starts his stay at his studio. There may be seven or eight plaques in each of the thirty studios, going back to the early twenties, when the colony

began. When I arrived at the Watson studio in May 1974, I went through the ritual of signing my name, along with the dates I was to be there. The row of wooden plaques faded to darker wood, as the signatures moved back in the years before.

I had not been aware in my two previous stays at Mac-Dowell that there were several ghost stories involving it. One very persistent story involved the ghost of Elinor Wylie. She was constantly reported being seen on the stairways of the main lodge. She was also alleged to be seen in the room she once slept in. The room was in the charming saltbox house set aside for women artists, in the days when women colonists were considered separate but equal. Those who later slept in the "Elinor Wylie Room" would persistently report strange noises and appearances. The reports would come from reasonably sane and sober people. Again I was intrigued in hearing about them because my interest had been piqued by the Eastern Airlines stories.

There were also many reports that the ghost of Edward Arlington Robinson liked to revisit his former haunts. He had done much of his writing in the Veltin Studio, far from the main lodge. It was a lovely, rustic cabin, built of native stone, with the usual huge fireplace and a view which swept over the pines to the distant New Hampshire mountains. Beside the doorway was a plaque, a quote from the poet himself. It read: "You will hear more from me after I am dead."

I had stayed there in one of my former visits and had not given the message on the plaque a second thought. But several others at the colony told me that there were many reports of Edward Arlington Robinson's revisiting writers or composers who were foolish enough to work at the studio late into the night. I never ran into this, although I had done just that many times. Perhaps I wasn't conditioned for it.

That raised a good question. Was the appearance of an apparition the result of suggestion? Suggestion was surely powerful; it was the base of hypnosis. In fact, hypnosis *was* suggestion. It was able to create, according to strict medical and psychological tests, both what were called negative and positive hallucinations in perfectly normal people. A negative hallucination was one where the hypnotist could suggest

to a subject that he absolutely could not see a person who was actually in a room. There may be four persons sitting across from them, but because of posthypnotic suggestion, the subject would see only three. Nothing in the world could convince him that a fourth person was there.

In the same way, a hypnotist could tell the subject that a person was in the room who wasn't actually there. The subject would swear on a stack of Encyclopedia Britannicas that the person was there in the room. I thought: Wasn't this a plausible explanation for anyone who sees a ghost or an apparition—that they were unwitting victims of suggestion? That their intelligence could be temporarily suspended by acidental hypnosis?

I felt very good about this theory. It could explain not only the Eastern Airlines phenomena, but the MacDowell Colony apparitions as well. It would clear up the whole question very tidily. I could forget about the idea of writing a ghost story and concentrate on my hard-line scientific study on the dangers of nuclear power, which was the epitome of respectable objective science, tragic as the story is. It was so odd to be working on that story while being nagged by the other about a ghost on a jet airliner. I couldn't balance the two—and yet somehow I felt there was a symbolism growing here that I didn't want to have anything to do with.

I again analyzed why I wanted to even bother to get involved with a ghost story. The answer seemed to lie in the idea that life after death is the most important philosophical question any man faces. Every other question, scientific or not, becomes insignificant compared to this. All the great religions are concerned with this question. Those who can answer their own questions by religious faith have no problem about this, but an enormous number of people need further evidence to answer their questions. I was one of those.

I tabled the idea of even checking the Eastern ghost story and nearly put it out of my mind. There was little time for socializing at MacDowell, but after dinner there were occasional get-togethers at the various studios. One evening I had some friends over for a few drinks around the fire. The subject turned again to the possibility of life after death, and what kind of form it might possibly take. Two of the guests,

Bill and Susan Moody, thought it would be fun to fool around with a Ouija board, just to see if some articulate messages might come through.

I watched as the couple placed their fingertips on top of the top of the planchette—the small triangular platform on three legs, with a circular window in it. This is supposed to stop over the various letters of the alphabet which are grouped in a semicircle on the board. The Ouija board has been around for a long time, and apparently Parker Bros., which makes them in this country, sells a tremendous number of them. I learned later that they are supposed to be the "kindergarten" of psychic development.

I've never seen any explanation for the planchette's moves around the board, how it stops at specific letters, apparently without the volition or consciousness of the two people operating it. Later I looked the subject up in an encyclopedia which said: "There are hints which cannot be ignored that the material which emerges by means of this type of device does not always originate in the subconscious of any of the performers; occasionally it seems to be due to some unknown kind of contact with distant events or thoughts of distant persons."

The commentary went on:

"The glass window moves from letter to letter, frequently spelling out gibberish, but sometimes words and sentences. . . . It was often assumed that the "messages" communicated through these devices must come from the dead, and much of the agitation against the use of Ouija boards in recent years seems to stem from a deep-rooted fear that they put the performers into perilous touch with either the dead or evil forces. Certainly the devices do sometimes produce material that is frightening, startling, embarrassing or obscene—wherever it may come from—but the tendency now is to look to the subconscious minds of the performers themselves as the source of the material.

The material that came over the board that evening in the Watson Studio at MacDowell certainly matched the theories

described in the encyclopedia. At first the letters spelled only gibberish, but they came fast, and it was difficult to keep up with writing them down. After a few minutes, the movements of the planchette seemed to become smoother and more stabilized. Bill and Susan Moody at the board alternately asked questions and continued to insist that the planchette was moving without any conscious effort on their parts. It stopped at letters so fast that they had no idea of what was being spelled out.

They were trying to get evidential material to check the board, information that they themselves didn't know, but which could be confirmed later. As the movement on the board settled down somewhat, the group began asking questions:

"Can you identify yourself?"

The planchette slid to yes.

"Are you someone who was here at MacDowell?"

Again the answer was yes.

Bill and Susan, still at the board, decided to ask questions which would have to be spelled out. The yes-and-no system could not provide any specific information to test the validity of the messages. "Please state whether you were a writer, an artist, or a composer," they asked, these being the three groups that were represented at the colony.

The planchette began moving in rather swift circles, then spelled out: POET.

"What is your name?"

The device moved to two letters and stopped: E.W.

"When were you here at MacDowell?"

The device moved down to the bottom row of numbers and spelled out: 1925-1926-1927.

I went over to the wooden plaques, and skimmed down the long list of signatures. The plaques over the fireplace had become so darkened over the years that it was difficult to read the names scrawled on the rough pine surface. I finally found the years indicated and looked at the names. Elinor Wylie, the poet, had signed into the Watson studio several times during the mid- and late twenties. I went back to the board. It would be interesting to see what followed in line with the

information about "E.W.," who had identified herself as a poet.

More letters were coming through. I began to write them down. They moved fast, so that it was hard to tell whether they were spelling articulate words or not. The question at hand now to the board was: "Will you talk to us?"

The device began circling under the two pairs of hands. Then it stopped over letters briefly, and moved on to the next: Y-E-S-I-F-Y-O-U-B-L-O-W-O-U-T-T-H-E-L-I-G-H-T-S.

This was a curious sentence: *Yes, if you blow out the lights.* We had no sort of light in the studio you could blow out; they were electrical. I wondered where this archaic expression came from. It was only later that I learned that during the twenties and the first part of the thirties, the only light in the studios came from kerosene lamps. The couple on the board kept asking me what was being spelled out, but it was difficult to tell them, until I had a chance to break down the letters I was scrawling on a pad.

We turned out three out of four electric lamps in the room, in compliance with the strange request. The question at hand was: "Can you give us the titles of some of your collected verse?"

The board went on to spell: HELP ME.

No one was familiar with any such title of Elinor Wylie's poems or volumes by that name. It didn't sound at all like a title she would choose. They asked, "Is that a title, or something you are asking for?"

The device hesitated, then spelled: SOMETHING I NEED. There was a creepy feeling in the darkened room. I was a little ashamed of myself for feeling squeamish. In fact, along with the others, I felt a definite chill. "What can we do to help you?" was the next question asked. The next letters formed quickly: HELP ME GET RID OF MY PAST.

Imaginary or not, the chill in the room was increasing. Bill and Susan stood up, and one of them went over and quickly turned the lights back on. Everyone in the room had had enough.

There were certain observations that could be made from the experiment. One was that there was no question that articulate sentences could come out on the board, without

anyone consciously forcing it to. This was in contrast to the first long minutes of total gibberish the device provided at the beginning of the session. Random spelling of words, like Julian Huxley's theory about monkeys punching at a type-writer, was impossible. Another conclusion was that the planchette moved by a force of its own, without being pushed or pulled by the hands of the people whose fingers rested on it. A third point was that the messages seemed to reveal the agony of a restless soul, but of course this could never be proved. Another factor was that there was some information provided (initials, dates) that no one in the room could re-member knowing. I knew that I had had no idea that Elinor Wylie had stayed at the Watson Studio over a period of years, and I was a little startled to find her name there on one of the six faded and tarnished plaques over the fireplace.

All this was inconclusive, of course. What dominated my mind was the nuclear research, which was like cramming for a final exam. I was lucky enough to get the book under control before I had to take off for the rest of the promotion trip. It seemed like an endless merry-go-round. The West Coast cities again, along with Miami, Dallas, St. Louis, Atlanta, and other points north and midwest. But on all these flights, I picked up more confirmation of the Eastern story from cabin attendants of several different airlines, including Eastern. The story was sticking to Eastern with remarkable consistency.

By December, 1974, I had completed the first draft of *We Almost Lost Detroit.* But there would be long weeks of checking and double-checking the facts with the editors and scientists. This was fortunately sporadic. I had time to relax a little, and also consider some other possible assignments as a relief from the constant work on the Detroit book that had been so demanding.

One of them was to write the script for a documentary film for the United States Information Agency on the subject of oceanography, and possibly producing and directing it later. I had always been fond of the subject, and it was a welcome change. The research and survey for the film would be demanding. It would cover the oceanographic institutions at Woods Hole in Massachusetts, the Scripps Institution of

Oceanography near San Diego, the University of Miami in Florida, and other locations. This project would be as far removed from a ghost story as any one could get.

Just prior to this, I had talked with the editors of the *Reader's Digest* magazine on doing an article on Uri Geller. He is the young Israeli ex-paratrooper who was presently startling scientists at several universities in both Europe and the United States with his capacity to apparently bend metals and start up broken watches simply by mental concentration. I had met him in New York previously through mutual friends. At that time, he had lightly stroked a door key, then taken his hand away. The key continued bending in my hand until it reached a forty-five-degree angle. He also held his hand over my watch, and it jumped ahead an hour and a half. I know a little about sleight-of-hand-tricks and was certain that was what he must have used—but I couldn't figure out how.

I didn't decide to go ahead on the article about Geller for the *Reader's Digest* until I made further checks. The whole story was so incredible. Here was someone who was apparently capable of changing the molecular structure of metal simply by concentrating on it. If true, this could change the whole face of physics—but only if true, only if verified repeatedly under laboratory conditions. I was getting myself into another story that I was half-trying to resist.

I was also moving into another hectic time of pressure. The oceanographic film required continuous study and travel. The finishing touches on the nuclear energy story required careful checking and rechecking. So did the Geller article. I was in the middle of stories on each end of the spectrum: the physical and the paranormal.

I was surprised when I accumulated the research studies at several universities and institutions on the Geller experiments. This was a scientific ghost story in its own right. At the University of London, several leading physicists were finding that Geller could run up a Geiger counter to a point 500 times background radiation by concentrating on it. He could dematerialize part of a vanadium crystal sealed inside a plastic capsule, simply by holding his hand over it. There were several other tests, all of them repeatable and startling.

At the conclusion of them, conducted in two different colleges of the university—Birkbeck and King's—three scientists came out with unequivocal statements regarding the future impact of the phenomenon. Professor J.G. Taylor, chairman of the department of mathematics, stated:

> I have tested Uri Geller in my laboratory at King's College with specially designed apparatus.
> The Geller Effect—of metal bending—is clearly not brought about by fraud. It is so exceptional that it presents a crucial challenge to modern science and could even destroy the latter if no explanation becomes available.

These were strong words. But those of Dr. David Bohm and Dr. John Hasted, of Birkbeck College were equally so:

> We feel if similar tests are made later, enough instances of this kind will probably accumulate, so that there will be no room for reasonable doubt that some new process is involved here, which cannot be accounted for or explained in terms of the present known laws of physics. Indeed, we already feel that we have gone some distance toward this point.

As usual, the *Reader's Digest* research department spent many weeks doing a line by line check on the Geller article. I was glad because it would serve as a double-check on the facts I had gathered for the piece. Geller was invited to come into the *Digest* New York office and let the researchers and editors observe his apparent capacity to violate the laws of physics.

There were a dozen or so of the magazine's staff at the meeting. Two of the editors were dyed-in-the-wool skeptics. Geller started his demonstration by lightly touching a key held out by a researcher. It began bending and continued to bend. As often happens, several other keys in the room began bending, although Geller was not near. One of the skeptical editors reached into his pocket, and pulled out his keys. His was one of those which had bent markedly.

Because of this experience, I became more willing to examine phenomena that I had never considered examining before. But I found that it was necessary to probe in depth; it could not be done superficially. When I had first heard of UFOs or Geller's feats, I simply did not believe them. Then I noticed another thing happening: I found myself blowing alternately hot and cold in my belief, even when the evidence was overwhelming.

The very idea of even considering the possibility of a ghost or apparition had been repugnant to me in the past. Yet I kept thinking, in view of the way my mind had opened up to several other events, that the story of the L-1011 might just possibly have enough to it to consider. I was beginning to make my mind up that it was something that really ought to be pursued—yet I was barely aware of that at the time. I knew that the only way I could even consider the idea was to dig deeply into the background and history of the whole subject —or not at all. Did the Elinor Wylie experience with the Ouija board suggest a possibility? I didn't know. Later I was to realize that I was heading a canoe for some very rough rapids.

The deadlines and pressures continued. Especially pressing was the research and survey for the documentary film on oceanography, which had slipped behind schedule. It was a broad and difficult project which involved conferences with United States Information Agency film executives and took me first to Washington, then on a general survey of various parts of the country.

I had some time to spare while I was there, and I decided to stop by the offices of the Federal Aviation Agency and its allied organization, the National Transportation Safety Board to find out the tragic background and details of the jumbo jet crash in the Everglades, which had been Eastern Flight 401, and to examine the roots of this strange story that had spread halfway around the world.

There was massive material available in the transcripts of National Transportation Safety Board hearings, the written testimony of passengers and flight attendants who survived, and the cockpit voice recorder that was recovered from the crash site in the Everglades. Here the complete conversations

of the ill-fated crew was recorded verbatim. I began to read the material and became utterly absorbed with it. There was a strange mixture of destiny, foreboding, and coincidence that gripped me from the start. Later, after I had personally interviewed many of the survivors, I began to sense many extraordinary circumstances that chillingly led into the strange events that followed in the wake of the crash. They began in the darkness of the Everglades and would continue far beyond that tragic night.

"The thought of death leaves me in perfect peace, for I have a firm conviction that our spirit is a being of indestructible nature: it works on from eternity to eternity; it is like the sun, which though it seems to set to our mortal eyes, does not really set, but shines on perpetually."

—Goethe

# Chapter II

The Everglades at night is drenched with the sound of frogs. In the darkness of this staggering primeval swamp, each kind has its own sound, from the narrow-mouthed toad to the sulfur-belly and the pig frog. They join in this throaty chorus among the mosquitoes and the water mocassins. Even the bellow of an alligator is drowned by it.

As the noisy sulfur-belly hunts crayfish, man hunts the sulfur-belly. Its legs are a delicacy. Hunting them becomes a passion in the forest of sawgrass, an addiction. Lonely air-boats prowl at night, but are lost in this blackness, a territory as large as the state of Connecticut or New Jersey.

Late in the night of December 29, 1972, Bob Marquis was guiding his airboat through the Everglades in search of frogs. The boat skimmed across the water and grass, its giant airplane propeller drowning out the noise of their song. The smooth, flat bottom of the boat glided with equal ease over the clumps of sawgrass and the shallow pools of the swamp. In his forties, Marquis was a former fish and wildlife officer. The Everglades was in his blood. His addiction to it had deep roots; its loneliness and blackness brought him no fear.

It was shortly before midnight, and he had some thirty pounds of frogs in the flat bottom of his boat. Clamped on his head was an eight-volt frogging light that helped him pick his way through the lush clumps and hammocks where willow, buttonbush, and myrtle grow among the sawgrass. Some called the Everglades "muck, misery, and mocassins." To Marquis it is a refuge, a love, a source of renewal.

Like most air-boaters, Marquis navigated by the seat of his pants. The trails he took were barely discernible. Even when the sawgrass was shoulder-high, the only clue to a trail might

be the slightest hint of depression in the leaves. He knew, however, exactly where he was: some twenty miles northwest of Miami, where the faint glow of its lights smeared the horizon. The terrain was, as ever, flat marshland, a soggy prairie covered with soft mud, much of it under six to twelve inches of water. In the deep spots and in some of the canals, the depth could suddenly change to a dozen feet—or even up to fifty or sixty.

Here he would cut his power, shift his weight carefully to the center, and move with caution. The slightest tilt could slurp the water over the shallow gunwale and swamp the boat unceremoniously, consigning it to a muddy grave. These awkward homely craft, half airplane and half scow, could skim over mud or water, up to more than sixty miles an hour.

Marquis was roughly ten miles from the spot he had launched his boat from its trailer off Route 41, known as the Tamiami Trail. He was somewhere near Levee 67A, one of the long, rough fingers of dirt and stone that spear through the endless river of sawgrass, for flood control. The weather was serene; the December night was a soft 72°. There were scattered clouds. The wind soughed at only seven knots.

From his perch in front of the screen that shielded the air-boat propeller, Marquis happened to glance to the north. Here he saw the lights of a large airliner, clearly discernible among the stars. It appeared as if it had just taken off from the Miami International Airport, lying to the southeast. The plane was low on the horizon, but it was hard to tell what its altitude was. It was moving southwest, perhaps five miles away from his airboat.

Marquis thought little about it. Jets were constantly taking off and landing at Miami. The Everglades was an integral part of the approach system. From the air, they looked like a vast black carpet, as black as the sea at night, and without lights. Without instruments it is impossible to tell whether the plane is 2,000 feet above the ground—or 20 feet. There is nothing to relate to, nothing to sort out, a sheet of black velvet. There is no well-defined horizon. Only the brilliant lights of Miami in the distance can give any orientation. But even then, the belly of the plane could, to the pilot's eye, be almost scraping the black carpet, or safely above it.

Since it was nearing midnight, and since Bob Marquis had a long trek back to the Tamiami Trail, his thoughts turned toward going back home. There was nothing unusual about the plane on the horizon, nothing particularly to catch his attention about it.

He was unable to know at that moment that he would soon be facing the most horrifying experience of his life.

Friday, December 29, 1972, was marked by the usual holiday cheer. Some of it was genuine, much of it forced and frenzied. In contrast to some joyous family reunions and preparations for the New Year festivities, the Air Force was reported bent on pulverizing Hanoi and Haiphong above Vietnam's 20th parallel, in the face of stern Congressional censure. One Republican senator bluntly said that Nixon must have taken leave of his senses. Truman was being buried in Missouri; the mayor of Detroit was saying that he wouldn't run again; Willie Mays was saying that he was going to play again in 1973.

In New York the chief cashier of the elegant St. Regis was shot and killed by a man he had recently fired. The winning number of the New York State Lottery was 367259, and those whose tickets matched that number would win $50,000.

In Miami preparations were being completed for the three-mile-long King Orange Jamboree parade, which would occupy over 50,000,000 people on NBC Television on its ninety-minute journey through downtown Miami to herald the Orange Bowl football game. It was the time when airlines were busy and frenetic, especially on the New York-to-Miami run, where chilled New Yorkers sought sun and warmth, and some Floridians were scurrying back home for the New Year holiday.

One traveler was Rosario Messina, a New York garment manufacturer in his forties. He had had to interrupt his Florida vacation to make an unwelcome three-day business trip to New York. His wife Sadie had not been at all happy about it. She had begged him to stay in Florida on vacation because she had a frightening premonition she could not shake.

Rosario was to return that Friday from LaGuardia airport.

20

He found, however, that he preferred a nonstop flight from Kennedy International—Eastern 401. It was scheduled to leave JFK at 9:00 P.M., a desirable flight in one of Eastern's spanking new Tristar jets, the L-1011. One of the new wide-body, jumbo-generation planes, this Lockheed version matched the Boeing 747 and the Douglas DC-10 in comfort and spaciousness.

Rosario was lucky to get on the flight; it had been reported sold out. One Eastern supervisor, Angelo Donadeo, found the only way he could return to Miami was by riding in the jump seat on the flight deck. As a technical specialist for all of L-1011s he was qualified to do so.

The giant planes were Eastern's pride. Fifty of them had been ordered as flagships of the Eastern fleet at between $15,000,000 and $20,000,000 each. "The quietest, cleanest plane in the skies," was the way one Eastern vice-president phrased it. He wasn't far from wrong. It bore the company's designation of "Whisperliner" gracefully and without embarrassment. In spite of the fiscal diseases of Lockheed and Rolls-Royce at the time, a dozen of the sophisticated trimotor craft had come off the line for Eastern, able to carry over 250 passengers each, in cushioned comfort.

Flight 401 would be handled by the L-1011 designated as Plane #310. Delivered in August 1972, it had already accumulated nearly a thousand hours of flying time, with over five hundred landings. Its computers could almost think for themselves; they could actually land the plane automatically, if desired. The passenger cabins were plush and inviting.

Both flight deck and cabin crews were in love with the L-1011s. Passengers came to feel the same way. Sound and vibration were literally a whisper. The cabins were airy, the lighting soft and inviting, the decor tasteful and subdued.

The plane that was to be the craft for Flight 401 came to New York on December 29 from Tampa. The cockpit crew was seasoned. Captain Bob Loft, in his mid-fifties, had nearly 30,000 hours of flying time, nearly 300 of them on the new L-1011s. First Officer Albert Stockstill—known as Bert—was nearing forty, had slightly more time on the new jumbo jet, but considerably fewer in overall hours. Second Officer Don Repo, just over fifty, was a veteran flight engi-

neer, with a passionate attachment to the L-1011 and all its intricacies. New as it was, he knew the plane by heart.

The cockpit crew would arrive at JFK from Tampa at shortly after 7:30 P.M., a comfortable enough time to prepare for taking Flight 401 back to Miami at 9:00, with its holiday passengers. A new crew of ten stewardesses would meet them at Kennedy to handle the cabins, replacing the cabin crew that accompanied Captain Loft on the flight from Tampa.

One of the stewardesses on Loft's flight from Tampa was Doris Elliott,* a slim attractive brunette, high-spirited and sensitive. Some two weeks earlier, she had been working a flight from JFK to Orlando, when she was hit with what she described as "a weird, sick feeling." It was overpowering. In her mind's eye, she saw clearly· an L-1011 over the Everglades, coming in on flight approach to Miami International. It was dark, late at night. She saw the left wing crumble and the fuselage smash into the ground. She heard the cries of the injured. She had to stop work in the cabin and sit down. ·

Two of her friends, flight attendants, immediately came to her side. They asked Doris what was wrong. She told them. She had had experiences like this before, and they had turned out to be almost totally accurate. Four of her former classmates had been killed at a railroad crossing, after she had foreseen the accident. They asked Doris when this new accident was going to happen.

"Around the holidays," she told them. "Closer to New Year's."

"Is it going to be us?"

"No," Doris said. "But it's going to be real close."

Doris regained her composure and finally was able to put it out of her mind. In fact, it was completely out of her thoughts when she arrived at Kennedy that December 29 in 1972, shortly after 7:30 that evening.

The cockpit crew—Loft, Stockstill, and Repo—went directly to Plane 310, the L-1011 that they were to fly to Miami. They would begin the preflight check immediately. They were to discover that a new assigned cabin crew of ten stewardesses had not yet arrived to handle the full comple-

ment of passengers that had been booked. There was not much time left; Flight 401 was to leave at 9:00. Considerable work had to be done before boarding. In a last-minute switch, Captain Loft's team of stewardesses—including Doris Elliott—was assigned to Flight 401.

The originally scheduled cabin crew was flying up to New York from Miami on Flight 26. They were late, and it looked as if there was little chance of reaching JFK for a turnaround on 401. They were a closely knit team and had enjoyed working together during the Christmas month.

In fact, just before leaving Miami, they had asked a friend to take a picture of them as a group. They were jovial and relaxed as the picture was taken. Of course there was the usual fooling around, including the V-shaped fingers behind the head to make horns, the exaggerated poses, the impish smiles. The two girls who were the butt of this lighthearted devilment were Patricia Ghyssels and Stephanie Stanich, both popular with their colleagues. When the picture was developed later, they would appear to be wearing horns on their heads, in the form of the V-shaped fingers of their friends. In airlines, cabin attendant teams are not universally congenial. The photograph would mark an exceptional occasion.

One of the stewardess group (whose name is withheld here) had not been in a jovial mood some six months before the picture was taken. She had consulted a psychic medium in the northwest sector of Miami, not far from the airport, and he had told her that she was to be in a plane accident before the year was over. She was going to think that she had been killed, but she must have confidence that she was alive, even though all around her there would be total blackness.

This scheduled cabin crew arrived at JFK at nearly 8:40 P.M. They scurried off their plane and over to Flight 401, which the standby stewardesses had already boarded. There was a congenial exchange of assignment as the original crew took over from Doris Elliott and the others. Her strange premonition didn't enter her mind again at that time. She left the plane with her two friends to pick up Flight 477, their original assignment to return to Miami via Fort Lauderdale. It

would follow Flight 401 down. They had, for the moment, also forgotten the premonition. It was to come back vividly to all three later that night.

The cockpit crew for Flight 401 entered the plane for the preflight check in fit and rested condition. Aside from the trip up from Tampa, they had each had over fourteen hours of rest. They had flown only slightly over two hours in the previous twenty-four. All were medically certified, the only limitation being corrective glasses for both Captain Bob Loft and Second Officer Don Repo for near vision.

On the morning of their scheduled flight for New York, Captain Loft had dabbled about his yard, doing some light clean-up. He had a pleasant home, matching his $52,000 salary. He was fiftieth in seniority among Eastern's 4,000 pilots. With a swimming pool at his home and a golf course next door, Loft was planning a convivial foursome the day after he arrived back from his trip.

Loft was every bit the image of the ideal airline captain. He was conscientious, a perfectionist, combining these qualities with a salty wit. As an outdoorsman, he had joined with some other pilots to own a hunting lodge near the Everglades town of Immokalee. Cool under pressure, he commanded respect from the crews who flew with him.

First Officer Bert Stockstill was also the prototype of the handsome, well-liked pilot. On the morning of Flight 401, he rose late, then went down to his workshop, where he was building a light airplane. He left for the flight up to New York about 12:30 in the afternoon.

Even those who knew Don Repo well had trouble in describing him. He had a rare sense of humor that was unpredictable. He was far from a stereotype. He had come up the line from aircraft mechanic to flight engineer. Later he qualified for a commercial pilot certificate. He was rough-hewn, popular, a perfectionist in his work. Repo had returned from a trip the day before his Flight 401 assignment, troubled by a light cold. He went to bed early to try to shake it. The next morning, he took one of his daughters to a doctor, dropped by his bank, and then drove to the airport shortly after noon.

All the crew were married. Loft had two children. Repo had four. Stockstill had none.

Aircraft #310, the Whisperliner that was waiting for them at the JFK ramp, had been in service for Eastern for some four months. She was graceful, sleek, polished. She carried Eastern's powder-blue and dark blue stripe along the banks of windows, stretching much of the length of a football field, then curving upward along the six-story-high tail. The belly of the plane was glistening, bright metal. The topside was a creamy white, with the Eastern logo along the side, near the flight deck.

She was equipped with three Rolls-Royce RB 211-22C jet engines, two on the wings, one astern in the tail assembly. The word "Whisperliner" was neatly printed in block letters along the pod of the engine in the tail mount. The crew in the cockpit sat two stories off the ground. On the ground, the craft looked like a huge, smiling, friendly dolphin, with the crown of the forehead curving down where the cockpit windows were. The black radar dome served as the snout. She would be well nursed. The special hangar for all the L-1011s was a $62,000,000 home in Miami, larger than the Orange Bowl.

The preflight check was routine. The craft had been well maintained, from both the company's procedures and the FAA requirements. Weight and balance were well within the required limits. The flight to Miami would require 42,000 pounds of jet fuel, and the plane was loaded with 85,000 pounds before takeoff. The Avionic Flight Control System was one of the most sophisticated in modern aircraft.

There were 163 passengers and 13 crew members boarding Flight 401 that evening. There was a large quota of "no-shows." Angelo Donadeo, the Eastern technical trouble shooter, decided to ride in the left jump seat behind Captain Loft, anyway. He had been sent to New York on a routine assignment and wanted to get back home for the closing on a house he had bought. He had no direct function as a member of the crew, but as a technical expert on the L-1011s he would be interested in continuing his observations.

Inside the cabin, last-minute preparations were being made by the stewardesses. The lighting was soft, splashing

down from the waffle-grid ceiling. There was little sense of crowding. Even near the tail section of the plane, there were eight seats across, in a two-four-two pattern, with ample room in the aisles. There were sounds of doors closing, the clump of the baggage compartment doors slamming in the belly of the plane. In the closets that divided the sections of the cabin, the electric doors slid down and closed.

From somewhere, the anonymous voice of the senior stewardess came over the intercom: the pleasant good evening, the welcome to Flight 401, the cabin altitude controlled for your comfort, the oxygen mask, as the other stewardesses went through the ballet of demonstrating them. As usual, there was also the ballet with the life jackets, the indicating of the escape doors, the warning to keep the seat belt fastened, and the suggestion to relax and enjoy the flight. Then the soft chime for the cabin attendants to take their places and the high whine of the jet engines as the plane began to taxi.

The Whisperliner left the ramp not too long after the scheduled departure time of 9:00 P.M. The holiday traffic was heavy. There would doubtless be a frustrating wait at the end of the taxiway, as the planes ahead in line took off. The huge craft lumbered out toward the runway on the black meadow of the field, picking a precarious path through the blue and white Christmas-tree lights that marked the taxi and runway paths.

In spite of the traffic, the delay at the end of the runway was minimal. At 9:20 P.M., Flight 401 was cleared for takeoff by the tower. Captain Loft advanced the three throttles, and the enormous ship rumbled down the runway.

Within moments, the L-1011 Whisperliner was airborne, and the lights of the runway were slipping backward from the plane. Below, the borough of Queens looked like a jeweled tapestry. The ceiling lights were dimmed, and soft baby spots highlighted the interior with pools of light. As the ship banked over the Atlantic, climbing, the NO SMOKING sign went off. The 28° chill of New York was about to be exchanged for Miami's balmy 75°.

The flight was smooth and uneventful, even though the seat-belt signs remained on until over West Virginia. The martinis, the Scotches, the Cokes were served, along with the packaged meals. The winds were favorable. Captain Loft

was making up the lost time. It appeared that the estimated time of arrival at the Miami ramp would be close to schedule: 11:32 P.M.

The mood on the plane was more buoyant than usual, perhaps because of the holiday season and the release from the chilled northeast. Barry Connell, a portfolio manager for Brown Brothers, Harriman, relaxed in his seat, reading a paperback. His wife Ann was beside him. She was an employee of Eastern, and they were riding on "space available" passes. The trip was relaxed and pleasant; the time slipped by swiftly. For a journey that would take two days by car, Flight 401 would cover the distance in less than two and a half hours.

Ronald Infantimo, a twenty-seven-year old Air Force veteran and student at Miami Dade Junior College, also sat beside his wife, enjoying the smoothness of the flight. They had tried to get an earlier flight, but it was booked; they settled for Flight 401. He was a serious student in aviation administration. They had been married just twenty days, had come up from Miami to New York for a honeymoon and a visit to his parents. Fara, his wife, worked for the Dade County school system as a secretary. They were very much in love. As the plane sped toward Miami, Fara asked her husband to change seats with him. Infantino obliged and moved in to the window seat. They were looking forward to a pleasant evening with relatives on New Year's Eve.

Rosario Messina, the garment manufacturer, considered himself lucky. He had gotten the seat he wanted on the non-stop Miami-bound flight, and would arrive back to greet his wife Sadie so they could continue their vacation together.

The passengers made up a cross section of life. There were accountants, housewives, lawyers, babies, businessmen, students, salesmen, and all the rest. There was even a tiny white poodle with a black-button nose, who sat patiently below the main deck, waiting to greet her master at Miami. Jerry Eskow, who had once been named Transportation Man of the Year by *Dun's Review,* was particularly pleased with the smoothness of the flight; so much so, in fact, that he took out a pad from his briefcase and wrote a letter to mail later to Eastern about both the L-1011 and the service on it. He was

lavish in his praise. His wife Joan had flown down to Miami the night before on the same flight. They made it a rule not to fly together, because they had four daughters, and were concerned about the possibility of accidents.

With the unusually high morale of the cabin crew, the service was good. As the craft began its gradual descent, the food and beverage carts were put away. The enormous galley in the belly of the plane, rimmed with stainless steel ovens, was in shipshape condition. Trudy Smith, who worked the galley that flight, put the finishing touches to it, squeezed in to one of the tiny elevators—barely bigger than a tall, slim dumbwaiter—and rose up to the main deck.

Even though the plane was not filled to capacity, serving 163 meals, along with the liquor and beverages, is never an easy job. By the time Trudy Smith reached the passenger deck, Flight 401 was coming in to the approach pattern for Miami International. She made her way aft, toward the lounge, and sat down to talk for a moment with Stephanie Stanich, one of the ten stewardesses in the crew. She was fond of Stephanie. They were close friends, often roomed together on layovers.

Forward on the flight deck, all was well. Miami was blazing in the distance to the south, contrasting with the black velvet carpet of the Everglades that seemed to go on forever.

The captain's voice, always comforting to the passengers, came on the intercom with a cheery note: "Welcome to sunny Miami," Loft said. "The temperature is in the low seventies, and it's beautiful out there tonight."

Shortly afterward, Captain Bob Loft, in the pilot's seat on the left-hand side of the cockpit, listened as the disembodied voice of Miami Approach Control came in over the radio: "Eastern four-oh-one. Left heading one zero zero, three from the marker. Cleared to IIS nine, left. Good morning."

It was not quite morning. It was in fact, just after 11:30 that night. The approach control voice concluded: "One-one-eight-point-three. Eastern four-oh-one. So long."

Within a few seconds, Captain Loft responded. "Miami tower, Eastern four-oh-one. Just turned on final."

There was a brief period of silence, then what seemed like

a radio leak when a voice from the tower said, "Who else called?"

There was no need for a response from Captain Loft; it was simply an indication that Miami Flight Control was busy with other craft in the area. Instead, he turned to his copilot Stockstill to lower the landing gear. "Go ahead and throw 'em out," he said. There was a familiar grind and shudder, as the huge landing gears began falling into place beneath the belly. Then, from Captain Loft: "Miami tower, do you read Eastern four-oh-one? Just turned on final."

"Eastern four-oh-one, heavy. Continue approach to nine, left." "Heavy" meant that Loft's plane was of the large jumbo jet class.

The shift had been made and acknowledged, from the Approach Control to the tower. Flight 401 could not continue its approach without being handed off to the tower for the final descent. Loft acknowledged: "Continue approach. Roger."

Then the checkoff for the final approach, a dialogue between Second Officer Don Repo, in the engineer's seat, and Captain Loft.

From Repo: "Continuous ignition. No smoke."

"Coming on."

"Brake system."

"Okay," Loft acknowledged.

"Radar."

"Up. Off."

"Hydraulic panels. Checked."

First Officer Stockstill, in the copilot's seat on the right, was counting. "Thirty-five. Thirty-three," he said marking the rate of descent.

Loft, his eyes scanning the instruments, turned to Stockstill. Only two of the three green landing gear lights were showing on the panel. "Bert," he said. "Is that handle in?"

Repo, his eyes on the engineering instruments, said, "Engine cross bleeds are open."

There was a moment of silence, a few brief interchange of words, before Stockstill said, "No nose gear."

"I gotta raise it back up," Loft said. "Goddamn it."

There was the sound of the flap position warning horn. A few more seconds passed. Captain Loft spoke again. "Now I'm gonna try it down one more time."

Stockstill acknowledged. In another few moments, an altitude-alert horn sounded. There was definitely something wrong with the nose gear. No one in the cockpit could tell immediately what it was. "Want to tell 'em we'll take it around and circle around and around?" Stockstill asked.

The plane was at 1,500 feet, dropping toward 1,000. The warning horns were corrected and stopped. There was little cause for alarm. The gear could be lowered not only by hydraulic pressure, but by hand-winding or free fall, where the sound would confirm the locking. Loft went on the radio.

"Well, ah, tower. This is Eastern, ah, four-zero-one. It looks like we're gonna have to circle. We don't have a light on our nose gear yet."

In moments, the tower acknowledged. "Eastern four-oh-one, heavy. Roger. Pull up. Climb straight ahead to two thousand. Go back to Approach Control, on one-twenty-eight-six." Loft switched his radio channel as the plane was handed back to Approach Control from the tower.

Sometime before, Loft had told a friend of his; "When you have a problem with the landing gear, nine times out of ten, it's the signal light that's off, and not the gear." He felt that way at this point.

With the flaps set at 22°, the plane was made ready to begin its gradual climb back up to 2,000 feet for the go-around. It was now 11:34 P.M., close to the moment that had been anticipated for touchdown. The plane had been directly on the glide slope for runway 9-L. Stockstill made a move to bring the landing gear up again, but Loft said; "Put power on it first, Bert. Thata boy. Leave the damn gear down until we've found out what we've got."

Stockstill agreed, as Repo said to Loft from his engineer's seat, "You wanna test the lights or not?"

"Yeah," Loft replied. "Check it."

Stockstill added, "Uh, Bob. It might be the light. Could you jiggle that—the light?"

Loft turned back to the radio, and said to Approach Con-

trol: "Okay. Going up to two thousand. One-twenty-eight-six." The plane had just dipped slightly below 1,500 feet, at 11:35 P.M. It was now climbing on up to a safe 2,000, where it could circle first north, and then west, in a wide racetrack pattern. Its speed was just above 180 knots.

The problem was either in the nose gear itself, or in the green light that signaled when it was down and locked. Before attempting to land, it was routine to have all three of the landing-gear signal lights reading "green across the threshold." At the moment, there was no gear-down-and-locked indication, but the sound had indicated it was.

The warning lights were housed in an assembly that sat across the throttles from the captain on the copilot's side of the cockpit. They were just below the handle that raises and lowers the gear. The light fixture that commanded the attention of the cockpit crew had a replacement value of $12. Like most instrument lighting assemblies, it was a little tricky to snap in the bulb, or its assembly, or to take either of them out. Don Repo, as flight engineer and Second Officer, was trained in its minor intricacies. On the other hand, the light was situated between the captain and the copilot, nearer the copilot. It would be more convenient for either of them to give it at least a preliminary check.

There were the options, regardless of the bothersome little light. They would try to change the bulb, of course. But at the same time, Repo could descend in to what is called the "hell hole," underneath the cockpit floor. There he could check the recalcitrant gear visually.

In the few seconds it took to begin the climb up to 2,000 feet, above the landing glide path, the crew was already checking the first procedure—replacing the warning light. At the same time, there was a lot to do in simply flying the plane in the holding pattern.

Stockstill announced, "We're up to two-thousand. You want me to fly it, Bob?"

Bob Loft, concerned with the radio communication for the moment, asked, "What frequency did he want us on, Bert?"

"One-twenty-eight-six."

"I'll talk to 'em," Loft responded.

At the same time, Repo was helping Stockstill check the warning light. "It's right above that—uh—red one, is it not?" he said.

"Yeah," Loft told Repo. "I can't get it from here."

Leaning into the control panel from behind, Repo gave the lamp assembly a tug. "I can't make it pull out either," he said.

Checking the endless minutiae of the new flight pattern, Loft asked, "We got pressure?"

"Yessir. All systems," Repo answered.

Captain Loft finally got back to the radio communication with Miami Approach Control. "All right, ah, Approach Control," he told them. "Eastern four-zero-one. We're right over the airport here, and climbing to two thousand feet. In fact, we've just reached two-thousand feet, and we've got to get a green light on our nose gear."

In seconds, the response came from Approach Control: "Eastern four-oh-one, roger. Turn left heading three-six-zero. Maintain two thousand vectors, to nine left final."

"Left three-six-zero," Loft answered. Then he swung the L-1011 Whisperliner to the north. It was exactly 11:35 P.M. plus half a minute.

Back in the cabin and shortly before this Albert Morris, a dealer in automotive transmissions, in his sixties, was congratulating himself on getting on Flight 401 as a standby. His original booking was on Flight 477, which stopped off at West Palm Beach. Flight 401 was a faster, more convenient non-stop. When the NO SMOKING sign went on, he brought his seat back up to the forward position and waited for the landing.

When the verbal reminder of the no-smoking and seat-belt signs came over the intercom, Ann Connell returned both her own and her husband's seats to the upright position. Their seat belts were already fastened. She heard the landing gear groan downward and the dulcet sound of the bell that sent the stewardesses to their seats. Glancing out the window, she was a little surprised to see the Eastern Airline's sprawling maintenance base at the airport receding in the background. They should normally be approaching it. Dorothy Warnock

was facing them on her stewardess jump seat at mid-cabin.

Feeling somewhat uneasy, she got up from her jump seat briefly, crossed over and looked out a window, just in front of the wing and the starboard engine. She saw nothing but blackness and assumed the plane was over the Atlantic. "Looks like we're circling," she commented. As the plane began heading away from the city lights and out over the vast darkness of the Everglades, Ann turned to her husband Barry and said; "If I didn't know any better, I'd think we were being hijacked."

The darkness beneath the plane was total. As the craft moved farther and farther away from the airport, Ann became somewhat concerned. She couldn't, in fact, decide whether the plane was heading out over the Atlantic or over the Everglades. There didn't seem to be any marked descent whatever, if at all. Nor was there any seeming change in direction. She then began thinking about the emergency exit. It was between her seat and Dorothy Warnock's. She also began wondering about the life rafts.

Her husband, Barry Connell, put down his paperback when the announcement came over that the plane would land at approximately 11:35. He was a little concerned when Ann pointed out to him that the approach to the airport seemed rather unusual. There seemed to be no question that the plane was heading away from Miami International, with no sign of returning in that direction. As a man who flew on business trips every other month or so, he was familiar with most normal landing patterns. Flight 401 was definitely not on a normal pattern.

Several other people around him were now commenting on the unusual nature of the approach. They included two stewardesses, Trudy Smith and Pat Georgia, in the double jump seats by the galley. Trudy Smith had left her conversation with Stephanie Stanich in the aft lounge when the NO SMOKING sign had lit up, then made her way to her position. As she had strapped herself in, she noticed a man walking down the aisle. She immediately jumped up to tell him: "You had better go to your seat, sir, or it may be the last walk you'll ever take." The man went immediately to his

seat. Trudy became aware that the approach was unusually long and mentioned it to Pat Georgia, who agreed. Sharon Transue, another stewardess, not far away in her seat, joined them in their puzzlement.

Sitting in her jump seat on the starboard side of the plane, Stewardess Mercedes Ruiz noticed the same problem from her position aft of the wing. She asked Pat Ghyssels, her colleague across the aisle, what was happening to the approach. Neither came up with an answer.

There was little outward sign of restiveness in the cabin. The lights were dimmed for landing; the engines were quiet. Ronald Infantino, after spending what he called "the happiest three weeks of my life," was happy to be beside his new bride and eager to get on with his studies. Jerry Eskow, the glowing letter to Eastern safely in his coat pocket, sat back on his seat and waited.

Forward in the cockpit, there was still the problem of the warning light. By 11:36 P.M., a minute or so after Loft had announced his northerly heading and holding pattern at 2,000 feet, the crew was beginning to get a little testy about the stubborn light.

"Put the damn thing on autopilot here," Loft said to Stockstill.

"All right," Stockstill acknowledged.

"See if you can get that light out."

"All right."

"Now push the switches just a little bit forward," Loft continued. "You got it turned sideways then." The gadget was giving all three of the cockpit crew trouble. It was obviously exasperating. "Naw, I don't think it'll fit."

On the jump seat, behind Captain Loft, technical specialist Angelo Donadeo invited the rest of the crew to ask him if he could do anything. But he remained discreetly in the background until that moment should come. In a crowded flight deck, an offer to help can sometimes be a hindrance. Loft and Stockstill, both seated nearest to the light, were working on the problem, each with a hand on the unit as the autopilot—a modern electronic wizard that could control whatever al-

titude or direction or speed that was punched into it—controlled the plane.

Loft and Stockstill each had his own autopilot system at his position, but only one could be used at a time. Each pilot had his own instruments to read the information as to what the autopilot was doing at the time.

Either autopilot could provide total control of the airplane, responding to the heading, pitch, or navigational control system put into it. The plane could be released from autopilot control by turning the engage lever to "OFF," or by pressing a button switch on either control wheel. In these ways, it could be completely overridden immediately.

But another safety feature was added into the autopilot design: it could simply be disengaged by a pressure of fifteen to twenty pounds on the control column, the steering yoke, by the pilot who needed to take immediate action in either altitude or direction. What was not evident at the time was that the automatic flight control system could be inadvertently disengaged by a rather insignificant bump on the control column. This could happen when a pilot might be getting up from or entering his cockpit seat, and accidentaly bump the steering column. If so, he could send the plane on a downward descent without immediately noticing it.

There was one other problem not noticed at the time about Plane 310, the craft that flew Flight 401 that night: the computers that held the plane on the proper pitch through the autopilot were slightly mismatched. Captain Loft's computer could disengage the autopilot altitude control with fifteen pounds pressure, while Bert Stockstill's would be disengaged with twenty pounds. There was more significance to this than met the eye.

Loft could disengage his computer. His altitude indicator would go out. This would show that he was no longer on automatic pilot, and he would have to take over manual control of the craft.

But the altitude indicator would remain *on* for Stockstill. This would give him the wrong impression, that the plane was still holding the proper altitude. He could not see the captain's indicator from where he sat, to crosscheck this.

35

Thus, one instrument might say the autopilot was holding the altitude. The other would say it wasn't. Neither pilot could see the other's indicator.

Because few people—if any—were aware of these anomalies, the pilots were not trained in looking out for them at that time. This could be critical; it could even be tragic. When there are so many different instruments to monitor at one time, especially in a high traffic or complicated approach, the visual sweeping of the proper instruments can be more than demanding.

There was no question that Flight 401 was making a complicated approach. In addition to trying to discover whether the landing gear itself was down and locked, or whether the green light was faulty, other traffic had to be carefully watched at Miami's busy international airport, where over eight thousand aircraft movements take place each day. And there were other planes in the sky now, but they were safely off to the left. To put Flight 401 on its safely monitored racetrack circling pattern, Miami Approach called Loft again: "Eastern four-oh-one. Turn left three-zero-zero."

"Okay," Loft replied, "Three-zero-zero. Eastern four-oh-one." Then he turned his attention back to the stubborn warning light. Stockstill continued to monitor the flight and help Loft from his position nearest the light. While he worked on the light, Loft decided to exercise one of his other options. He turned to Repo, and said; "Hey, hey. Get down there and see if that damn nose wheel is down. You better do that."

Stockstill was still struggling with the light bulb—"peanut sized," it was referred to in maintenance. "You got a handkerchief or something so I can get a little better grip on this?" he asked. "Anything I can do it with?"

"Pull down and turn to your right. Now turn to your left one time."

Nobody felt an emergency situation. But it was getting preposterous, especially when the crew was convinced that there was nothing really wrong with the nose gear. "It hangs out and sticks," Stockstill said. "This won't come out, Bob. If I had a pair of pliers, I could cushion it with that Kleenex."

Repo, getting ready to go down in the "hell hole" where the landing gear well was, paused a moment. "I can give you

a pair of pliers," he said. "But if you force it, you'll break it,—just believe me."

"Yeah, I'll cushion it with the Kleenex."

"Oh, we can give you pliers," Repo repeated.

Miami Approach, monitoring the flight carefully, came in on the radio, at 11:37 P.M. "Eastern, uh, four-oh-one. Turn left heading two-seven-zero."

"Left two-seven-zero," Loft acknowledged. Then he gave up on the light. "To hell with it," he said. "To hell with this. Go down and see if it's lined up with that red line. That's all we care. Screwing around with that twenty-cent piece of light equipment we got on this plane. . . ."

The crew chuckled. With the options available, they were confident the problem would be quickly solved. The light was jammed, and nothing could be done about it for the moment, at least. The visual check would more than suffice. Even that would be redundant, after the free-fall process.

Down in the nose-wheel well, the light could illuminate the landing gear so that it could be viewed through an optical sight, like a telescope. It was located in the forward electronics bay, just forward of the wheel-well. If two rods on the linkage showed that a red line on each lined up together, it would indicate without question that the landing gear was in safe and proper position.

Second Officer Repo opened the trapdoor, and climbed down the ladder into the hell hole. There was room enough for a man to stand down there, and for two to squeeze in. It housed a battery of black boxes containing the complex avionics systems of the plane. On the flight deck, Loft and Stockstill still struggled with the warning lamp. Extra time was needed before the plane turned back for a new final approach. Loft called Miami Approach again.

"Eastern four-oh-one will go out west just a little further, if we can here, and, ah, see if we can't get this light to come on here."

"All right, uh, we got you headed westbound there now, Eastern four-oh-one."

"All right," Loft replied. Then he turned to Stockstill and said, "How much fuel we got left on this plane?"

Stockstill checked the gauges. "Fifty-two five," he said.

The Whisperliner had burned over 32,000 pounds of jet fuel on the flight.

Loft, still working on the lamp said; "It won't come out. No way." Then, to Stockstill: "Did you ever take it out of there?"

The noise in the cockpit from an air vent made hearing difficult at times. "Huh?" said Stockstill.

"Have you ever taken it out of there?"

"Hadn't till now."

"Put it in the wrong way, huh?"

"In there. Looks square to me."

"Can't you get the hole lined up?"

They were trying to reinsert the lamp assembly. It wouldn't fit. Another plane appeared below them, over a field near the Everglades used for practice takeoffs and landings.

"I think that's over the training field," Stockstill said.

"West heading. You want to go west, or—"

"Naw, that's right. We're about to cross Krome Avenue right now."

They were in the process of crossing over Krome Avenue, a strip of a road that separated the last of thinning-out lights west of Miami, and marked the beginning of the full black carpet of the Everglades swampland. It was a few seconds after 11:40 P.M. Ahead of the plane was total darkness, again, stretching far to the horizon. Within two minutes, the plane would be over this wilderness. The plane was on automatic pilot. The altitude was set for 2,000 feet. Captain Loft was leaning across the throttles, still trying to help Stockstill with the "peanut" light.

Although he was flying the plane during the abortive attempt at working on the light, Stockstill was the only crew member who could reach the light assembly conveniently. Although he had loosened his shoulder strap, Loft still had difficulty in leaning over to it. He had his left arm on top of the glare shield and was leaning across with his right. Specialist Donadeo, on the jump seat behind the captain, still could do little to help without getting in the way. He stood by, waiting to help if needed.

There was, however, at this point, an almost imperceptible

38

decline in altitude, as the plane began dipping below 2,000 feet. But nothing to indicate this showed up on Stockstill's autopilot annunciator. He could not see the one on Loft's panel from where he was sitting.

Stockstill didn't need to loosen his shoulder harness to get at the warning-light assembly. He put his left hand on it and tried to pry it loose again.

"I don't know what's holding the damn thing in," he said. "Always something. We could've made schedule."

Loft had already recycled the landing gear, and there was no question in either his or Stockstill's mind that the nose gear was down and locked. Repo, below, was almost sure to confirm it when he checked the red line indices through the telescope. It actually was not even necessary to do that; the free-fall recycling was a tested procedure in itself.

In the two minutes and twelve seconds that followed Stockstill's comment that the plane could have made schedule, several things happened. One of the most important was that the soft and gentle C-chord chime, which warned of a drop in altitude, sounded at 38 seconds after 11:40 P.M., as the altitude of the plane fell off ever so slightly to 1,700 feet. There was no sensation of the plane's descending, nor over the blackness of the Everglades was there any visual suggestion. The warning chime, which lasted half a second, came from a speaker located at Second Officer Repo's panel. Repo was below in the hell hole, getting ready to visually examine the nose gear.

The altitude warning signal was designed to remind the pilot to level off at the altitude he was assigned and to stay there. In this case, it was the 2,000 feet Flight 401 had been cruising at. There was no visual warning light with it. The volume of the chime is very low. It would be difficult for anyone with a headset on to hear it above the noise of the cockpit, especially when the crew members were so preoccupied with the problem at hand.

There was no indication that anyone at all heard that C-chord chime, which was softer than a suburban doorbell. There was also no further indication on Stockstill's autopilot annunciator that the plane had left its assigned 2,000 feet altitude.

At the precise moment that the chime sounded, Loft was saying; "We can tell if the damn nose gear is down by looking at our indices." He was referring to the red line again. But he added: "I'm sure it is," Stockstill confirmed.

"It free falls down," said Loft.

"The tests didn't show the lights worked, anyway," Stockstill added.

From Loft: "That's right."

"It's a faulty light," said Stockstill.

They both agreed. It was time now to get Second Officer Repo back up, and come in for the long delayed landing. But Repo was already coming up the ladder from below. Partway up, he raised his hand into the cockpit area and said, "I don't see it down there."

"Huh?" Loft asked him.

"I don't see it."

"There's a place in there you can look and see if it's lined up," Loft said.

"I know. A little like a telescope."

"Yeah."

"Well—"

"It's not lined up?"

"I can't see it," Repo replied. "It's pitch-dark and I throw the little light—I get, ah, nothing."

At this point, Donadeo felt that he could be of some help without getting in the way. He unfastened his safety belt and rose to join Repo in the hell hole.

Someone asked; "Wheel-well light on?"

It was still hard to hear in the cockpit. "Pardon?" Repo asked.

"Wheel-well lights on?"

"Yeah," Repo said. "Wheel-well lights always on when the gear is down."

"Now try it," the captain said.

Donadeo crossed to the hell-hole door. Repo disappeared down the ladder as he approached. Donadeo squeezed through the two-foot-square door and climbed down the ladder to join Repo. The compartment lights were on down there, and Donadeo began walking aft, toward the bulkhead and the periscope that could view the nose gear. The visual

checking was actually a redundant operation now, at 40 seconds after 11:41 P.M., because the free-fall looking of the nose gear was certain.

Back at the Miami Approach, the controller noticed that the alphanumeric data block on his radar display showed Flight 401 had an altitude reading of only 900 feet instead of the assigned 2000, but momentary deviations in altitude information on the radar display are common. He would have to wait for at least another scan on the radarscope to verify this puzzling reading. At the same moment, the controller was occupied in orchestrating two airliners southeast of West Palm Beach, two more on departure for Bimini, and two others west of Miami approaching over the Everglades, all over a span of some seventy miles. As he monitored all six of these planes, Flight 401 was cruising far out over the Everglades.

The controller had time, however, to radio: "Eastern, ah, four-oh-one. How are things coming along out there?"

Captain Loft responded immediately. "Okay. We'd like to turn around and come—come back in." Then, to Stockstill: "Clear on left."

"Okay," Stockstill said. The display on his automatic pilot panel showed that the plane had not diverted from its 2,000-feet assignment. Below, on the flat black Everglades, there was no visual hint whatever that the plane was not at that altitude. The speed of the plane over the last several seconds had been picking up: from 174 knots to over 188—some 200 miles an hour. The throttles were pulled back a little to adjust for this.

The increase in speed, however, was not coming from the power of the engines. The angle of descent was increasing, bringing with it a corresponding increase in speed. The automatic pilot still read out its 2,000-feet assignment on Stockstill's side of the cockpit.

Miami Approach Control came in over the radio again: "Eastern four-oh-one. Turn left, heading one-eight-zero."

Loft responded: "One-eighty ."

It was almost 11:42 P.M. At this moment the plane was now only 600 feet above the swamps. It was falling at the rate of 500 feet every twenty seconds. Following the command to

change direction, Stockstill gently turned the wheel to the left, at the rate of 4° per second. The left wing dipped down to a 28° angle.

Just five seconds after 11:42 P.M., Stockstill spoke sharply: "We did something to the altitude."

"What?" Loft said.

"We're still at two thousand, right?" Stockstill asked.

There was no direct response. Loft yelled: "Hey, what's happening here?"

It was nine and a half seconds after 11:42 P.M.

"Man is immortal; therefore he must die endlessly. For Life is a creative idea; it can only find itself in changing forms."

—Rabindranath Tagore

# Chapter III

Nearly twenty miles away from the Everglades, a varied and eager group of friends and relatives was waiting outside Eastern Gate 87 at Miami International Airport. The computerized TV screens were flashing the usual departures and arrivals. The faces were upturned and anticipating. The reaction was good. Flight 401 was cleared for landing, the bright green figures showed on the screen. Practically on schedule. Joan Eskow, who by family rule had flown down the night before on the same flight, was pleased. With her three teenage daughters already down in Miami for vacation, they would be joined by her husband Jerry, on schedule.

Sonnie Rubin, a retired chiropractor from North Miami, was particularly happy when she saw the figures on the screen show that Flight 401 was cleared for landing. He was waiting with his two grown daughters at the airport to meet his twenty-four-year-old son Steve, who was flying down on 401 with his wife Rochelle, nearly eight months pregnant. A grandchild was in the making. The family reunion planned for the New Year would be all the more joyous.

The family of Fara Infantino was waiting patiently for her and Ronald to arrive. Kathy Delarosa, Fara's sister, had the New Year's Eve celebration nicely planned at her home on South West 17th Terrace. Fara's mother would be there to celebrate with the young bride and her son-in-law also.

Waiting at the gate at the airport, Sadie Messina still could not fight back the feeling of ominous fear she had when her husband Rosario had left for New York. She could not explain why. Her two sons were with her, and she was waiting anxiously on the concourse. At some minutes after 11:30, as she waited by Gate 87, she was startled to hear a

familiar whistle. Her two sons heard it also. She was startled because it was the very special one that her husband always sounded when he came home, a family code signal. It came from behind her back, which was to the gate. She turned abruptly. The gate was closed. There was no one there at all. Her heart sank. She was sure now that Flight 401 had crashed, yet there was no sign whatever at the gate that the plane was even delayed. If she was sure, she was the only one who thought so. The bright green letters on the TV monitor still showed its cleared-for-landing message.

Bob Marquis, still on the quest for the sulfur-belly frog, continued to pick his way gingerly through the sawgrass and muddy waters of the swampland. The tiny eight-volt frogging lamp strapped to his head threw a slender pencil of light ahead of him. He guided the airboat expertly, steering it by the tall lever beside him, which guided the air-rudders to port or starboard. The ingenious scow would respond to the slightest pressure on the accelerator under his right foot. There was nothing to be snagged by the sawgrass or muddy roots. The airplane engine and propeller, framed by what looked like a huge birdcage, were high above the water and mud. The rudders were mounted behind them, steering the strange-looking craft by the flow of air streaming back through them.

Except for the considerable roar of the engine, the night was quiet, inviting, and beautiful. The airliner Marquis had seen was still in the distance, still on the horizon. The only thing unusual about it was its rather low altitude.

Something drew Bob Marquis's attention away from—and then back to—where the low airliner had been flying. But the plane was not where he expected it. Instead, he saw a brilliant reddish-orange flash which seemed to be about five miles away. It was hard to tell. It seemed to stretch the length of three football fields. It glowed for five or six seconds. Then suddenly all went black again, back to the undisturbed darkness of the Everglades.

In the radar room below the glassed-in control tower at Miami International, Charles Johnson, a veteran of fifteen years' service as an FAA controller, watched the radarscope

carefully to get another reading on Flight 401's altitude. He was not unduly upset at the moment. Captain Loft had showed no sign of concern on his last transmission, just before 11:42 P.M. Loft had simply responded to Johnson's question as to how he was coming along, by saying he'd like to turn around and come in for the final approach. This was a casual, normal response with no emergency evident. To Johnson this meant that the landing gear problem had been solved, and all was well. Although his radar data showed 401 at 900 feet, Johnson was aware that pilots with a landing-gear problem often come in at an abnormally low altitude to reduce the stress on the landing gear, which might otherwise jam. He was also reminded of one time when the altitude reading for a flight he had once monitored showed a plane on his scope reading 90,000 feet when it was actually at 10,000.

It is the practice of FAA controllers everywhere not to bother pilots with trivial matters. Pilots, in fact, resent any nonessential interference with their flights from the tower, unless it is clearly and unquestionably an emergency situation. With faulty readings on altitude radarscopes not uncommon, Controller Johnson needed extra sweeps on his radarscope to double-check whether there *was* anything worth alarming Flight 401 about.

Meanwhile, Johnson turned his attention to a Lan Chile plane, Flight 451. It was requesting a change in altitude. A Bahama flight also wanted approval for a change in course. The exchange took 41 seconds. He turned back to Captain Loft's signal from Flight 401.

He was surprised to find that he was reading a void. He spoke into the microphone: "And, ah, Eastern four-oh-one," he said. "Are you requesting the emergency equipment?" He wanted to find out if Captain Loft wanted fire trucks to stand by on the runway if the landing gear failed to function. There was no reply to his question.

Almost immediately after he spoke, both Lan Chile and National Flight 611 came in with questions. It took a minute to clear them up. Then he came back on the air to Flight 401: "Eastern four-oh-one, I've lost you on radar, and your transponder. What's your altitude now?"

He waited twelve seconds, then spoke again: "Eastern four-oh-one, Miami—"

He never finished the sentence. National Flight 611 came in on his signal, loud and heavy:

"Approach, this is National 611. We saw a big explosion, looked like it was out west. I don't know what it means, but I want to let you know."

On the heels of this message, the Lan Chile pilot came in: "Lan Chile 451," the pilot said. "We saw a big flash. It was a general flash, like some kind of explosion."

At that exact moment, Eastern Captain J.L. Tomkins, was conducting proficiency tests in a plane just over the jetport training field near the Everglades. His attention was suddenly drawn to a large kidney-shaped pattern of orange flames, surging up from the black Everglades. They seemed to last for two or three seconds. Then there was total blackness again. He immediately radioed the tower at the training field, then changed his heading back toward Miami International. There seemed to be a column of heavy smoke rising in the air from the place where the orange flames had flashed. But there was no further light. Abeam of the smoke on the way back to the main airport, he could see nothing whatever down below, where the smoke seemed to be coming from. No flashes, no lights, no activity.

Simultaneously, controller Richard Schultz was directing the close-in traffic from the local tower. He had been the one who handed off Flight 401 to Johnson at the time the warning-light problem first was discovered. At shortly after 11:42 P.M., Schultz was occupied with several final approaches and takeoffs. N173W, a private plane that had just taken off, came in on Schultz's frequency.

"Miami tower, one-seven-three whisky."

Schultz responded. "One-seven-three whisky. Miami."

"Are you missing an airplane off your scope?"

None of the recent Flight 401 activity had been monitored by the local tower, since Controller Johnson, as the area man, was responsible for that. "Not to our knowledge," Schultz replied. "What do you see?"

"There was a big flash from a tremendous flame. Yessir, a

47

big flash. Looked just like an airplane drove right into the ground. He had high-intensity strobe lights on his wingtips."

Schultz asked him to stand by. Down in the radar room, Charlie Johnson, was in the process of shifting over to special duty for handling the obvious emergency. Schultz lost no time in confirming the fact that Flight 401 was without question down in the Everglades, in a remote and inaccessible location. He came back on the radio to N173W.

"One seven-three whisky," he called. "When will you be coming back to Miami?"

"Tomorrow," was the reply.

"Okay, sir," Schultz said. "When you get back to Miami, would you call Miami Tower on the telephone and describe in detail what you observed, sir?".

"Roger. Now, if you like."

"Well, uhh, we're a little busy right now."

A few moments before the radio reports flooded into the approach and airport tower at Miami, Eastern technician Angelo Donadeo had just finished squeezing into the cramped quarters of the hell hole of the Flight 401 Whisperliner, to join Second Officer Don Repo. It was a tight squeeze, but there was room enough for the two of them to walk aft without bumping into the avionic equipment in the bay. He began heading toward the periscope device to try to see what the problem was in checking the red-line indices on the nose gear. He wasn't sure, but he thought he sensed a slight reduction in altitude. At the point that he was passing the bulkhead, everything went black. He did not even remember hitting the bulkhead with his head. He felt no concussion. He was unconscious.

The next thing that he could remember was that he was down on the floor of the hell hole in a sitting position. He saw water coming up through the floor. He heard Don Repo, near him, moaning. He began yelling for help. Repo joined him. They were both in pain and in agony, trapped in total darkness and unable to move. They felt the water rising.

Sue Tebbs and Adrianne Hamilton occupied the two

stewardess jump seats in the first-class forward cabin, their back to the cockpit entrance, on the starboard and port side, respectively. Sitting backward, they faced the passengers. On the go-around, Adrianne, the senior flight attendant on 401, had felt no sensation of the plane's pulling up to its 2,000 feet altitude.

She had listened as the landing gear had moved up and down two times and knew the plane was circling over the Glades. From her position, she could see out the first-class windows. She thought she saw fog or clouds, she wasn't sure which.

Then she felt the plane touch down. She thought it was the landing. But almost immediately, she felt herself being thrown violently to her left, toward the center of the airplane. Then she knew the plane had crashed. All the lights went out at the moment of the impact. She felt water rushing over her. She put her head down and closed her eyes. Beside her was a service center. She tried to protect herself from hitting it. She found herself hanging from her seat by her seat belt. She was hit by a powerful smell of jet fuel.

She released her seat belt and slipped to the floor, which was on a rakish angle. It was extremely slippery. She tried to walk on it, but the pain in her back and the slickness of the plane floor caused her to fall down the slant, to the starboard side of the plane.

She looked up, and found that she was looking up at the open sky. There was no moon, but the stars were bright. Everything else was black.

She could see enough, however, to realize that the nose section of the plane where she was sitting had split off from the rest of the L-1011. She could see what was left of the toilet. The pain in her back was paralyzing. She could barely move.

Beside her on the tilting floor was Sue Tebbs. Her feet were resting on the skeleton of the open fuselage. Sue was in great pain and unable to move. It was too dark to tell how high they were off the ground. Adrianne heard sounds coming from the cockpit, in the nose section behind her. It was the only portion of her section that was still completely encased.

They were yelling for help. From down in the hell hole, she heard a voice calling out that water was coming in. She could hear moans and screams in the distance.

Far back aft in the tail section, Beverly Raposa and Stephanie Stanich had been seated in their stewardess jump seats, facing forward, their backs to the bulkhead at the rear of the plane. Beverly had noted that the plane seemed to be going to circle and mentioned it to Stephanie, without concern. For some reason she felt that the go-around was abnormally quiet. Then, suddenly, she noticed what seemed to be an increase in power. She could feel the plane bank to the left. As it did, she felt a tremendous jolt. Then the cabin seemed to be filled with a huge ball of flame, orange and pink. It lasted only for a fraction of time.

There was a thunderous crash, then the sound and roar of a tornado. Her seat was thrown violently to the left, and then to the right. She could see things flying all about her. She saw her arms go out in front of her, waving grotesquely from side to side. Her legs and head were thrashed viciously back and forth, but her body was held in tightly by her shoulder harness. There was a rush of wind. A liquid that seemed like jet fuel swept over her like a waterfall. Then there was total blackness.

When she came to, Beverly was still in her seat, penned in by something on top of her and something to her right. She could not tell what it was. There was no sign of Stephanie anywhere. Beverly's seat was leaning far to the right almost on top of her. To her left, there was only open space. There was no light anywhere. She wasn't sure what was on top of her. It felt like one of the inflated escape chutes, but it might have been the service console. Her right hand was trapped and she couldn't free it. With her left, she lifted the object holding her down, then managed to take a deep breath and press her harness buckle with her left thumb.

Whatever had been pinning her still held her in. She pushed hard. She didn't know quite where she was, but above her she could see the stars. Suddenly she felt herself falling to the left. She landed in thick mud. She must have blanked out momentarily, but then she came to and struggled to her feet.

She was standing in the marsh. The smell of jet fuel was everywhere. She cried out a warning almost immediately: no one was to light a match. She could barely see anything, but she made out the nebulous outlines of some people standing in the distance. She started to grope her way toward them, but she could hardly move through the sawgrass—six feet high in spots—and the sharp metal pieces of the shattered fuselage. Her feet sank into the mud, and she cut her leg on a jagged section of the plane. She kept moving, however, painfully stumbling toward the vague shadows of people in the distance.

Stewardess Mercedes Ruiz, sitting opposite from Pat Ghyssels behind the wing section of the fuselage, had not been perturbed about the go-around because it was such a common thing. It also added up, at times, to a little extra flying time and more pay. She finally picked up a *McCall's* magazine to get back to an article she had been reading. It was about people who find themselves feeling low in holiday seasons, like Christmas.

Then—she remembered nothing. She came to in her seat in the middle of darkness, in the wetness of the swamp. Her seat belt was unfastened. She was very cold, and she smelled jet fuel. She was bleeding from the back of her head. Pat Ghyssels, whom she had been sitting across from only moments before, was nowhere to be seen.

Looking up from his paperback book, Barry Connell had sensed a slight increase in engine thrust and a slight upward shift of the nose of the aircraft. It did not seem abnormal. He felt a strange jar on the left of the plane. Then—suddenly—a loud, grinding impact that sent the huge craft skewing crazily along the ground. As it did, the brilliant flash of light went through the cabin, traveling from the forward part of the plane all the way to the rear. It seemed to travel just below the ceiling height. The fuselage spun as the plane skidded, but it did not cartwheel. It felt like a roller coaster or wild whip ride. Then the fuselage began breaking up. There were sounds of metal tearing apart. A cold blast of air rushed in. Jet fuel began raining down heavily.

The moment it happened, Connell reached over and

grabbed his wife. She was on his right, by the window. He pulled her toward him, pushed her head down with his, and tried to keep them in the center of the two seats to reduce exposure to the impact. Then the chunk of the plane they were on skidded backward and came to rest. There was no part of the upper fuselage left. The cabin floor tilted crazily at a 45° angle. Debris was everywhere.

Connell was hanging by his seat belt, tilted toward his wife beneath him. He struggled with it, freed it, then toppled down over her, to his right. He released her seat belt. Then he helped her as they forced their way out through the debris, where the fuselage skin had once been.

He looked for the stewardess, Dorothy Warnock, who had been in the jump seat just in front of them. He could vaguely make out in the darkness that there was nothing left of the seat where she had been. The body of the aircraft seemed to have disintegrated. The galley, however, seemed to be intact, to his left. Then it struck him: the fear that someone would light a match and ignite the jet fuel, which was everywhere. His first impulse was to get his wife and run. But there was no place to go.

He helped his wife and several other passengers off the remnant of the cabin floor, and down to the thick pile of debris. Both Barry and Ann Connell had lost their shoes. One woman they helped down from the wreckage was desperately looking for her husband. He had been sitting right next to her, but now could not be seen or heard anywhere. The Connells tried to look for him, but it was hopeless in the dark, the tangled wreckage, the torn and jagged metal, and the water-covered mud beneath them. There were about eight of the survivors clustered there. Everyone was drenched in jet fuel.

In front of them, barely discernible in the glow of the Miami skyline far on the horizon, they could make out what was left of their section: a fence of grotesquely tortured steel. Two of the stewardesses were with the group. It was hard to tell which ones they were. The Connells finally recognized Dorothy Warnock, who with her colleague, tried to keep up the spirits of the group. They were giving encouragement, comforting two of the group who seemed to be injured more

than the others. They could make out another cluster of survivors on the other side of the wreckage. They, too, were standing, not daring to move, waiting. Some were screaming in pain; some were bitter and acrimonious.

One of these was Al Morris, the auto transmission dealer. He had suddenly seen the forward part of the plane folding back toward him, and the seat tops coming together like dominoes. He had squeezed out from the wreck through a crack in a door and a window. He helped several of his fellow passengers out. He could hear others all around him calling for help. He organized his small group into yelling for help in unison. Voices from another group, somewhere in the darkness, yelled back for them to shut up, that help would come. Morris cursed them and Eastern, and kept his group yelling. The two groups, in a macabre feud, kept yelling back and forth at each other in acrimony, as the moans and screams of the injured and dying swelled around them. Wandering aimlessly around them, the tiny white poodle whined and whimpered, her fur soaked in kerosene.

Sitting next to his new bride Fara, Ronald Infantino had continued to wait for the long go-around to end, when Flight 401 would come in again for its final approach. His three-week honeymoon visit to New York had been one of the highlights of his life. His studies that would prepare him for aviation administration stretched out ahead of him when he returned. Fara made this all the more meaningful. Relaxed, with his seat belt on, he suddenly found that everything went totally black. There was no sensation of impact, no sign of what was happening to Fara. He felt a strange, tumbling sensation. When he came to, he could hear screaming, everywhere around him. He found himself screaming as loudly as he could.

He was on his back in the water. A section of a seat held his head and shoulders partially above it; the rest of his body was submerged in the swamp. His seat had been stripped of its fabric; only the metal remained. He had been completely stripped of all his clothes by the force of the impact. Only the elastic from the top of his socks remained on his ankles. He

reached back and felt the upper part of his right arm. His fingers sunk deeply into a wound there. The arm seemed to be barely hanging by a thread. The pain in his right knee was excruciating. The cold on his naked body was becoming unbearable.

And Fara. Fara was nowhere to be seen or heard. He struggled to get up, to see if he could find her. But he couldn't move. In fact, he felt himself going deeper into the water, up over his chest. The bare frame of the chair was the only thing that stopped him from sliding down under the water, and drowning in less depth than that of a bathtub. The thought that Fara was somewhere near and alive kept him fighting for survival. He continued to scream, joining a chorus of others.

Just before the impact, Jerry Eskow felt a violent vibration, followed by a rasping scraping sound. The plane seemed to be splitting up in front of him.

The next thing that Eskow was conscious of was that he was strapped to his seat, which in turn was resting in the middle of a deep mudhole. There was a pile of twisted metal everywhere around him, with tall sawgrass in between. Near him, out of sight, was a woman survivor. She was screaming that she was drowning, and that she couldn't hold on much longer. Eskow was helpless to aid her. Both his pelvis and one knee was broken; he could not move. He tried to shout encouragement to the woman.

His coat and shirt were ripped off. In the coat pockets were two coveted tickets to the Orange Bowl—and the glowing letter of praise he had written to Eastern.

The moment that Bob Marquis saw the orange flash from his airboat, he knew that the airliner had gone down. He estimated that it was about five miles away. He gunned the throttle of the boat, pushed it to its top speed of forty miles an hour, and plunged through the darkness and the high sawgrass with nothing but the eight-volt frogging lamp on his head to guide him.

To his left, he could make out the blurred outline of Levee 67A, which could act as some sort of guide to the site of the ball of fire. But it was dark in that direction now; even the black column of smoke was dissipating. The Glades, difficult

enough to navigate in during the day, were twice as difficult at night.

Near the levee, he swung the roaring eighteen-foot airboat to the right, then skimmed out along, beside the levee toward the northeast. There were really no navigational guides to go by now; simply a sense of direction and a knowledge of the strange water-and-grass terrain of the Glades. He swung his head from left to right, his lamp picking a precarious path. A hidden stump, a lumpy hammock, could spin his boat out of control and catapult him into the marshes.

After running about ten minutes at top speed, he cut his 150-horsepower engine, as the airboat wallowed to a clumsy stop. There was no sign anywhere now of the brilliant orange flash he had seen. The black smoke was gone, too; not a flicker of light was to be seen—only the dim, low outline of the levee to his left. It was nothing more than a long, thin pile of dirt, some six to eight feet high, with two ruts running along the top where a jeep could precariously ride on a rough, bouncing trip.

In the silence, he stopped to listen. He could hear people in the distance. They were screaming and yelling hysterically. It was hard to tell how far they were. Perhaps a quarter of a mile, perhaps more. He was not even certain of the direction the voices were coming from. He started the engine and moved ahead toward the place where the voices seemed to be coming from. Then his boat suddenly ground to a stop. He jumped off and found that the shallow hull had jammed into some thick bushes. He tugged at the bow, then shoved the hull back in the water. He listened again. This time the voices were nearer, and he could sense their direction.

Now they were louder, and he knew they were directed at him because they must have seen the light strapped to his head. It was the only light at all in the entire area. Everything else was totally black. Before he saw anyone, his light reflected off the pieces of wreckage. The place was a shambles. Parts of the plane were everywhere. He was the only one on the scene who had not been on the plane.

He heard one scream, louder than the others, near him. He turned his head and his lamp with it, toward the sound. In the pencil of light, he saw a face. It was all that showed above the

water, like a disembodied head. It was screaming and kept dropping into the water and out again. Marquis, half in shock and hysteria himself, jumped out of the boat and sloshed through eighteen inches of water to reach the man. He was screaming that he couldn't hold his head up much longer. Marquis grabbed him, pulled him up awkwardly to a piece of wreckage, gently eased him down on it. The man looked as though both of his arms and legs were broken. Marquis felt like throwing up. He thought, "That's one there. There's got to be others around just like that."

He swept his head around as the lonely headlamp swung across the scene. There were four or five people right in front of him, strapped in their seats, tilted over into the swamp water. He rushed to them, straightening them up so they could breathe. He felt utterly lonely, helpless, frustrated. There was no one else to help, and the chorus of cries was now thunderous because his lamp was the only thing visible on the entire scene. He kept yelling back words of encouragement, telling them to calm down, to take it easy, that help was on its way.

He moved as fast as he could and concentrated on one thing: saving people from drowning in the shallow water. But some were already drowned. He began stumbling over dead bodies lying face down in the ridiculously shallow water. They had already drowned; it was too late. Some of the dead were sitting up, strapped to their seats, scattered in the sawgrass. They looked like mannequins. And many of them were naked or half-naked from the blast of the impact. At times he would see flesh a short distance away, go toward it, then find it was the stuffing of a seat cushion. He dragged the drowning up to the shallow bottom of his boat, as many as the hull would hold. But there were still more. The screams and the moanings were not stopping. They were growing louder. He looked to the skies and prayed for help. Then he turned his light back toward the people among the wreckage, on the swamp.

At the Coast Guard Air Station at the Opa-Locka Airport, the report came in from Miami Approach at approximately

56

11:45 P.M. Within seconds, the helicopter scramble alarm was sounded. Charles Cunningham, an aviation machinist, jumped out of bed and went immediately to the launching pad, where helicopters HH-52 and HH-52A were standing, along with another chopper and an amphibious aircraft. Lieutenant Mike McCormack, the duty pilot, was already in action, along with the other crewmen at the base. Lieutenant Bill Hodges, at the home of a friend, received a phone call from the duty section ten minutes later, and lost no time heading for the air station.

Mike McCormack's chopper was the first off the pad, at 11:55 P.M. He headed west, out over the Miami Lakes Country Club, and then into the thick darkness of the Glades. There were no lights visible ahead, nothing to mark the scene visually. Miami Approach had advised that Flight 401 had disappeared from the radarscope about eighteen miles west-northwest of Miami International.

There was the faint glow of starshine, but there was no moon. By 12:10 A.M., McCormack began sweeping the flat wilderness with his ''Night-Sun'' light, from a 500-foot altitude. He saw nothing at first, only the flat expanse of tall sawgrass soaking in the wide, vegetated sea of water. The Kansas plains could be no flatter. Then he saw it in the distance: the faint, flickering pinpoint of light from the frogging lamp on Bob Marquis's forehead. It was the only sign of civilization as far as the horizon stretched.

From below, Marquis saw the helicopter approaching. At last, he thought, at last. Suddenly cheers went up from the scattered clusters of passengers standing on the debris. The cheers mixed with the groans and screams of the injured and the dying. Marquis removed his lamp, waved it to the sky, as the helicopter continued to approach.

From his pilot seat in the helicopter, Lieutenant McCormack looked down. From this vantage point, the wreckage appeared to be total. The debris was peppered everywhere, reflected in the light of his ''Night-Sun.'' The pieces seemed to stretch in a swath as long as a quarter of a mile, as wide as a football field. He could make out two large pieces among the hundreds of small ones. They were the tail section and part of

the cabin where the wings had been attached. They were little more than open clam shells.

He continued to sweep with his night light. A leg or an arm would appear, sticking out of the mud, immobile. Then, near the larger sections of the plane, he saw several islands of people. They were slowly waving their arms. Cautiously he dropped the chopper to slightly below fifty feet. He orbited the scene gingerly, trying to get a total picture. Then, very carefully, he settled the helicopter lower, attempting to find a solid enough spot for landing near the wreckage.

From his airboat, Marquis watched the craft settle. Suddenly without warning, jagged pieces of metal began spewing through the air, like shrapnel. They clattered against other pieces on the ground, spun out by the rotor wash. Marquis screamed and waved the helicopter off with his lamp. McCormack pulled up fast, circled, then tried to come down again to another spot. Again the shrapnel began flying, whizzing dangerously close to Marquis and his airboat, and the survivors.

Each time McCormack tried to bring his rescue craft down, the same thing happened. He moved far off to the side. He dropped down again, this time far enough away so that the debris remained still. But directly under the landing gear was deep muck. The craft would sink into it and become helplessly mired. The best that McCormack could do under these circumstances was let one wheel barely touch the surface, and work from a tiptoe position. This would not be enough. Marquis waved the craft over toward the levee. McCormack tilted the helo, and slid across in the air to the dike, some 500 feet from the wreckage.

Marquis skimmed across the swamp in his airboat to join him. They tried to plan a rough strategy. Marquis would continue to place as many victims as possible on flat chunks of metal able to support them and give whatever aid he could. McCormack would radio for vehicles to come out on the ruts along the top of the levee, a long, grueling journey from the nearest road, six or eight miles away. Then he would seek a firm landing place as near as possible to the crash, without blowing up the shrapnel, and take on as many survivors as the

craft would hold. Slogging on foot from the levee to the crash site would be almost impossible. The water in some places was five feet deep; in others, only six inches. The footing was treacherous, especially at night.

Coming up now through the sky was HH-52A. It had just been airborne as McCormack's chopper reached the site. It arrived in the area at 12:18 A.M., forty minutes after Flight 401 had impacted. Copilot Bill Hodges, of the second craft, saw the lights of the first chopper on the levee. It was easy to spot in the blanket of total darkness around it. There was also the light of Marquis's lamp. The airboat could be made out beside the dike, where the first helo rested.

As they flew over the disaster, heading toward the levee, Bill Hodges looked down over the scattered wreckage. There could be few, if any survivors, he was thinking. In his craft were a medical corpsman and Petty Officer Don Schneck, the structural mechanic. Schneck was dropped off on the dike, near the first chopper. He was told to run over and catch the airboat out to the wreckage, 500 treacherous feet away. The corpsman would be dropped directly by helo, after a safe landing spot was located nearer the survivors.

Schneck grabbed an emergency hand radio as he jumped out and ran to the airboat. He got in with Marquis. Within seconds, the propeller roared and the boat aquaplaned back toward the scene of the crash. Schneck jumped off near the debris, near the nose section where the flight deck and hell hole were still encased in the L-1011's sheathing. He had a flashlight with him, the kind used to taxi an airplane to a ramp at night. There was a yellow wand on the end of it, and it made a small, concentrated shaft of light. He played it ahead of him as he sloshed through the water and muck, trying to avoid the deep holes. He could have used a better light, but he had asked a crewman to grab him a light before he left the air station, and this was the only one that could be found.

As he slogged toward the debris, he tried the emergency radio in his hand. Evidently someone had forgotten to tell his helo pilot that he had it, and the receiver was not turned on back in the chopper. It turned out to be useless. Schneck kept calling the helicopter as he stumbled through the mud. No

response came back. Then somewhere near him in the darkness, he heard a man's voice calling, "Coast Guard! Coast Guard!"

Schneck moved toward the voice. He found a man beside his wife. She was still in her plane seat, although it sat alone in the swamp. The man pleaded with him to help his wife. She had a deep laceration in the groin. Schneck improvised a tourniquet. He applied it immediately, and it seemed to stop the bleeding. He turned his attention to the man. He seemed all right, but began to become hysterical when he saw his wife's wound in the beam of the flashlight. Schneck tried to calm him down. Then he gave him the radio and told him to keep calling back to the helo. Schneck knew it was useless, but it would give the distracted survivor something to do.

When he had done all he could for the woman, he again began walking toward the sounds of the injured. Then he heard a woman's voice calling. It was strange, because it seemed to him that the voice was coming from up in the air, well off the ground. He called to her to keep talking, so that he could trace where she was. He finally found her. She was on a section of the fuselage that was stuck in the ground, and she was on the top of it. It was sticking up quite high in the air above him.

She did not seem to be injured. She was standing high on the wreckage, and she was scared and shaking. Schneck told her to sit down, that she was safer there than anywhere, in a high and dry place. She calmed down a little and then followed his suggestion.

Almost immediately afterward, Schneck turned to his left and came across his first body. It was a man, lying face down in the water. There was nothing Schneck could do, but it shook him up severely. There were other cries for help, however, and he kept going.

In front of him, his light picked out a large, molded section of the plane. It towered over him as he stood in the swampy water. It was pitched at an angle, and it was extremely hard for Schneck to tell what section of the plane it was. He ran his light over and up and down it. Then he recognized it as the cockpit section. It was lying like a dead beached whale.

The black snout of the radome had been knocked off. The

angle of the pitch of the nose section seemed to be about 45°, but he could not see the windshield from where he stood. He passed his flashlight along the lower side of the section. He could hear two men's voices inside, calling for help. He quickly looked for a way to get into the flight deck. He found a couple of small holes and poked his light through them. In among the smashed cockpit, he could see someone moving. Very slightly. But moving.

At this moment, he heard Adrianne Hamilton's voice. She was calling, ''Come around the other side.'' Schneck struggled through the sawgrass to get around to the sound of the voice.

Several minutes before, stewardess Adrianne Hamilton had seen the light of the airboat approaching. She continued to hear Repo and Donadeo calling for help. Adrianne moved as much as she dared and yelled to them that she saw an airboat in the vicinity. It was on its way to them, and they must relax. But it seemed to take hours to reach them. The flickering light moved and stopped, moved and stopped, as the boat approached. Now, with the light near enough for someone to hear, Adrianne called again.

The first person Don Schneck came upon when he got around to the other side of the wrecked nose of the plane was Sue Tebbs. She was lying just aft of Adrianne Hamilton. Both were in great pain. Schneck gave Sue Tebbs a superficial check and found a fracture of the lower left leg. He moved her to a piece of debris that was high and dry. Back near the cockpit, Adrianne Hamilton told him of her back. Schneck's extensive first-aid training told him that he should not move her, but there was a heavy beverage cart dangling above her. Adrianne was worried about it. Schneck checked it and satisfied himself that it was secure. He reassured her about it. Schneck was used to fueling planes, and he worried about the jet fuel. He found himself constantly checking for any smoldering fires. He thought he saw a faint glow several feet from the edge of the bulkhead. He went to it quickly, interrupting his investigation. It was under a life jacket from the plane. When he turned it over, he found a little survival light burning, not the glow of a smoldering fire. He was relieved. He brought the weak little light back to Sue Tebbs

and gave it to her to hold, a faint source of comfort in the mass of devastation.

There was other debris hanging over Adrianne, and it looked loose. He started pulling it away and throwing it into the Glades. It was a tangled jungle. He pulled as much of the loose material away as he could. It seemed to be near the bulkhead that led into the cockpit.

As Schneck pulled the last loose piece away, the top of the head and shoulders of one of the flight deck crew was revealed. It was the First Officer. Schneck checked his eyes and put his hand on the man's neck to check the neck pulse. There was nothing that could be done. He was dead.

Schneck poked his light into the flight deck area and swung it around. The crew seats were uprooted. Then the light struck another crew member. He was lying on the floor on his back. Schneck did not know whether he was alive or dead. But then he started to move a little. Schneck told Adrianne to stay where she was and then went into the cockpit.

He cleared one loose chair out of the way, and moved some more debris to get to the man, to see if he was pinned down. The uniform told him it was the captain. He had a lacerated left ear and broken ribs. His legs seemed all right. He seemed to be in shock. Then he struggled, as if he were trying to get out of the plane.

Schneck told him to stay still. "We'll be getting you out of here pretty quick," he said.

Schneck was still having trouble trying to adjust to the scene. The captain tried to move again.

"You made it this far," Schneck said. "If you can just hang in there a little bit longer, we will get you to a hospital."

Then the captain looked at Schneck and said, "I am going to die."

Schneck argued back, trying to keep him going. He told him it was important for him to stay still until help came.

Below him, in the hell hole, the voices rose again. The water was still coming up there. They were crying, "We don't want to drown."

Schneck had done all he could for the captain in the upper cockpit, if only lending moral support; he had no first aid

supplies with him. He crawled down the twisted ladder to the hell hole. Donadeo was aft, his feet propped up against a bulkhead. He told Schneck he was in pain, and Schneck did not think it was a good idea to try to move him. He loosened Donadeo's belt and tie and opened his shirt to try to make him more comfortable. Schneck checked him for fractures, but could not find any. There was a laceration on the inside of his left leg.

Just forward of Donadeo, the Second Officer seemed to be angry. Schneck took this to be a good sign. If a man is mad enough, he was thinking, he will fight whatever way he can to stay alive.

The most important thing that Schneck could do was to reassure the men they were not going to drown; the water was only a foot or so deep. He was growing more and more frustrated; there was so little he could do. Right at the moment, he wanted to prepare a way to get the men out. The ladder was in the way, and it was partially jamming Second Officer Repo under it. Schneck pulled it out and put it up in the cockpit. Then he pulled himself out of the hell hole and threw the ladder out into the Glades. He found that the hatch door that led down to the hell hole was in the way. He could not get the two men out the way it was set. He kicked at it and kept kicking until it was freed. Then he threw that over, too.

As he did so, the captain on the upper deck began moving around again, rolling over one of the fallen seats in pain. Schneck was certain that if he continued, it would cause further injuries. He put both hands firmly on the injured man's arms and held him down. Schneck spoke very forcibly, and the captain calmed down.

Schneck then went out to Adrianne Hamilton again. He asked her how many people were on the plane. When she told him there were 176, he couldn't believe it. He had seen only a handful as he approached the location. He looked out desperately to see if he could locate the medical corpsman, but he was nowhere evident. If he could at least get morphine, he thought, that would help.

With just two Coast Guardsmen, a frog hunter and 176

victims the prospect of doing much good was agonizingly slim. Next to Adrianne, he noticed that Sue Tebbs's leg had begun bleeding badly. He was cautious about using a tourniquet because his training had taught him that they should be used sparingly. But the situation called for it, and he applied it.

As he did, he saw the light of the corpsman, who had struggled through the swamp toward them. Schneck suggested morphine for the crew members in the forward compartment. When the corpsman—Charles W. Johnson, almost the same name as the Miami Approach controller—came out, he and Schneck tried to figure out what to do about getting the injured out of the flight deck section. Adrianne was unfortunately in the way of the small opening in the cockpit bulkhead, the only way they could get the men out. If they pulled the injured out through that way, they would have to take them out over her. They were uncertain what to do; they were afraid to move her. She had no feeling in her legs. Should they wait for a backboard?

Schneck went to Adrianne, put his hands under her shoulder blades, and moved her very slowly, tenderly. He assured her that if her back really hurt, he would stop. He moved his hands down toward the small of her back, and when he finally reached there, she said, "It hurts—but it is not extreme."

He picked her up gently, like a baby, and carefully put her down next to Sue Tebbs. He asked her to talk to Sue to keep her spirits up, because Sue looked very pale and he was afraid she was going into shock.

Then Schneck looked up to the sky and saw lights approaching. There were several helicopters. Army and Air Force, as well as Coast Guard. They were heading directly toward the site. Now as they began to settle, the metal didn't fly from the rotor wash. It had had time to sink into the soft mud, and at least one danger was gone. But everywhere there were bodies. It was hard to find a landing place.

On the surface, the faint lights of half a dozen airboats skimmed like waterbugs across the swamps, toward the wreckage. Some headlights could be seen in the distance, bouncing laboriously over the bumpy ruts of the long, narrow levee. But it was still black. It was still impossible to see

where the cries for help were coming from, still almost impossible to crawl toward the screams through the scattered knife-edge metals, greased with treacherous jet fuel, and the tangled sawgrass and mud.

But at last help was on the way, and Coast Guardsman Schneck didn't feel quite so lonely.

"The objective world exists. It is not an illusion. It is real not in being ultimate, but in being a form, an expression of the ultimate. To regard the world as ultimately real is delusion."

—Radhakrishnan,
*Eastern Religions and
Western Thought*

# Chapter IV

Near the Eastern ticket counter, the closed-circuit television screen that announced that flight arrivals and departures still showed Flight 401 as delayed. The same message blazed on several computerized screens throughout the Eastern section of the sprawling terminal of the airport. As it grew past the estimated time of arrival, there was some anxiety among the friends and relatives of the passengers, but it was moderate.

Didi Welch, on duty at Gate 87, was used to delays. Every airline in the business faced them daily. She waited at the gate agent's post on Concourse 9, confident that she would get some news of the L-1011's arrival at the ramp. As the minutes dragged on, she began getting inquiries. By midnight the inquiries were increasing, and she regretted that she had no direct information. She was in the dark as much as they were. As the questioners began to get more restive, she tried the tower, but was unable to get through on the phone. She did her best to placate the more insistent ones, and promised them she would give them more information the minute she had it.

Up in the tower, the scene was grim. Freed from his routine to organize the rescue efforts, Controller Johnson had notified the Coast Guard less than three minutes after the crash. The rest of the calls followed in rapid order: the 44th Aerospace Rescue and Recovery Squadron, the Dade County Public Safety Department, the Florida Highway Patrol, the Public Health Service, the Ambulance Service, the Miami Fire Department, an army reserve unit at Opa-Locka, reserve squadrons from Homestead and Patrick Air Force bases.

The rescue effort snowballed from there. A special Miami

Coast Guard coordination center took over to assemble doctors and paramedics with helicopter crews. Help was summoned from St. Petersburg, from Cape Kennedy, from all over the state. As each unit was notified, it in turn notified others. A half dozen hospitals in the area set their prepared emergency plans into motion. Strangely enough, three days before the disaster, the Palmetto Hospital in Miami had held a disaster drill. The fictional situation set up for the drill was precisely what was happening at the moment: the crash of an airliner in the Everglades.

Standing on the fractured eggshell of the forward section, Coast Guardsmen Schneck felt a psychological boost when he saw the other helicopters approaching, even though they were forced to search laboriously for places to land where there were no bodies, few fragments, and reasonably firm mud. An army helicopter approached him precariously. He watched for the shower of shrapnel from the debris first, but it failed to materialize. Then, an inch at a time, the chopper settled within thirty feet of him. He saw the figures of four men climb out from the chopper, blowing in the stiff breeze of the rotor wash. They were carrying backboards for the injured.

They took Sue Tebbs first, holding the backboard high. Another army rescuer picked up Adrianne Hamilton, as Schneck helped to slide her off the metal island where she was lying. The mud was like quicksand. The short thirty feet to the helicopter was a tangled and treacherous obstacle course. Suddenly the army man carrying Adrianne stepped into a hole. He lost his footing and began to sink. Schneck was beside him. He managed to grab Adrianne just as she started sliding into the water. He held her up and regained his footing as the army man struggled to pull himself out of the hole.

By the time Schneck got halfway to the helicopter, he thought he would collapse. He could not believe that he was exhausted so fast. On each step he would pull up his legs from the suction of the mud that gripped his every movement. He yelled to the chopper crew for a stretcher. Two of the crew

climbed off the ship, stumbling toward him with a back-board. Schneck placed Adrianne on it and went back to what was left of the cockpit.

On the way back, he stumbled into the figure of a man. He was moving around some of the bodies in the swamp, bending over them, moving them slightly. Schneck did not want anyone not qualified to move the injured, and asked him what he was doing.

"I'm a doctor," the man replied. He had arrived in the helicopter.

Schneck was relieved. "Good," Schneck told him. "There are men in the flight deck that really need help."

Schneck led the doctor through the mud, through the debris, toward the hell hole. There was still not enough light, only the flashlights that the men carried with them. The doctor made his way into the cockpit first. Schneck followed him. As the doctor was groping his way down to the hell hole, Schneck stopped to look at the captain.

"Don't worry about that man," the doctor called as he went below. "He's gone."

Schneck couldn't believe it. All the shock of the efforts he had made hit him. He had tried hard. There was so little he could do. Schneck bent down and examined the captain again. For some reason, he just couldn't believe the doctor. He looked for any of the vital signs. They weren't there. Captain Loft was dead.

But there were men below—Repo and Donadeo. More army rescuers from the helicopters had joined him now. Schneck picked the two smallest because of the tight squeeze through the hatch and the narrowness of the area where the two injured were lying below.

Two rescuers tried to lift Donadeo out first. Schneck stood above the hatch. He was forced to stand in an awkward position. Donadeo was heavy. The two army men had their hands under his arms, and lifted him to the cockpit deck. He struggled but couldn't do it.

He told the others, "Set him back down." Then he studied the situation, looking down into the hell hole. Then he said firmly to Donadeo, "You're going to have to help me get you out if you want to get out."

They tried again. Schneck leaned down and put his arms under Donadeo's armpits. Donadeo grabbed Schneck with both arms, in spite of the serious injury to his back. Somehow they got him up.

They had less trouble with Second Officer Repo, although he was obviously badly injured. Both were taken to the waiting helicopters and whisked to Hialeah Hospital. There were more choppers coming in as others left the scene with the injured. But the light was still the problem. Rescuers were still groping through the dark with only flashlights to guide them. The helicopters needed their "Night-Sun" lights for finding places to land, as first priority; later they would be used for locating the injured. The struggle to move even a few feet through the muck to a helicopter was exhausting and distressing. The closer the helicopter could get to the injured, the more help they could give. Yet the uncertain terrain foiled attempts to land close.

The choppers still could not hover directly over the wreckage. Even though the metal debris had sunk deeper into the mud, the noise and the blast of the rotor made it almost impossible to work directly under them.

After Repo and Donadeo were removed to the rescue helicopter, Schneck remembered the woman who had first called to him from the high piece of wreckage. He struggled through the swamp toward her and found that another rescuer was painfully making his way up through a forest of metal to the woman.

Everywhere he turned, he could see groups of people in the background, faintly visible in the darkness. They waved slowly, painfully, incessantly. Schneck looked for the larger pieces of metal, slogged to them, looked for people to pull free. He noticed that slowly the crew of rescue workers was growing. They seemed to be working smoothly, quietly, without a central command, but in great instinctive harmony. A game warden on the scene warned them to work in pairs.

By the time Schneck reached the tail section, one of the few recognizable sections of the plane, there were many rescuers around. It was good that there were. A man was trapped underneath the heavy section, unable to move. There was a rapid consultation. Within moments, a score or more

rescuers moved without instruction. The enormous tail was lifted; the man was pulled out.

As Schneck carried on his macabre work, Bob Marquis did likewise. Neither was aware of his growing exhaustion. Both were fighting back an inner hysteria and shock, but ignored it. There was too much to be done.

In one of the small islands of people, slowly waving their arms for help and recognition, was Stewardess Beverly Raposa. She had seen the first flickering light of Bob Marquis's airboat as it approached, at the time when there were no other lights whatever in the vicinity. The approach of the lighted pinpoint was agonizing enough in its slowness. In spite of the calls of the group for help, it stopped, moved, stopped again at a great distance from them. But it represented hope, and so did the first helicopters when they arrived.

The time between the arrival of the rescuers by swamp, by air, and by tortuous levee, and the time that the rescuers were able to get to many of the isolated groups, seemed an eternity of frustration and helplessness. Beverly Raposa, competent and conscientious, found it particularly frustrating. She wanted to help, to find others who were lost among the debris and muck. Yet every time she tried, it was futile.

A little boy was missing. She tried to get off the precarious piece of fuselage where her group was standing to look for him. She stepped off. She sank. She fell. She cut herself again. She had no flashlight, even though one was with her at the time of the crash. It was in her purse, somewhere buried in the tangled mess of the tail section.

She wondered about Stephanie Stanich, the stewardess who only moments before the crash had been sitting across the plane from her, waiting for the landing. Stephanie was nowhere to be seen; there was no sound of her voice calling for help. Beverly was deathly afraid, deeply shocked by the carnage all around her. Yet she knew she had to overcome her fears.

Her first instinct had been to yell out quickly and firmly for no one to light a match, regardless of the need for light. She was drenched in jet fuel and swamp water. So were the others. In the darkness, it was a natural impulse to seek light

of any kind. A lighted match, she was sure, would incinerate everyone. No one lit a match or a lighter.

After her abortive attempts to strike out from the metal island they were standing on, Beverly knew that something had to be done to keep up the morale of the people. It was now bitter cold. Feebly, she began to sing a Christmas song, "Frosty the Snowman." Hesitating, the others began to join in. But the words eluded them. Beverly tried another. This time they did better. "Rudolph, the Red-Nosed Reindeer" and "Jingle Bells" brought the group alive. Beverly urged them to sing as loudly as possible. They did so. When they finished their Christmas repertoire, they began over again and kept it up. In between the songs, the moans and screams were heard around them, nearby and in the distance. But there was nothing Beverly or the others could do, except wait. They watched as the helicopters and airboats and shadows of individual rescuers slowly worked thier way toward them, then moved away with other victims before reaching their location. It took until three in the morning before five nameless rescuers reached them with a medic, more than three hours after the crash. And it wasn't until that time, as Beverly was lifted off the debris, that she realized how badly her back was injured.

Stewardess Trudy Smith was also concerned about Stephanie Stanich. As her friend and often roommate on layovers, Stephanie had been the last person she talked to, before she went up to her jump seat at mid-cabin. It was hopeless, of course, to try to find her. Immediately after the crash, Trudy remembered being helped up by her jump-seat mate, Sharon Transue, who had never flown an L-1011 before, and had traded a trip assignment to get Flight 401. Both of them had hung in the air by their seat belts; both crashed down onto the wreckage when they released their buckles. Both worried about an explosion from the fuel that had flooded their clothes and the impenetrable darkness around them. Like others, Trudy didn't know the extent of her injuries then: smashed vertebrae in both the neck and lower back. Sharon was luckier; her X rays would be negative. As the rescuers began to come slowly into the scene,

they could do little more than try to remain calm in the face of the chaos all around them and help the few passengers gathered with them stay calm, too.

One of the passengers was a twelve-year-old boy trying desperately to find his father, who was nowhere to be seen or heard. The boy's hands had been singed and blistered by the brief fire that had flashed through the cabin. Trudy took off her jacket, bundled it around the boy's hands, and tried to comfort him. She had to restrain him from moving off into the dark of the swamp to look for his father.

Stewardess Pat Ghyssels was the last person that Mercedes Ruiz spoke to before the thunderous roar of the crash filled her ears. It was all Mercedes remembered of the actual crash: the noise so loud she couldn't believe it was real. She thought it was a dream. She lay on her back, and even in pain, the stars looked beautiful above the darkness of the Everglades. But she felt close to death: in fact, in her unconsciousness, she felt she had died, then crossed back to life again. But Pat Ghyssels was nowhere to be seen.

When stewardess Dorothy Warnock had heard the sickening rushing sound of the crash and felt a waterfall come over her in what seemed like slow motion, she thought the plane might have crashed in the Atlantic, perhaps on a sandbar. She thought of the life rafts, but then realized they were in mud and swamp. She was surprised at the cold; she could faintly see her breath. She found herself in the group with Barry Connell and his wife Ann, as the unexpected sound of Christmas caroling came faintly across the glades.

Their island of despair began to follow suit, singing as they tried to comfort two members who were obviously in serious pain. The woman whose husband was missing lay bleeding with a leg wound. Barry Connell took off his coat and covered her with it. Only the distant glow from the Miami skyline gave them enough light to make out the shadows of people close in the group.

The first sound of Bob Marquis's lonely airboat brought hope and encouragement. And when the helicopters began passing overhead, with their "Night-Sun" lights, there were brief flashes of illumination that helped them to try to find the missing husband of the woman who had been sitting with

74

him, one row behind the Connells, only minutes before. Three and a half hours later, the rescuers reached them. In the helicopter, they were flown to the Hialeah Racetrack, where police cars were waiting to take them to the hospital. The woman's husband had not been found.

The same story was repeated throughout the jungle of jagged fragments and matted sawgrass. When the rescuers reached Jerry Escow, the transportation executive, he knew he was injured, but not the extent, which included broken knees, wrist, and pelvis. Near him he could hear a woman calling out that she was going to drown if help didn't come soon. She must be close, Escow was thinking, because of the nearness of her voice. Yet he could not move and lay helpless himself.

It seemed hours before a group of rescuers reached his side. He immediately told them to go to the woman, who needed help more than he did. They did so. But they failed to return right away, and he lay in despair of their ever coming back. As he lay there, he thought: If I ever survive this, I'll be born again. They did return, and he survived.

Lying in the water, his naked body chilled in the coldness of the Everglades, Ronald Infantino continued calling for his wife Fara. There was no sound in return. He could not stop screaming. Out of the darkness, a woman stumbled by. She was searching frantically for her husband. She saw that Infantino was shivering. Holding back sobs, she took off her jacket and placed it over his chest. Then she disappeared as quickly as she had come into view.

Then he saw it: the wavering light of a flashlight coming toward him. It got closer, closer, and finally came down near his face. But he still couldn't stop screaming. All around him, others were screaming, too. Even when he reached the hospital, where the doctors began piecing his dangling right arm together, his screams went on. And always he carried the thought that Fara must be alive.

Al Morris, still bitter and resentful under the terrible trauma of the crash, finally saw a helicopter land not more than a couple of hundred feet away from him. In moments, a man struggled to reach his side. The man took off his coat and put it over one of the survivors near Morris, then turned to him.

Morris recognized him immediately. It was former astronaut Frank Borman, recently appointed one of the vice-presidents of Eastern. Borman assured him he would do everything possible to help. Morris's resentment faded quickly.

As Borman stood there, Coast Guardsman Cunningham's chopper finally found a safe landing place nearer the wreckage. Borman sloshed quickly over to it, then led Cunningham, the co-pilot and a corpsman to the group where Morris was huddled.

They squeezed as many of the injured as they dared into the chopper. There was the boy with the burned hands, still crying out for his father. There was a year-old baby. There were six altogether; old and young, frightened and injured, cold and soaked. As the craft readied itself for takeoff, Cunningham dropped four personal survival arc strobe lights in the landing zone, so they could find it again when they returned to rescue others.

The loaded helicopter rose, banked, and skimmed back across the Everglades toward Miami. It was back almost immediately after discharging the survivors at Hialeah Racetrack. The strobe lights made it easier to land. Within moments, the helicopter had taken off again with a load of ten more survivors.

The informal rule set up by the FAA was to leave the dead, search for the living, and get them out as soon as possible. There was nothing that could be done about the dead that night. As the night wore on, the Coast Guard automatically slid into the role of coordinator for the giant rescue effort. But all the others played key parts in what turned out to be an amazingly smooth effort of men and equipment, working together with almost impossible communications between civil and military units. Slogging through the swamp to the victims and carrying them to the rescue craft became murderously exhausting to the rescuers. Carrying a victim for just twenty feet could take five or ten minutes, as rescuers sank into the water and mire, and tried to keep the victims from sinking into the water with them. Every step was treacherous. Fractured, jagged metal was everywhere, gouging both rescuer and victim alike. Finally an idea was developed. A human chain was formed, like a bucket brigade, stretching

several hundred feet from the crash site to the levee. Victims were passed from arms to arms along the human chain. It was painful to the injured, but better than falling into the swamps and water with an intended rescuer, who could be hopelessly bogged down himself.

Dr. Jim Hirschman, the Rescue Medical Advisor for the city of Miami, was dropped at the scene of the carnage by a Coast Guard helicopter the moment he could get out there. The communications were bad, but the work of the rescue workers was prodigious. Hirschman found that the walkie-talkies brought to the site by some of his team were inaudible at the Miami base stations. He found that it was almost impossible to communicate with his associates at the scene. By necessity and instinct, the men were working in groups of twos or threes, searching for the living, carrying equipment, setting up bases for field stations with access to airboats and helicopters.

Hirschman was separated from a fellow doctor and several of his paramedics almost immediately, and they never did get back together. But they worked in conjunction with the army, Air Force, and Coast Guard helicopter crews, which were constantly taking off and landing, and finally being able to set up gasoline-powered generators for lighting the scene.

With radio communications faulty, it was necessary for the rescuers to wallow through the mud to get to either a helicopter or survivor. The effort was wasteful and costly. A command post was needed. But even without it, the coordination was incredible.

For every organization involved, the first priority was rescue. Eastern Vice-President Frank Borman was an early arrival at the site, wearing a jump suit reminiscent of his days as an astronaut. At the same time, Eastern officials were setting up a method of notifying the bereaved whose families and friends had gone down in the Everglades.

It was a clumsy start, springing from the enormity of the tragedy and the urgency of immediate rescue work.

The breaking of the news to the people waiting at the concourse gate was an urgent priority, too, but a difficult one. Preparations had to be made to prevent utter chaos. Quickly,

a medical team of Eastern doctors was contacted to report immediately to the Ionosphere Lounge, the VIP room, which would be set up as the central point for reporting on the survivors and the dead. Special phones were set up. Eastern personnel from customer assistance, sales, ramp agents and other departments were called in to man the phones and try to ease the pain of the bereaved.

It was a complex job and it took time. The preoccupation with the planning meant a delay for the Eastern officials to send a contingent down to the concourse where Didi Welch was alone at the desk, still unaware of what had happened. In the attempt to plan an organized method, there was a delay of almost an hour before key officials were able to formulate a viable plan, and make the necessary decisions to go ahead with it.

It took considerable time to confirm conclusively that Flight 401 actually had gone down. It took more time to confirm its exact location. Eastern officials realized that false news of a crash—if it hadn't occurred—would create as much havoc as the actual news of the crash. They had to be absolutely sure of their facts before the announcement was made at the waiting gate on the concourse. Didi Welch was contacted and told that the flight was still on a holding pattern, in order to buy time to make these confirmations. They also did not want Didi alone at the gate to make the official announcement to the waiting group.

In the confusion, Didi was all but forgotten, but the pressure on her for more news was becoming unbearable. Her desk on the ramp was surrounded by nearly a hundred people, each of them wanting to know why the plane was supposed to be still in a holding pattern and when the flight was going to arrive at the gate. By now, it was nearly an hour past the announced arrival time.

Didi Welch, at the focal point of the whole tragedy, knew less than the man on the street at that time, because the news was already out on the radio with the first, sketchy report that Flight 401 had crashed. Didi and the friends and relatives crowded around her didn't know this, but she did know that she had to get more information and get it quickly.

She picked up her phone and called Jim Dunn, a friend of

hers in crew scheduling. Jim was working late at his desk. Just moments before, a friend of his in crew scheduling had burst into the office to say that 401 had gone down.

"Jim," Didi said on the phone, "I'm down at the ramp, and I can't get anybody on the phone who can tell me when 401 is going to get in."

Jim was startled, because he had just heard the news. "You mean they haven't told you?"

"Told me what?"

"That 401 is down. Crashed in the Everglades."

"Good God, no," Didi said.

"Call the tower and say you know. I'll be right down," Jim said. Then he picked up the phone and called the tower. "Did you know Didi is all alone down there?" he said.

Walking down the long concourse toward Gate 87, Jim could see the crowd milling around the ramp agent's desk in the distance. Didi was hidden by them. They were quiet and orderly, but obviously pressuring for news. The closed-circuit TV screens still blazed in their green phosphorescent letters that 401 was delayed.

As he approached the gate, a man was standing by a pay phone in the corridor. He suddenly dropped the phone. It dangled, swinging on its cord, against the wall. The man rushed toward the crowd at Didi's desk.

As he did, he was screaming, "You've been lying! You've been lying! The flight has crashed in the Everglades! My wife just heard it on TV!"

The man dropped on his knees to the floor and grabbed his head.

Jim Dunn saw the crowd freeze for a fraction of a second. It was almost a tableau. Then it was as if somebody pulled a switch, as if an electric shock had suddenly gone through a fishbowl.

There were screams as everyone seemed to go crazy at that one single moment. They dropped and rolled on the floor. They bounced themselves off the walls. They lay on the floor in total hysteria, screaming, crying, sobbing. It was as if they were in the crash itself. Alone behind the ramp agent's desk, Didi, was dazed and stunned by the suddenness of the impact.

A team of over a dozen Eastern representatives entered the scene just at that moment, relieving Didi Welch of her loneliness, and trying to comfort and console the unconsolable. Gently, sympathetically, they began to guide the people down to Concourse 2, toward the Ionosphere Lounge, where the doctors and nurses were already waiting and a central information phone had been set up.

In the lounge, Sadie Messina's anxiety was reaching the breaking point, from the moment she had heard, back at the gate, the familiar family whistle her husband always sounded when he came home from work. And yet there was hope. Her husband Rosario's name was not on the passenger list, when it was finally prepared and posted. Eastern officials helped her phone the Eastern counter at Kennedy, to see if he had missed the plane and was waiting there. There was no response to the paging. Then they checked every other airline flying from New York to the Florida area. His name was not on any list. She clung to the hope that he had taken another flight, gripped a cup of coffee tightly, and waited.

While the initial total burst of frenzy had died down, replaced by the tension of waiting, sounds of hysterical crying would rise and fall in various parts of the room. Some fainted, some half-collapsed. Officials would guide the worst of these to the Braniff VIP lounge, where the Eastern doctors and nurses could work with less distraction. There was no airline rivalry now. Braniff, Delta, National, United, all the others offered any help they could give.

Joan, the wife of Jerry Eskow, waited, and prayed. Finally the first list of survivors arrived from the command post. Eastern executives were making up a list as to who was waiting for each particular passenger. A voice from the lounge desk came over the speaker:

"May we have your attention," it said. "We will announce the names and location of those survivors as they come in. Eastern representatives will assist in any way possible to arrange for friends and relatives to go immediately to whichever hospital is involved."

As the names of the first survivors were called out, there were shrieks of joy from isolated parts of the room, then a sudden dash for the door, to find whatever hospital was

involved. When the name of Jerry Eskow was announced as being taken to the Hollywood Hospital, north of Miami, Joan Eskow collapsed.

Others were not so lucky. Sadie Messina waited as list after list of survivors came in. Rosario's name was not among them, and he was, it turned out, a passenger on the flight. Nor was the name of Fara Infantino announced, although her husband Ronald would not know that for many hours. He was undergoing hours of intensive surgery at the Hialeah Hospital, where the thought that Fara was still alive kept his hopes and courage up. The wound in his arm was deep, and the doctors worried about this, as they did about the deep wounds of others. Such an injury provided a fertile ground for the possibility of gas gangrene. This complication was dreaded, as bacteria would ferment the sugars in the tissues to create a gas which then would spread rapidly through other tissues. The major treatment to stop it was the removal of the limb or all the tissue involved—sometimes a hopeless situation.

Victims poured into the hospitals, as the helicopters flew them in from the Everglades wilderness. Emergency staffs were waiting and handled the flow with amazing smoothness under the pressure of the situation. Under the direction of Dr. Richard English, the work of the Palmetto Hospital was unusually smooth, because of the recent disaster drill held there only days before.

The victims were bloody, dirty, and grimy, soaked with the kerosenelike fuel of the jet aircraft and the Everglades muck. Clothing was in shreds, and many were totally naked from the wind blast, which would strip clothes, shoes, watches, and jewelry on the impact. The survivor list grew, but not fast enough. It became slowly apparent that there were more dead than living. The first lists that were compiled showed only a dozen survivors at Mercy Hospital and about a score at Palmetto Hospital, out of the 176 total on the plane. There were other hospitals yet to be heard from, but no one knew how many names would appear on the ''Missing or Presumed Dead'' list.

The list of the presumed-dead was not yet confirmed; it could be assumed only by the absence of the names from the hospital lists. In the Everglades, only the living were being

evacuated. The dead were being left where they were until daylight made it possible to find the bodies and bring them out. At the site, Bob Marquis continued to help find the living and bring them to the helicopters or the ambulances on the levee. He had no idea how long he was working, nor did he feel any real exhaustion.

It slowly became evident that there were no more cries and screams for help from any part of the scattered debris. All that was left were the silent and the dead. Making a final round in his airboat, Bob Marquis looked up at the sky. The first streaks of dawn were showing over the edge of the flat, wet prairie of the Everglades. Marquis turned his boat toward the Tamiami Trail, zigzagged through the twisting, matted saw-grass trail and reached the sandy ramp where his car and trailer waited. He loaded the airboat on the trailer, and drove toward Miami, toward home. At the same time, Coast Guardsman Schneck was satisfied, along with the rest of the army of rescue workers, that there were no more living left to evacuate. He didn't look at his watch. He, too, looked up at the sky and saw the sun coming up. He could leave the site now, but the scenes that had happened that night would never leave him.

In the growing daylight, fresh workers arrived at the Glades to look for the bodies, tag them, and slide them into heavy black plastic zippered bags. The list of confirmed dead began to grow, slowly at first, then at greater tempo as the sun climbed higher in the sky on Saturday morning. The bodies were numbered, and whatever there was in the way of clothing and identification were slid into the bags with them. Helicopters continued to settle and rise, bringing the bodies to ambulances and hearses, which in turn took them to the county morgue at Jackson Memorial Hospital. The morgue was not very large, hardly enough to hold more than a score of bodies. Large refrigerated trailer trucks were rented and rolled into place in the hospital parking lot. Families and friends were urged not to come there until they were notified.

They came anyway, wanting to make sure that the final waiting was over. Some had to be restrained from trying to enter the trucks, where fingerprinting and attempts at identifi-

cation were being made by county officials and FBI specialists.

The news of the crash of Flight 401 hit Doris Elliott and her crew mates the moment they stepped off Flight 477 at Fort Lauderdale, en route to Miami. Doris had all but forgotten her strange but intense premonition that an L-1011 was going to crash in the Everglades during the holiday season. She was stunned. The memory of her tragic forecast flooded back to her. When she got home, she woke her roommate.

"Do you remember what I told you two weeks ago?" she said.

"God, Doris, I remember it like yesterday."

"Almost the exact time and place," Doris said.

"Two other girls were there with us when you said it."

Doris sat up, and dropped her head in her hands. "I wish I hadn't seen that in my mind. I wish I hadn't *mentioned* it!"

"It's not your fault," her roommate said. "You can't take on the guilt for it."

"I know," Doris said. "But I'm sick. I'm absolutely sick."

"We almost were on the flight ourselves—before they rescheduled us."

"I knew that was going to happen, too," Doris said. "I knew it was going to be close. Remember?"

"I remember."

"You know something?" Doris said. "I wish I wouldn't get these pictures in my mind."

But Doris Elliott's vivid premonition, confirmed by three other flight attendants, was only one of many stranger events that followed in the wake of the tragic Flight 401.

"Death opens unknown doors."
                                        —John Masefield

# Chapter V

The rising of the sun on Saturday morning had unveiled the full horror of the scene. Ripped and pulverized metal sprawled for a third of a mile from where the left-hand wingtip slashed the swamp. Only two small pieces of metal marked that point. Then three giant swaths followed fifty feet away, as if a three-bladed plow had gouged the soft mud and sawgrass, forming three canals. At the end of the canals were the first fragments of small engine parts, and an oil cooler. Beyond that was an engine-mount frame, part of the port engine fan case, and an oil scavenge filter. Two football fields away from the point of impact was a section of the left-hand wing and the port engine itself. And beyond that was the piece of wreckage that had demanded so much attention from the crew the night before: the nose landing-gear strut assembly, lying alone like a dismembered claw of an eagle.

The more intact structures were far from the point of impact. Twelve hundred feet away was the large eggshell that once had been the midship cabin, over the right-hand wing. Beyond that was the forward fuselage and the flight deck, where Coast Guardsman Schneck had worked so feverishly to save lives in the cockpit and hellhole. Nearby was the empennage, the tail section, remarkably intact in contrast to the rest of the plane. There was also another large fragment, the fuselage housing the galley area, a wide and spacious compartment beneath the main cabin, served by two narrow elevators and lined with handsome stainless-steel ovens. The scattered wreckage stretched for exactly 1,600 feet from where the wing first touched.

The daylight also revealed the character of the desolate

terrain. The pools of water, for the most part half a foot to three feet in depth, were not isolated pools, even though they looked that way. They were part of the continuous river that makes up the Everglades, almost as wide as the entire state of Florida. It could be called neither land nor water. The sawgrass was an intruder in the river, as well as the metal and jet fuel sprayed across it near Levee 67A.

In among this were the bodies of the dead, many of them ripped with strange, long slashes. Later it was discovered that these ribbonlike wounds were caused by the edges of the sawgrass. The removal of the dead was slow. The identification of the bodies, many of them without clothing and identification, was slower. The major investigation effort at the site by the National Transportation Safety Board staff would have to wait until all the dead had been removed.

Meantime, the grim statistics were reaching a stabilization point, but the figures still fluctuated because of the difficulty in identifying the dead, and because of duplicated counting in some cases. The first basic summary showed incorrectly that 80 had incredibly survived the crash and 97 were dead. By late Saturday, the count had shifted. Only 77 survivors could be accounted for; 28 of these were in serious condition. The rest ranged from fair to good.

There were horror stories behind these numbers. A driver of a panel truck gagging and sickened by his cargo: a van full of severed arms and legs. An undertaker, preparing the body of a pregnant woman, the fetus pushed far up into the chest cavity, a sight he in all his experience had never seen and could hardly bear. The body of a child, covered with mud, beside a doll in the Everglades swamp.

There were ugly stories, too. The body of an attractive girl, who turned out not to be a girl, but a transvestite. A husband traveling under an assumed name with his mistress. The looting of bodies and an erroneous report that the crime was done by some of the Miccosukee tribe of the Seminole Indians who live in the area. The report was quickly withdrawn by the perpetrator of the story.

This tribe, which can live, if needed, by hunting for the deer, the turtle, the frog, fortified by figs, avocado, wild grapes and plums, has rigid taboos about stealing and a

deep-abiding respect for the spirits of the deceased. They bury their dead in watery mounds and embrace a belief in the inevitable. They believe strongly in the Great Spirit. Their morals are higher than the white man. And in the mystical ambiance of the Everglades, they frequently report the sighting of ghosts.

They fear above all death by hanging, since they feel it will imprison the soul in the body forever. Otherwise the spirit leaves through the mouth and is free to continue its existence. So intense was the belief in all that had to do with the dead, that the Miccosukee tribe explained that their school-house could not be used to lay out the dead from Flight 401 because they would have to burn it afterward. Yet they helped in the rescue work without stint.

These feelings, this mood, these mores hang over the atmosphere of the Everglades, where the Indian legends merge with the roar of jets. The events that were to follow later in the tragedy of Flight 401 were to blend the ancient with the modern jet age in a pervading and inexplicable way.

But the dominant question the day after the crash was *why* the tragedy took place at all. Investigators of the National Transportation Safety Board—the NTSB as it is known—began their off-site part of the intensive probe even before all the bodies had been cleared from the wreckage. At that time they knew little of the details of what had happened inside the cockpit just before the crash. The information was fragmentary. The scene was one of disjointed confusion.

At the start of the investigation, they knew simply that Flight 401 had disappeared from the traffic controller's radar screen at almost exactly 11:42 P.M.; that weather conditions and visibility were excellent; that it was the first fatal accident involving the new wide-body jumbo jets. It also carried the potential of matching the record for the worst single aircraft crash in history, with its total of 176 passengers aboard. Exactly that number had been killed when a Soviet jet exploded on crashing near the Moscow airport. The fact that there miraculously were many survivors of Flight 401 saved it from equaling that grisly record.

But the event did mark the first fatalities among the jumbojet series. Up to this date, none had been recorded involving

the Douglas DC-10, the Boeing 747, or the Lockheed L-1011. All of the craft in this series had won great respect from crew members. Except for minor bugs, the L-1011 was regarded as a masterpiece of modern engineering.

The investigation of the causes would pose massive problems and require careful analysis. There would be an exact history of the flight to re-create, a study of injuries to be compiled, a long look at the survival aspects, an assemblage of many of the critical parts of the plane, a thorough review of the flight recording instruments and the tape recordings of the conversation inside the cockpit, as well as the dialogue with the approach control tower.

All of this would take time, skill, and exactitude on the part of the NTSB's bureaus of aviation safety and technology. They would be searching not only for the reason for the L-1011's crash, but for what could be learned in the way of future safety.

The focus of the investigation would center on what was called the digital flight data recorder system, a new system that would print out extensive information about the history of the flight. This, together with the Fairchild cockpit voice recorder, would give a picture of what had happened from the technical point of view with unprecedented accuracy.

The technical crew of the NTSB retrieved the shockproof instrument box and tapes that would help unravel the mystery. It was intact in the tail section, as was other elaborate electronic gear which seemed basically undamaged. Then they set about the painstaking job of bringing major pieces of the plane out of the swamp and over to the Opa-Locka air base. Here parts of the plane would be reassembled in order to reconstruct a partial mockup. As this was being carried out, a committee called the Human Factors Group would try to trace what happened to both crew and passengers in the accident and what they had observed. They would have their hands full.

There was the painful job of interviewing survivors, even those who lay in pain on their hospital beds. There would be many questions to be answered from the point of view of future air safety. What section of the plane were most of the survivors in? Were the seat belts effective, even in the face of

the tremendous impact of the crash? Were the seats themselves some protection? Did the fuselage and frame of the plane protect some from injury? What injuries were most prevalent? Could there be more survivors if certain changes were made in the design of the plane? What was the seating pattern? What did passengers and crews notice just before the impact that would give a clue to the reason for the crash?

Miraculously, the prognosis for most of the survivors was reasonably good. Stewardess Mercedes Ruiz was interviewed on her hospital bed, her scalp badly lacerated and her pelvis broken. She would recover and return to flying. The same was true of most of the other flight attendants. Adrianne Hamilton, Sue Tebbs, Pat Georgia, Trudy Smith, Sharon Transue, Dorothy Warnock, Beverly Raposa all suffered badly—but would recover in varying degrees as time wore on. In spite of their pain and discomfort, they patiently answered the questions brought to them by the investigators. But none were able to trace the cause of the crash. The consensus of their recollection was the suddenness, the unexpectedness, the shock of the impact coming without warning of any kind.

But two of the flight attendant team would never join with them again. The body of Stephanie Stanich, who had sat just a few feet away from Beverly Raposa in the tail section of the plane, was found strapped in her jump seat, a considerable distance away from the wreckage. There had been hope that she would be found alive because some thought they had seen her walking away from the site in a daze, but the hope was tragically unfounded. Pat Ghyssels had sat just forward of her, on the port side of the plane, opposite Mercedes Ruiz. She, too, had died, adding to the agonizing grief of her injured crew mates. But in spite of their own personal recognition of this, the investigators would have to press on.

The flight crew, of course, held the key to the exact cause of the crash. But here the investigators would be stymied. Captain Loft and First Officer Stockstill were dead. Second Officer Repo lay on his hospital bed, hovering on the edge of death and unable to speak coherently. His prognosis was not good. The outlook for technical specialist Angelo Donadeo

was better, although he was in great pain and under heavy sedation.

The basically known facts immediately after the crash were flimsy. There had been a problem with the landing-gear warning light. The plane had circled to check it out. It was preparing to come back in for a normal landing, since the problem with the landing gear seemed to be resolved.

The ground controllers stated that there was no concrete warning of an impending crash, aside from what appeared to be a false radar reading. The crew of Flight 401 showed no evidence of any special difficulty or alarm. The final message to the tower from the crew was that they were turning left to a heading of 180°.

Although he had blacked out immediately on impact, Angelo Donadeo struggled to recall for the NTSB investigators those final moments in the cockpit and hell hole. He remembered the problems with the warning-light bulb and assembly, the frustrations of Loft and Stockstill as they tried to take out the unit and put it back in. He recalled many other details. But because there was no indication of an emergency up to the last fraction of a second, there was little of importance to attach to the details at the time. The entire accident had happened almost totally without warning, even to the flight crew. For those who died or those who survived, there was a sudden moment of truth, with less warning than that given a drowning man who sees his death suddenly impending with blazing clarity.

Technical specialist Donadeo recalled the calmness in the cockpit during the last moments of the flight, punctuated only by irritation at the stubborn warning light.

"As I can recall," Donadeo told the investigators, "the light assembly had been removed, and I don't recall who removed it. When I had turned around, I noticed that the Second Officer had the light assembly in his hand. He had snapped the cover open, examined something, resnapped the cover shut, and I had turned around and looked in some other area, and I don't recall who actually reinstalled the light assembly."

After the crash, the assembly was found inserted in its

housing at a 90° angle from its proper insertion. The fact that the assembly would not snap back in properly had irked and distracted Captain Loft and First Officer Stockstill. Minor as this was, it could add to the other distractions which in turn could have drawn attention of the crew, at the expense of not noticing that anything was going wrong with the flight.

There was still more distraction affecting Captain Loft and First Officer Stockstill when Second Officer Repo reported from the hell hole that it was impossible to see the red lines that had to match up on the nose gear to visually indicate that it was down and locked. This added another delay as the plane circled, getting ready to come back into the landing pattern.

Angelo Donadeo also reported that there were problems of hearing in the cockpit, probably the essential reason for none of the crew's being aware of the warning chime that indicated they were starting to lose altitude. "I had an air vent alongside me," Donadeo said to the Safety Board probers, "and I had to strain in order to hear."

Donadeo, who was the only person who had been on the flight deck who was still able to talk, had another key recollection, which involved the automatic pilot. He helped search for a clue as to what happened that might possibly have knocked the automatic pilot out of kilter. Not generally known at the time was that only a very slight pressure was needed to disengage this automatic control, which in turn could start a totally unexpected descent. What actions the pilot or copilot took during the time Flight 401 stayed in a holding pattern were critical, down to the smallest detail.

First Officer Stockstill, the copilot, had been forced into an awkward situation. He was in charge of flying the plane, but at the same time, he was the only one near enough to the stubborn warning light to do anything about it. Captain Loft was freer to maneuver, but he was in an awkward position, too. He could barely reach the troublesome light. Donadeo, sitting behind him in the jump seat, had noticed Stockstill's left hand on the light assembly panel, with Loft trying to help him. Did Loft jolt the steering column or accidentally change the throttle setting?

"The captain had either released or removed his seat belt—I couldn't see," Donadeo said, "and then reached across the pedestal, and was trying to assist the First Officer with the installation of the light assembly, or remove it, I don't know which. He was forward of the throttles. His left arm was over the top of the glare shield, and he was leaning across with his right arm forward of the throttles."

Perhaps here was the key to the mystery. What seemed to add up was a combination of circumstances imposing themselves on a crew trying calmly and diligently to solve the problem at hand. But there was not enough evidence to tell. The only other possible source of direct information was Second Officer Repo, the flight engineer. But Repo was in critical condition on his hospital bed, barely coherent, and barely able to talk to his family. Repo, with his robust sense of humor and intense love for the planes he flew, could therefore not offer any solution to the cause. The medical outlook was not good. He lingered some thirty hours after the crash; and finally died of multiple injuries early Sunday morning. He was the last of the assigned flight crew to die. Of the others, only Captain Loft had clung precariously to an hour or so of life before he succumbed in the cockpit. Nothing in their last communication to the tower indicated they expected anything disastrous at all. Only the stunning impact of the crash could have let them know it had happened.

The same was true of the passengers. The investigation would turn to them for any possible enlightenment, but there could be little hope for any. Al Morris, who was to live in spite of a broken rib cage, could only recall the seats coming toward him, and how his frustrated anger at Eastern was tempered by the appearance of Frank Borman in the middle of the Everglades. He was to recover. Ironically, he had been one of the passengers who had switched to Flight 401 from another reservation. His wife did not know until four in the morning that he was in the crash.

Jerry Eskow, whose letter of praise never reached Eastern, remembers only the crash and the debris and the fact that he felt born again. He would recover slowly and painfully from his multiple fractures and lacerations and donate over $1,000

to the Miami hospital that helped him toward recovery. His wife had taken a plane the night before, and she, perhaps, might not have been so lucky.

Barry and Ann Connell would be eternally grateful. They, too, had been scheduled for a different flight. In addition, they almost missed Flight 401 entirely. Beyond that, they were offered seats in the first-class section, where very few passengers survived; but they refused the offer. They lived, and their injuries were light. The outcome buttressed their abiding faith in God.

Ronald Infantino suffered not only the loss of his bride Fara, but an agonizing recovery period. When gas gangrene set in, he was flown to a special hospital in Panama for high-pressure oxygen treatment. This deadly infection can develop when the organisms of the *Clostridium* family which live without oxygen produce toxins in dead tissue. The toxins kill the muscle fibers around them, and more dead tissue is created. The invasion goes on as the tissues ferment to make the bubbles of gas that give the dreaded disease its name.

Infantino survived miraculously. He recovered slowly. He still had no feeling in his right hand, and his legs gave him trouble. The accident affected his whole life and philosophy. The nurse who took care of him in the long recovery program over many months inspired him with a fresh belief in God, a belief so deep that it permeated his life. He went on from his studies in aviation administration to start his own successful commuter airline. Its symbol is a cross. His religion was superficial before; but it is deep now. Eventually he remarried the nurse who helped him back to health and introduced him to a new concept of Christianity.

The fate of the passengers marked the fragility of life and the ironic twists that affected their individual destinies. The question of why some were killed and some survived would never be answered. Yet there were clues hidden in the pattern of death, injury, and survival that might have realistic bearing on what future aircraft design could be developed to ameliorate or soften the tragic losses.

As chairman of the Human Factors Group, Gerry Walhout directed the intensive study of the results of the crash, its

detailed effects on passengers and crew, and the factors that affected the outcome. The analysis was cold and detached. It would never reflect the sorrow, the grief, the pain, or even the joy of survival.

The final figures were cold, shocking—but also perplexing that so many survived in a plane that was almost totally destroyed. Some sections—like the cockpit area and galley—remained relatively intact. In these, nonstructural equipment like electronic equipment, oven units from the galley—even the galley elevators—was salvageable. In fact, some of this costly equipment was still in usable condition.

In the final figures, a total of 99 of those aboard the plane were killed. There were 77 survivors. Of these, 60 cases were serious; 17 had minor injuries, or none. The soft mud and waters of the Everglades were credited for the reasonably high survival rate and for the prevention of fire breaking out in full force, beyond the initial flash as the fuel vapors ignited.

For those who did survive, this lack of fire was merciful; but it could not prevent the injuries. The most prevalent of these were leg and rib fractures. There were also spine and pelvis fractures and some burns during the brief flash fire. The fatalities were found to be most frequently the result of flailed chests, and blunt impact injuries.

Walhout's investigating team determined where the surviving and deceased passengers had been seated in the airplane, in the hope that the survival aspect could be traced and accounted for. Over forty passengers and flight attendants were interviewed and traced to the exact seat they were sitting in at the moment of impact.

A random checkerboard pattern emerged on the seating diagram that revealed a fateful tapestry governed more by destiny than design. In Row 15, six had survived, sitting side by side across the beam of the plane; two had survived unhurt on the right. In Row 18, the passenger in seat E was killed; his seat mate in seat F survived. In Row 33, everyone was killed. Many who lived stayed strapped to their seats; but the same was true of many who died.

Each passenger seemed to notice something different

about the crash. The passenger in 7-C felt the plane nose up and heard a roar of the engines just before the impact, as did several others. In 15-H, the passenger felt the airplane shaking violently, and coming apart. Then he noticed his seat partner seemingly on the ceiling. Not everyone remembered the flash of fire.

The strength of the seat belts, the sturdiness of the seats and of the body structure of the giant plane were credited for saving many lives. The safety board has several guidelines that determine survivability in an accident. These include a relatively intact environment for the occupants, crash forces which do not exceed the limits of human tolerance, adequate occupant restraints, and sufficient escape provisions. Under these qualifications, the accident could not be classed in the "survivable" category. Yet 77 still lived.

The seats were of a new design. Energy absorbers in the support structure cushioned the forces of the crash. Each of the seats that was bolted to a platform and attached to the basic skeleton of the plane stayed together. Where it didn't, many passengers survived because they were thrown clear of the wreckage at reduced velocities.

The checkerboard pattern that emerged on the diagram was hard to fathom. Aside from these conclusions, it could not explain why many had died at this moment, and some had not. In a fraction of a second, the lives of 176 persons were shockingly changed; some to die, some to gain a new faith in God, some to suffer the rest of their lives.

The damage, of course, was more than physical. Nightmares plagued a great number of survivors. They were vivid, real, and persistent in almost three-dimensional clarity. And although the crash was over in a single excruciating moment, it continued to live, as if it were real, on the screens of the minds of dozens who were on the flight. They were more than dreams. "They were as if I were reliving the scene in total," was one report. "It was not a recollection. I was there again. The scenes were as real as concrete."

The Human Factors Group was not assigned or equipped to move into the area, yet it was one of the most important aftermaths of the crash. If thoughts and dreams were as real

as concrete, wouldn't this forever haunt the mind and uncon-scious of living victims and those whom they loved? What urge was it that kept the spirit of all those passengers and crew members who survived on the edge of being indomit-able?

Some mentioned that they felt that they had died, and then returned to life. Recent studies by serious scientists such as Dr. Elizabeth Kubler-Ross and Dr. Raymond Moody have shown that patients whose vital life signs have stopped, and who later recover, report vivid experiences where they have been greeted by friends and relatives who have died before them. For the first time, science is taking seriously the possibility that we live after death.

Dr. Kubler-Ross and Dr. Moody are not the only scientists involved with the serious study of whether we live after death. Dr. Ian Stevenson, of the University of Virginia Medi-cal School has conducted extensive laboratory experiments with mediums and in the field of reincarnation with limited but interesting results. Dr. Karlos Osis, of the American Society for Psychical Research has completed an elaborate study entitled *Deathbed Observations by Physicians and Nurses* in 1961, which closely paralleled the more recent studies.

They deal with the subject rationally and cautiously, but bring a fresh, modern viewpoint to an area neglected by science for such a long time. Because they indicate hope instead of gloom, they represent a more enlightened view of a subject that is usually looked at with fear. The fact that three separate scientific studies indicate that comfort, not fear, is the dominant emotion in most dying persons can bring solace to those who have suffered the loss of loved ones.

There were other inexplicable events following in the wake of the crash. Sadie Messina, who had stood by the gate waiting for the flight her husband was on, not only heard the familiar family whistle alone that night. Her two sons who were with her heard it, shortly after 11:30 P.M., at a moment that could have marked the time of impact, or close to it.

Hers was a close knit family. She was devoted to her

husband Rosario. "We were so very, very close—closer than two people could ever be. The whole family—my two sons, Rosario and me. I loved him and he loved me more than two people could ever love."

The premonition she felt before the flight, before Rosario's trip to New York, was not based on her own instinct alone. Rosario had told her with sad conviction some time before that: "Sadie, I'm going to die. I'm going to die young, and I don't want to leave you."

Sadie Messina faced a world of loneliness after her loss. She would see his face often at night. It was real, she says, not as if in a dream. It was as if he were in the room. "I see his face often," she says. "And he is never smiling. I don't think he is at all happy."

One night as she prepared to go to sleep, she felt a presence beside her. She knew immediately that it was Rosario. He took her in his arms and held her. She never wanted it to end. In the morning she felt as if her limbs were frozen. She tried to move but couldn't. The doctor discovered that she was temporarily paralyzed, a condition she gradually overcame in spite of her loneliness and melancholy.

The incidents seemed to punctuate not only the fragility of life, but the durability of thoughts and ideas. Was there the remote possibility—as Sadie Messina almost felt—that the dead could not only survive after death, but could return as an articulate entity? But where was the geography, then, where a nonphysical entity could exist as an individual form, fully conscious of his self and his surroundings, communicating not only with others on that plane, but on rare occasions with the physical world he had left? Was there a clue to this in the dreams that were so striking and real they could barely be distinguished from reality?

The tragedy of Flight 401 would continue to exist in the minds and dreams of those who survived, an indelible reality that could never leave them. But what about those like Rosario Messina, or Second Officer Repo, or Captain Loft, who had died? Could thoughts and dreams continue among those who were no longer alive after the crash?

But these questions were not being asked in the days immediately following the holiday disaster. There were the

solemn funeral services to endure and the desperate work of the hospital to keep the living alive.

The flight crew was buried on the same day, shortly after the crash. Services for Captain Bob Loft were held at a United Presbyterian church; services for First Officer Bert Stockstill were held in his home town of St. Martinville, Louisiana; a requiem mass was held for Second Officer Don Repo. He was popular, well-loved. The church was filled to overflowing.

Even before the printout of the flight recorder and the transcription of the voice tapes, theories were being formed. The consensus was that the crew was distracted by the problem with the warning light, and that somehow the plane had diverged from its altitude in a way that was unnoticed by the crew. Yet the crew was experienced and competent, with thousands of hours of flying time. There was the warning chime that would sound when the plane diverged from its assigned altitude of 2,000 feet. There was the autopilot which had its own annunciator signal to indicate the altitude it had been set for, to say nothing of the standard altimeters.

Slowly the evidence was gathered, the tapes transcribed, the printouts assembled, the data analyzed. The fault, wherever it lay, had to be found, as in all air crashes.

One supervisor in charge of clearing the major parts wreckage arrived at the scene as the bodies were still being taken out of the area. He would return to the site every working day for five weeks to complete the job, using skilled riggers and special loaders adapted for the marshy terrain. It was a grueling job, but he took it as part of something that had to be done. But a year later he began waking up with nightmares that haunted him; not about the fear of flying, but about the scene of the wreckage itself.

From the probe, clues might be found that would save others from a similar tragedy. Gradually possible causes were eliminated. The crew was trained and qualified; there was no doubt about that. The autopsy on Captain Loft revealed a small, benign brain tumor, but careful analysis of what happened showed that this had nothing to do with the accident. He was functioning perfectly, and a first-class

medical certificate issued only a few weeks before showed that his eyesight needed correcting glasses only for near vision. Don Repo required the same correction, but neither of these affected their capabilities in flying the plane. Bert Stockstill had no limitation placed on his medical certificate.

There was no basic trouble with the aircraft. Plane #310 was fully certified, there was no malfunction of the structure or the power systems, and it met every possible government regulation. The L-1011 was then, and is now, a favorite of the pilots who fly them. Its performance is magnificent. And— ironically—the postaccident examination showed that there was nothing wrong with the nose gear.

But gradually the subtleties began to emerge. The C-chord chime that warned of the departure from the assigned altitude of 2,000 feet was so faint that it could barely be heard on the cockpit voice recorder tape. Further, it sounded only in one speaker—near Second Officer Repo's seat—and Repo was down in the hell hole when it sounded, trying to peer through the telescopic sight to look at the nose gear.

But why was it dark there in the wheel-well, so that the diagnosis of the problem was delayed? Another factor emerged out of the complex subtleties of the probe: there was no light switch down in the hell hole. The switch was on the "eyebrow panel" (a panel immediately above his eye level) of the captain's side of the flight deck. The crew apparently was misinformed. They thought the light that would illuminate the nose gear went on automatically when the landing gear was down. All this could contribute measurably to the distraction of the flight crew as it circled over the Everglades.

There was also the problem that the only warning that the plane had left its assigned altitude was the half-second C-chord chime that was barely audible and had gone unnoticed. If the plane had been at a higher altitude than its 2,000 feet assignment, an amber warning light would have flashed to show that the plane was slipping out of its assigned altitude. This warning was eliminated from the lower altitudes because of the proliferation of the panel lights that flash as the approach is neared, where more distraction can be created.

The critical point that emerged in the investigation lay in the operation of the autopilot. Weeks after the Flight 401

disaster, a representative of the Air Line Pilots Association questioned an L-1011 technical expert during the hearing on the accident:

QUESTION: Were the crew members taught that with the autopilot engaged in command mode, altitude hold engaged, that a slight bump or pressure on either steering yoke would disengage the altitude hold portion, would or could disengage the altitude hold portion of the autopilot?

ANSWER: They were not taught that. As a matter of fact, I don't think that very many people were aware of this until after the accident.

QUESTION: I agree. If there is a disconnect of this sort, an inadvertent disconnect, or however you want to call it, what indication is there?

ANSWER: Your indication would be the annunciator in front of your particular seat. The prism would flip over; you wouldn't have the altitude showing.

QUESTION: Does the light in the altitude hold selector switch go out, or does it stay on?

ANSWER: It should go out.

QUESTION: And I believe you have just said what the indication was in the annunciator panel.

ANSWER: Right.

QUESTION: Is there any indication in the AFCS (Avionics Flight Control System) warning annunciator panel?

ANSWER: I don't think so.

QUESTION: Does the autopilot aural disengage warning light sound, the wailer?

ANSWER: No, sir.

QUESTION: Does the autopilot engage lever drop in this case?

ANSWER: Negative.

QUESTION: What is the primary indication that the altitude hold has engaged when the altitude switch is pushed?

ANSWER: The way we teach it and use it, if you push the switch in to switch light and watch the annun-

ciator for the prism to flip over, showing the altitude, this informs you that you are in effect in altitude hold.

QUESTION: Are you aware that there have been cases where the AFCS mode annunciator on the corresponding side to the engaged autopilot indicated altitude hold disengagement while the opposite side mode annunciator panel still indicated that the altitude hold was engage?

ANSWER: I have heard this, but I have not personally seen it, so it would be hearsay.

QUESTION: Are you aware that the First Officer cannot see the captain's annunciator panel if they are both in the correct position in their seats?

ANSWER: Affirmative.

QUESTION: Assuming that these cases are correct, could you agree that this is a highly undesirable fault in the annunciator system?

ANSWER: I have to think about that for a minute.

QUESTION: The one says it is on and one says it is off, and one pilot cannot see the other's?

ANSWER: We have other redundant characteristics. It would still be undesirable, though.

But all this remained an enigma because the copilot's own system should have been in use, since he had taken over control of the plane. If so, the annunciator should have shown that the plane was no longer on autopilot control.

Coolly, logically the long search continued over many weeks, with attention centered on why the plane went into its slow and unexpected descent. The logic boiled down to four possibilities. First was the possible physical incapacity of Captain Loft, which extensive checking showed was not a factor. Second was the autopilot problem, which could have been a major cause. Third was the question of flight-crew training, and there were some critical loopholes in this. Last, there were the flight-crew distractions, which were so intense that they could have been a heavy contributor.

What finally emerged was a tragic contribution to the ancient axiom of engineering known as Murphy's Law: if anything *can* go wrong, it *will*. The crash was not the result

of a single error. It was "the cumulative result of several minor deviations from normal operating procedures which triggered a sequence of events with disastrous results," as the National Transportation Safety Board eventually put it.

But the fault had to be placed somewhere directly. The ultimate safety-board decision was that the flight crew failed to monitor the flight instruments during the final four minutes of flight. In failing to do this, the unexpected descent was not noticed until it was too late. The reason for the failure was obvious: the problem with the landing-gear warning light had drawn attention away from the one major job that had to be done—the flying of the airplane.

The decision had to be reached, but the circumstances were such that a simplistic placing of blame was the easy way out. It left a lot of open questions. Why wasn't the flight crew adequately instructed that a slight nudge could dislodge the autopilot? Why was the altitude warning chime designed with such a low volume, and in a place where the captain and copilot could barely hear it even under normal circumstances? Why should there even be the possibility that the copilot could be led by a false annunciator signal into thinking that his autopilot altitude was still holding? And while the approach controller needed three full scans to determine whether an altitude reading was wrong or not, what could be done to improve this system so that clear warning could be given when noticed on the scope? Why was there no light switch down in the hell hole, so that Don Repo could have made an immediate and swift visual check of the nose gear?

While the flight crew was buried with the cold finger of guilt pointing at them, the circumstances were such that a large number of airmen could say, "There, but for the grace of God, go I."

In fact, the final recommendations of the National Transportation Safety Board were such that they implied that the guilt should have been dispersed over a wide area. In the future, a light switch would be required down in the hell hole, near the optical sight that viewed the nose gear. If this had been available at the time of Flight 401, Don Repo could have finished his job in a matter of moments, and Flight 401 could have come in promptly for a smooth landing.

The next recommendation from the safety board would require that a flashing light would warn the crew of any divergence from the altitude set for the autopilot to maintain. This would buttress the gentle C-chord chime that had been inaudible to the crew of Flight 401. If the recommended light had flashed over the Everglades, there is little doubt that the unexpected descent would have been checked and the flight would have come in safely.

The board also requested a review of the ways to set up a procedure for an air traffic controller to warn quickly when a marked deviation was noticed on the radar screen. If this system had been in effect, Flight 401 would have had time to avert the accident. Out of the investigation also came a program to install a terrain-avoidance radar system, warning the pilot as he dangerously approached any land or hills or mountains beneath him, in time enough to take defensive action. A new computerized system for the ground controller known as the Minimum Safe Altitude Warning System was put in development by the Federal Aviation Administration. It would continuously monitor aircraft altitude to make sure that any planes would be at a safe altitude above the highest point in the area. This development grew out of the Everglades crash. If it had been installed on that holiday evening in December 1972, the lives of nearly a hundred people would have been saved, and the crew would not have died in the shadow of a guilt which surely was not altogether theirs.

Any crewman whose plane is in a crash for which he was even faintly responsible is bound to feel guilt, especially if he took pride in the performance of his job. All three crewmen of Flight 401 took an immeasurable amount of pride in both their jobs and in the new L-1011, a plane that all three had revealed that they loved and respected.

But the story of Flight 401 did not come to an end at the close of the safety-board hearings. What was to follow would be, to many, a strange and revealing series of events of unusual impact that went beyond the modern jet age and into the unknown.

Gradually the stories of the L-1011 disaster in the Everglades began slipping from the front pages of the Miami

newspapers. There was the tragic aftermath: the claims for damages that could never ease the anguish, the implementing of the procedures and recommendations that would quite realistically assure that an accident of that type, at least, would never happen again. Eastern Air Lines, both as a corporate entity and as individuals, did everything humanly possible to assist the victims, demonstrating ably that in times of stress a corporation does indeed have a soul.

The L-1011 sister ships of Plane #310 were given lavish engineering and maintenance attention, so that the growing fleet became the favorite of pilots and flight engineers, in spite of minor bugs that can infest any aircraft at times. The chain of circumstances that led to the accident was now effectively blocked. The plane would go on to become one of the safest and best in the air.

It was a graceful, beautiful craft. In spite of the lingering memory of that December evening in 1972, flight crews and flight attendents bid enthusiastically for its schedules. The enthusiasm was not ill-founded. The L-1011 was quiet and roomy. In fact, the big jet engines were the quietest in the world of aviation. Its wings were designed with direct lift which eliminated annoying ups and downs on approach. The entire rear stabilizer moved with the controls, rather than just the aft section of it. This provided surer, more deft control. And it was economical: it burned only 51 gallons of fuel per passenger, compared to 65 burned by the older jets.

It was reported that the ill-fated flight crew—Captain Loft, First Officer Stockstill, and Second Officer Don Repo—had been as much in love with the craft as the other flight crews. Repo, especially, had an intense attachment for it. A sturdy, virile man with salt-and-pepper sideburns, he was popular with both flight crews and flight attendants. "He had a lot of nervous energy," one stewardess described him. "He was a very conscientious person. But he laughed a lot with us, and he was soft-spoken. I never heard him raise his voice."

Captain Loft was well thought of by his associates, too, but was considered more subdued in spite of his occasional salty language. Bert Stockstill was more communicative with the cabin crews, but Loft always dominated the scene with his athletic stature and sense of command. All three were profes-

sionals of the highest caliber, according to their peers. They took an inordinate amount of pride in their work. The tragic web that entrapped them could not be considered a reflection of their capabilities. Pilots who flew with them swore by them. Some of them felt that if the trio remained conscious of what had happened, it had cut into their deepest souls. One terrifying moment had engulfed them so suddenly, that they, along with the others on the flight, had no time to comprehend the enormity of the event.

In a moment of crisis like this, where life suddenly changes into death, or the immediate certainty of death, those who have not been through it cannot experience or imagine what the mental and emotional shock would be to the person's being itself. There would possibly be incredulity, utter amazement, perhaps the thought: this-can't-be-happening-to-me. Then the struggle, the will to live, the fight to prevent death, where the force of will can sometimes overcome the hopelessness of the physical destruction. Even with the body shattered and death near, deathbed observations of doctors and nurses have indicated that patients have been known to recognize the condition and to deal with it in whatever way there is possible—including the acceptance of the inevitable.

But the question was what part of the dying person is doing the recognizing? What is it aware of, under these sudden unexpected and intolerable conditions? A new scientific trend leans toward the conclusion that the consciousness of the self is not the brain or the mind. It is associated with them, but apart from them. Consciousness is being considered more a sensor or an observer than an integral part of the system, just as a stream of electrons are part of—but separate from—the wire that conducts them. Electrons are indestructible; a wire is not. Would the consciousness, the Energy that is the motivator and activator of the brain and nervous system simply disappear at death? Or would it continue in a non-molecular and nonatomic entity in a form of energy that physics has not yet discovered? Many minds of wisdom and stature think so, but none communicates the idea so incontestably that all accept it. There is controversy and censure

even for those who wanted to probe the idea with an open mind.

But this question would have a direct bearing on what was to happen later on the L-1011 sister ships of Plane #310, and that would have a profound effect on many people in the aviation world and outside it.

"Anthropology has taught us that the world is differently defined in different places. It is not only that people have different customs; it is not only that people believe in different gods and expect different post-mortem fates. It is, rather, that the worlds of different people have different shapes.

"The very metaphysical presuppositions differ: space does not conform to Euclidean geometry, time does not form a continuous unidirectional flow, causation does not conform to Aristotelian logic, man is not differentiated from non-man or life from death, as in our world.

"The central importance of entering into worlds other than our own . . . lies in the fact that the experience leads us to understand that our own world is *also* a cultural construct. By experiencing other worlds, then, we see our own for what it is and are thereby enabled also to see fleetingly what the real world, the one *between* our own cultural construct, and those other worlds, must in fact be like."
(italics added)

—Walter Goldschmidt,
in his introduction to
*The Teachings of Don Juan:
A Yaqui Way of Knowledge*

# Chapter VI

When the Scandinavian Airlines flight attendant brought up the Eastern Airlines story to me in the spring of 1974, I knew little about the theory of ghosts or apparitions. This was foreign territory to me. The idea of attempting to communicate with the dead was a vague and remote possibility described in some literature on parapsychology, some of it fairly convincing, other not convincing at all. While I never scoffed at the idea, I couldn't buy it without a lot more evidence demonstrated than that which I had run across. I didn't know then that some surprising events were going to develop, and that they were going to have a strong and serious influence on my entire outlook.

At that time, I was completely absorbed in writing about stark reality—the great potential danger of nuclear power plants and their proliferation throughout the world. Accidents had been happening frequently in these plants, but they were being soft-pedaled to the extent that the public knew little about their dangers.

I had gone to Nigeria in 1973 to begin research on the story of the Lassa virus, which shortly before had just been isolated in the laboratories at Yale University. After one laboratory technician at Yale was fatally stricken with the disease and a leading virologist had barely scraped through alive, it was decided that the virus was so deadly that it could no longer be studied at Yale. All the vials full of blood specimens from the victims of the virus were incinerated, except a small batch which was sent to a new maximum security laboratory at the Center for Disease Control in Atlanta. This was a story of science at its best, and I became completely absorbed in it.

At Nigeria's University of Ibadan, both American and Nigerian scientists tried to figure a way to combat the terrifying disease. It was a large university with an equally large medical center that was impressive under any standards. During one serene evening there, with the African sunset blazing over the rain forests to the west, I chatted with the Nigerian doctor in charge of medical and surgical research at the university. He was a quiet, intelligent man with a soft, musical voice. He had studied medicine at the University of Pennsylvania and was fully trained in modern research techniques.

"It is strange," he told me, "that modern medical science has often overlooked what could be learned from primitive practices."

"How can our sophisticated knowledge be matched by someone who's untrained?" I asked him.

"I'm not demeaning modern medicine by any means," he continued. "It is just that in the headlong rush toward developing miracle drugs and complex instruments, I feel that medicine has left large pockets of unexplored territory. Modern science is miraculous, but incomplete."

I was interested because in the various stories I was doing, there always seemed to be a point where modern, objective science came to a dead end, and frankly admitted it. Doctors could work effectively up to the time of death. Psychiatrists could help patients with equal effectiveness, but they were a dead end as far as deep psychosis was concerned. Physicists were reaching a dead end as far as particle physics were concerned, because they began to find insoluble paradoxes at the end of the line. The very observation of matter beyond the electron or proton changed the behavior of the particles, so that they could not be observed or traced in their normal activity.

After I finished the research on the Lassa virus study, I was going directly to Brazil to research the strange story of Arigo, the peasant surgeon. His miracle cures had been verified by both American and Brazilian doctors, with whom he cooperated fully.

But the doctors could go no further than this. They had no

scientific explanation as to how he was able to operate without pain, fear, bleeding, or postoperative infection. He could cut through the viscera without using hemostats to clamp off the blood vessels. He could roughly shove a kitchen knife up under a patient's eyelid and extrude the eyeball grotesquely to treat a case of retinoblastoma, or cancer of the eyeball. The patient would be fully conscious, yet would not flinch as the unsterile knife came toward the eye. There would be no pain, no bleeding. I became more convinced that there were many phenomena beyond our comprehension. Could ghosts be one of them?

The cultural construct of Brazil was different from that of the United States. It would be a form of arrogance for either country to say that the philosophic outlook of the other was either more, or less valid. Many of the most educated and cultured Brazilians accepted spiritism—the belief in the reality of communication with the dead—as a matter of course. They rarely questioned it. People of all walks of life were mediums there, acting as channels of communication with spirits, according to their precepts.

In Brazil I discovered the studies of the late Luis Rodriguez, a brilliant student of the psychic, a former successful pharmaceutical manufacturer. He had spent years trying to find a bridge between modern psychiatry and primitive techniques for treating psychosis, just as the United Nations scientists were to do later in their Nigerian studies. His theme was that Freud, Adler, Jung and others simply did not go far enough in their probing into the depths of the human psyche.

Interestingly, Freud once expressed regret for not moving into the study of the occult. In a letter to the Advisory Council of the American Psychical Institute in 1921, he wrote:

I am not one of those who, from the outset, disapprove of the study of so-called occult psychological phenomenon as unscientific, as unworthy, or even dangerous. If I were at the beginning of a scientific career, instead of as now, at its end, I would perhaps choose no other field of work, in spite of its difficulties.

Rodriguez was concerned with the failure of psychiatry to get at the source and roots of neurosis and psychosis. He blamed it on the taboos set up by the scientific method. At times it seemed that these taboos were even stronger than those of medicine men. "Thou shalt not touch" was a frequent scientific attitude toward even examining such things as mediumship, ESP, psychokinesis, clairvoyance, apparitions, reincarnation, and other aspects of the unexplored. The very word "occult" was a turn-off. In my timid and cautious look at the stories I was getting myself into, I shunned the word and still shun it. It simply didn't fit into the vocabulary of journalism, to say nothing of science.

Rodriguez had a theory that every person was psychic, but more often than not failed to realize it or develop it. Some were, of course, more psychic than others; just as some artists, musicians or mathematicians are more talented than others. The more talented psychics were those who fell into the category of mediums.

Mediumship is an emotionally charged word. It conjures up images of crystal balls and tea leaves. This is abhorrent to modern thought. The more enlightened picture of a medium is that of one who acts as a channel for unknown forces and personalities which are not part of the structure of his conscious mind. Of course, there could be good mediums or destructive mediums; talented or untalented.

Rodriguez's theory of psychosis was that it was nothing more than symptoms and syndromes signifying that the victim was in the process of becoming an intense and overwhelmed medium, that neither he nor the psychiatrists recognized. There was a full-blown scientific study by Dr. Raymond Prince, of McGill University in Montreal, that supported this theory. Coincidentally, it involved the medicineman healers in Nigeria, but was separate from the U.N. studies. Dr. Prince had found that the village healers treated their psychotic patients not only through the channels of mediumship, but by recognizing that their symptoms were outside forces flowing through them. The healer set about to guide these forces into developing mediumship instead of

psychosis. It was, in one sense, a process like Freud's sublimation.

Rodriguez commented on this in a letter to a friend:

> This development eradicates the psychoneurotic or psychotic condition that heralded the flowering of the mediumship facility. This is the reason why mental diseases do not exist among these primitive people, who may be counted in the millions.
>
> Mental diseases are, therefore, the fruit harvested by overcivilized man due exclusively to a condition of ignorance maintained by an exaggerated sense of sophistication and hallowed cultural superiority.

What interested me was that his theories might have some direct bearing on the explanation for Arigo's incredible achievements. Later, his theories would also bear heavily on my probe into the ghosts of Flight 401. Rodriguez had six clear postulates that I examined in relation to the Arigo story, and which I didn't realize at the time, would apply to the Eastern Airlines story as well.

He claimed there were basic hard facts about man's cosmic existence. I couldn't agree they were proven facts but I did find his tenets provocative:

1. That man is an incarnate soul.
2. That this soul was not created at the time of birth.
3. That it has had many other lives on earth, and that others will consequently follow.
4. That contact between the incarnate and discarnate persons has been taking place since man appeared on earth for the first time.
5. That the psychic faculty known as mediumship is the method devised by nature to establish this necessary and enlightening contact.
6. That primitive people all over the world are well acquainted with these simple facts of life.

I quoted more of his letter in the book I finally completed on Arigo:

What I have learned is that it behooves us to improve the nature of this contact by enhancing its reliability, and separating it from the superstitions involved in religious creeds, doctrines, or dogmas, from rites and rituals. Likewise, not to waste time with obdurate skepticism that retards progress by postulating pseudoscientific explanations that explain nothing.

Rodriguez was aiming at mediumship as the root of the matter. I was aware of the great number of charlatans that had been exposed in the past. This made navigation difficult. If a channel is filled with rocks, does that make navigation impossible? Not quite, but it does require extreme caution. I was careful to use it in my further research in Brazil.

When I had begun to get intrigued by the Eastern Airlines ghost story, I wasn't fully aware why. Perhaps it was because of the futility of the everyday world. Wars, politics, venality, and outright blindness on the part of otherwise intelligent and informed people perhaps help serve as a catalyst to look beyond the ultra-confused world everyone was facing.

Now I kept asking myself where did the truth lie? Scientific progress was reaching a stage where in one sense, it was irrational. Aside from the unthinkable nuclear war potential, where the United States and Russia were exactly twenty-eight minutes away from mutual incineration and extinction, the peacetime development of the nuclear industry was building up to a similar threat. The question of life after death was coming into sharper focus for young as well as old.

What intrigued me was that the story of the aftermath of the L-1011, even if it turned out to be allegory or folklore, symbolized the contrast between the onrush of a shaky materialism and the possible reality of the spirit and life after death.

The investigation of the facts of the crash itself had been simple: lengthy straight interviews, the study of the FAA and NTSB documents, and other records. But what would it be like to try to track down a ghost story? How could you go about it? What specific devices did psychics use to try to contact the dead? Were any of them really successful, or were they myths? Could, for instance, Second Officer Don

Repo, the flight engineer reported to have reappeared on the Mexico City flight, be communicated with? If so, could it be established by hard evidence that could be tracked down and followed up? It was a crazy idea, but a challenge. I couldn't visualize what was to ultimately happen. It would turn out to be far beyond my tentative speculations.

"Interesting if true—and interesting anyway."

—Mark Twain

# Chapter VII

In the middle of March 1975, I packed to go to Miami to continue the research on the oceanographic film for the USIA. The University of Miami's work in this field was outstanding. It occurred to me that as long as I was going there, that I could make at least a tentative exploration on the Eastern apparitions. On the other hand, I would be much too busy with everything from whales to plankton to think about it. But perhaps I could find someone in Miami to help with the research and make some preliminary stabs at the project.

I tried to fight off the idea because it was distracting. I knew I was vacillating and that irked me. Just before I took the plane, I was due to receive an award from the New York Academy of Sciences for the book *Fever*. What would they think if I mentioned I was considering writing the story of a ghost? Again I put the Eastern idea out of my mind and concentrated on the research in oceanography, in the respectable realms of science and documentary filmmaking.

I took off for Miami in mid-March at 9:00 P.M. on Eastern's Flight 401. The L-1011 Whisperliner was indeed a beautiful bird. The engine nacelles, two on the wings and one high in the tail section, looked big enough for a man to stand in. Mechanics and baggage loaders were scurrying around underneath the belly, checking the umbilical cord for the ground electrical system, snaking the baggage trucks up to the loading door, sliding the containerized freight over the rollers into the freight door, hauling the food trays into the galley.

Inside, the high-arched ceiling glowed with a pleasant softness. The seats were widely spaced and inviting. We would be flying at 30,000 feet. The weather in Miami was warm, with scattered and broken clouds. I settled back with a

premixed Gordon's martini, took some reference material on the oceanography film out of my briefcase, and tried to concentrate on it.

It was difficult to do. My mind kept going back to Flight 401, over two years before, when 176 people sat back on the same comfortable flight, and never reached their destination. I had no fear of that accident repeating itself. It had been a freak combination of circumstances that would now be almost impossible to duplicate. As flight crews will tell you, the main fear they have of flying is the limousine trip to and from the airport. I was feeling a sadness for the people of that ill-fated flight, and especially for the crew which was snarled in a web of improbable circumstances.

There was no sign of Repo, and I didn't expect that I would be that lucky. But without exception, the cabin crew knew of him. After the drinks had been served and the meal trays cleared, I went up to the topside galley and chatted with some of the flight attendants about Repo and Plane #318. We were on #305, but still Plane #318 was a sister ship from which several stories had emanated.

As I had found before on other flights, the reactions of the stewardesses were varied. Some would refuse to talk about the subject. Others would laugh and joke about it, but confirm that they didn't like to work in the lower galley alone. Others told of girls who flatly refused to work in the lower galley at all. Some mentioned cockpit crews who refused to fly #318, not because of lack of safety, but because they felt uneasy. Some would be intensely interested and want to know what I had learned about the story. And many were very much afraid that if they told me what they knew, they would jeopardize their jobs or be sent to the company shrink. This, I was to find, was a dominant factor with everyone from Eastern I talked to.

Their reactions and fears would later turn out to be a major stumbling block. This was understandable, even though I assured them that their identity would be protected. They would have no way of knowing that I would do that. Even with those who joked and laughed about the story, there was a dead seriousness about it. Too many of their friends were convinced of its validity, either directly or indirectly.

Tracking down the details under these circumstances seemed to me to be an almost impossible research job. Eastern had approximately 5,000 flight attendants, and only a handful of them had had direct experience. I knew no one at Eastern through whom I could get names and phone numbers, and company policy was strict in not issuing them to anyone, even within the company.

On the Flight 401 that night, however, was a stewardess who was completely intrigued with the story. It turned out to be Emily Palmer,* a flight attendant who had collected several stories in detail and said that she would get them together for me at a later date. She would also talk to some of her friends who had had direct experience to see if they would be willing to be interviewed. She was a tall, striking brunette with great enthusiasm and wit. She emphasized that Repo was certainly a good ghost, who had been continually pointing out possible malfunctions to the flight crews, and who was eager to help. She thought Eastern's attitude was ridiculous, especially with the implied menace of a psychiatric referral in the offing. This, she thought, was the main reason why the crews did not want to talk.

I told Emily that if I decided to do the story, I would get in touch with her and take her and her husband to dinner the next trip to Miami. She urged me to write the book. There were too many sane and respectable crew members involved for it to be a myth, including captains, and First and Second Officers.

Her enthusiasm was contagious, but I would have little time to even think about the story on this trip. Such a story would be a heady experience, dealing with a transcendental world I knew little about, although some of my previous books had reached out toward the edge of reality. I was thinking that I preferred subjects like the new deadly virus in *Fever,* or the harsh reality of *We Almost Lost Detroit.* In spite of the difficulty of the subject matter, they were within clean grasp. The facts were facts; there was nothing misty about them. Yet they had plenty of inherent drama that made them interesting to write.

I was happy about the award from the New York Academy of Sciences for *Fever* because it reflected that the book

clearly got across what science could do at its best. The worst phase of science was the attitude that sometimes revealed a lack of social awareness (as in the proliferation of nuclear power, inviting a potential catastrophe), or scientific prejudice that stubbornly refused to even consider exploring the little-known realm of the paranormal.

Science knew much, but understood only a fraction of a vast unknown geography. The human brain—the main tool that science used for its observations—was little understood in itself. Its capacity to observe was limited by the finite circuitry, which in turn was trying to comprehend the infinite. The machinery of the unverise reached out beyond the exquisite but limited tool that was trying to take it apart to examine it. The mind certainly went beyond the brain, but both met a paradox when reaching out toward the infinitely small or infinitely large. Whatever seemed indivisible could be divided again. Whatever could be multiplied, could be multiplied again. With the brain and its limited circuitry as its only tool, science was like a radio trying to tune in to television pictures. To go beyond its limitations, science would have to make a quantum, transcendental leap which would combine desirable objectivity with tolerance for imaginative and creative assumption.

There was little doubt in my mind that the idea of a ghost or an apparition was something that neither a scientist nor a journalist could ever pin down—except from the point of view of interesting and provocative evidence. Evidence is not proof. But it approaches proof if it is convincing and logical. If it approaches proof, it is not at all dissimilar to the mathematician's tool in calculus, where the symbol '$X \to 0$'' is often used to say ''as X approaches zero.'' The ''X'' never reaches zero, but it is a workable and convenient assumption.

I was getting intrigued again about the Eastern story as these thoughts went through my mind on the flight. Could the story be treated as the device of calculus, never reaching its goal, but approaching it in a provocative way? Could the idea of a direct communication really work? I would have to think about it some more.

I did. When I got to Miami, I went to my hotel and lined up my appointments at the University of Miami's oceanographic

institution. Then I called a girl I knew who was a journalism student in Miami. She had written me previously about doing research for any projects I might have in the Florida area. Her name was Rachelle Faul, and she had a bright and perceptive mind. She wasn't afraid of legwork. My first thought was that I could get her to check several time-consuming areas in the oceanographic research and survey.

We had dinner together. As we talked, she brought up the fact that she was extremely interested in the psychic field and had done a considerable amount of study in it. I told her about the Eastern Air Lines story. As I did, I made a decision on the spot. I would assign her to explore the Eastern story, and I would do all the oceanographic research myself. If there seemed to be any evidence that we could locate Eastern employees who would talk, and gather other data from the Federal Aviation Administration that might support the story, I would come back to Miami after the oceanographic script was completed, to further dig into the strange story of the Eastern ghost.

We laid out a rough plan. I warned her about Eastern's employees being very reluctant to talk. Inside information would be very difficult to get. The fear of getting laid off was very real to them. I had very few suggestions to make, because I had not given much attention to the story. My decision even to just test it out was made on impulse. We roughed out some key questions that needed to be answered. What happened to Plane #318? There were rumors that it had been sold to TWA, or that its number had been changed. What were the names of those who reported seeing apparitions? How could we get in touch with them? How could we learn of any flightdeck crews who had experienced the phenomena? What clippings were in the newspaper morgues? What information would the FAA have? What records, reports, documentation would be available?

It would probably be useless to go to Eastern public relations, because we already knew what the company line would be: a group of hysterical employees who should visit the psychiatrist. However, we would try, anyway. I had one lead from Sharon Henning, the Pan Am stewardess. She knew an Eastern flight attendant named Liz Gallagher.* I called her

later from the hotel room, but she was able to confirm only that several of the girls she worked with on the L-1011s refused to work in the lower galley. She was pleasant, but knew of no direct leads. Emily Palmer was off on a trip and would not return until after I left.

I had to leave the entire initial probing in Rachelle's hands. My mind was too full of plankton and ocean upwelling to give it much thought. It was so much easier to research in a subject you could grab hold of. Even though man had never reached the bottom of the sea, it was much more tangible. I feared that I was throwing Rachelle a curve.

But she took it in good spirits and proved to have a knack of getting along with people. When we got together two days later, she had completed a lot of legwork and gathered a lot of information of a general nature, but practically nothing but secondhand reports from Eastern. There was plenty of technical material from the FAA about the crash itself, to supplement what I had reviewed in Washington.

Practically everyone she talked to knew about the stories of the apparitions, but they were reluctant to talk about them. It didn't seem very promising. There simply didn't seem to be enough to go on. There were a few clues, however, that could possibly lead to something. Rachelle had a close friend, Betsy Wilkes, who previously had been a flight attendant for Eastern. Along with Rachelle, she was an avid student of the psychic and would be glad to help if she knew of anything. The problem was that we couldn't reach her and my time was growing short on this trip. Also, Rachelle had another friend, J.R. Worden, who along with the other two, was active in the Spiritual Frontier movement. As such, all three had experienced some form of mediumship, in greater or less degree. Worden also knew a lot of people who worked with Eastern and might be able to come up with some ideas.

But none of this was at all concrete. I had to leave Miami the following morning to fly directly to Edmonton, Alberta, en route to the West Coast for more oceanographic research. The occasion in Edmonton was the taping of a Canadian television program to be syndicated nationally concerning my book *The Interrupted Journey*, which had been published nearly eight years earlier. There was renewed interest in the

subject, with many new UFO reports over Canada. The program producer felt that the story of Barney and Betty Hill was a case that had never been solved and was most interesting because of the high caliber of the Hills and the psychiatrist involved. There was also interest because the case might possibly indicate contact with alien beings. Betty Hill was being flown out from New Hampshire, and Dr. J. Allan Hynek from Northwestern University, where he was chairman of the astronomy department. I had not seen either for some time, and it would be good to say hello to them again.

The trip from Miami to Edmonton is probably the most dreary flight you could take; but oddly enough, Northwest Orient had a direct flight, with no change of planes. There were stops at Chicago and Minneapolis, however, to make it a long haul. However, I was glad for the chance to rest up, and spent most of the first part of the flight sleeping. At Minneapolis there was a change of crews, and when we took off for the last leg to Edmonton, I suddenly remembered that I had forgotten to do my usual checking to see what the Northwest crews knew about the Eastern phenomenon.

One cabin attendant, Elizabeth Manzione, knew about both the Eastern apparitions and the Barney and Betty Hill story, and was extremely interested in both. Elizabeth was a bright, attractive brunette with a tremendous amount of enthusiasm. She volunteered to do some further research among various Eastern ramp agents and flight attendants whom she often ran into on her various trips. I was anxious for any material I could get and told her that it would really be appreciated. She said I'd be surprised at how much material she could dig up, and that I shouldn't underestimate the power of a woman as far as detective work is concerned. We both laughed, and she went on about her job.

Before the Canadian television taping the next day, Professor Hynek and I had lunch together and talked about the problems that come up when you get into unexplored territory. Professor Hynek had been the official scientific consultant for the U.S. Air Force since the early days of UFO sightings. Through this work, he became the only scientist in the country who was in on every detail of the early Air Force probes into the subject. At first he had been sure that there

would be a logical explanation for the sightings, and that they could be easily cataloged and explained. But as the evidence mounted over the years, and the quality of the reports from military and commercial pilots, police, FAA supervisors, and other officials who literally risked their jobs by reporting UFOs was high, he began to wonder whether the casual write-off of the phenomenon was valid.

The problem with the UFO phenomenon was the same as that concerning the paranormal field. The quality of the evidence was what counted. But because the field was so ephemeral, it attracted a lot of static at a high noise level, making it extremely difficult to separate the valid from the invalid. It could be done, but it took a tremendous amount of time to study the evidence and weed out the bad from the good.

"I might be getting myself into another story tougher than UFOs," I told Hynek.

"The problem I see with anything like this," he said, "is the general assumption that we know everything that's possible to know, and that everything beyond our present scientific knowledge is simply nonexistent, or we would already know it. Fifty or a hundred years from now, scientists will be laughing at a lot of our theories, just as we now laugh at some of the theories of a century ago."

This might be a key, I was thinking, in exploring anything so ephemeral as an apparition. In the new reawakening among so many people to the potential of the psychic world, the current yardsticks based on the past and present might have to be reexamined. There seemed to be so much new in the wind. The Barney and Betty Hill story, which we discussed at length at the TV taping that night in Canada, was far from answered, one way or the other. There were residuals resulting from it that were puzzling. In her regression under hypnosis, Betty Hill recalled that a large needle was pushed through her abdomen, and she was informed that this was a pregnancy test. No doctor in his right mind would use that sort of technique at that time, in the early sixties. Nearly a decade later, a new test was announced in the medical journals for checking amniotic fluids during pregnancy. It used the identical technique, never used before.

Betty Hill had also drawn a star map, under hypnosis, which she recalled she had been shown by the "humanoid" being on the UFO. Several years later, working from a model of this map, astronomers located a new constellation.

In spite of the general scientific resistance, there was so much going on in the outer edges of science that it was hard to keep up with. Scientific studies using electroencephalograph techniques were being developed at the University of Washington to study transcendental meditation. Other universities were studying Kirlian photography, a method of measuring energy emanating from the body. Biofeedback research was burgeoning. Jonas Salk was saying, "A new transformation is occurring in the circumstance of human life. . . . Man's past performance should not be taken as the only basis for judging his future." Wilder Penfield, who pioneered in new techniques for the treatment of epilepsy, reviewed his career in his Princeton University Press book *The Mystery of the Mind.* In it he said that he started out to prove that the brain is responsible for the mind. As he studied thousands of patients, experimenting with electrical stimulation of the brain, he finally concluded that the mind was totally independent of the brain. "The mind stands above the content of consciousness at any moment. It is an independent entity. The mind directs, and the brain executes. The brain is messenger to consciousness."

If the mind was an independent entity, what happened at death? This remained the overriding question for everyone. This was why the L-1011 incidents were more than a ghost story, more than a curiosity. They reflected a vast, little-explored area in a realm that man yearned to know more about.

It wasn't until June that I was able to get back to Miami. Meantime, Elizabeth Manzione, the Northwest cabin attendant, was proving her theory on the capability of women detectives. She sent report after report gathered from Eastern Airlines personnel at nearly every airport where Northwest shared the ramps with Eastern. There were several, including LaGuardia and Kennedy. Many of her reports were scrawled on air-sick bags, the most convenient form of stationery at the time. She explained that she might forget the details if she

didn't get the facts down quickly. The bags had a tendency to bulge in the file, but they contained a lot of information. And they were instrumental in my deciding to continue on with the research, now that the script for the oceanographic documentary was completed.

In Miami, Rachelle Faul had not been idle. Together with J.R. Worden, they had scoured their Eastern contacts and had come up with some very interesting information. First, through the Spiritual Frontiers group they belonged to, they had learned of an FAA executive based in Atlanta, who was extremely interested in the L-1011 phenomenon because it had been reported by flight crews who were capable and reliable. I had never visualized technical people as mediums, and this information was rather startling. What was even more startling was that J.R. had tracked down two Eastern pilots, Stan Chambers* and Rich Craig,* who were also mediums. They were both based in New York, both members of a Spiritual Frontier group there, and both had been on Miami layovers during the time I was away. Incredibly, J.R. told me that when the stories of the L-1011 apparitions grew to alarming proportions, the two captains and their wives, who were also mediums, had conducted what they called a "soul rescue" mission to exorcise the planes. They would be willing to talk to me, J.R. said, when I returned to the New York area.

I had to stop J.R. at this point to try to absorb all this. "How did you ever pick all this information up?" I asked him.

"Well," J.R. said, "the Spiritual Frontiers Fellowship is a pretty tightly knit group. They're seriously interested in the psychic as part of religion, and on the whole, they're a literate and intelligent bunch. I'd say the members are mostly successful in business or the professions. We're not as nutty as you might think."

I laughed with him, and he continued. "We're frequently in touch with members in other parts of the country. We have a real common interest, and you can't talk to just anybody about the paranormal stuff. It isn't something that's easy to dig. So what happens in Boston or Atlanta or New York gets heard about in Miami or anywhere else."

"You say the pilots are willing to talk with me?"

"They said anytime you got back to New York and they weren't off flying."

"What about the FAA executive?"

"Rachelle tracked him down," J.R. said.

"I was talking to this friend of mine in the Spiritual Frontier group in Atlanta. She put me in touch with him, and I called him. He'd be glad to talk, he said. He's very interested."

"None of them, however, want their names used," J.R. said. "They don't think people are ready to absorb the idea that pilots and technical men can be mediums, too."

"It *is* hard to visualize," I said.

"There's been too much mystery put around this idea," J.R. said. "Mediums are just people who have developed their psychic awareness more than others."

I studied J.R. and Rachelle sitting across the hotel room from me. They were both mediums, and they couldn't act or look more normal. Rachelle, in jeans, would blend into any college campus. J.R., in a crew shirt and corduroys, looked like any engineer or executive on his day off.

This was getting interesting, I thought. I would look forward to learning more about this. "Anything else turn up?" I asked.

"It's really tough to drag information out of the flight attendants" Rachelle said. "They're running scared. Same with the cockpit crews. I've talked to several of them, with the same story. They know all about the stories, but they either don't want to talk because they might get fired, they say, or they know the stories only secondhand."

"I talked with a mechanic who told me he's observed a lot of interesting details you might want to look into," J.R. said. "His name is Garry Lewis.* He was working temporarily in Miami, but he's back in New York. He's another who doesn't want his name mentioned, but he'll talk with you."

There seemed to be good leads shaping up, thanks to J.R. and Rachelle. But it wasn't going to be easy. There were endless blind alleys and false leads. Rachelle went to the airport ramps and the stewardess lounge at Miami International to make a cold-turkey canvass, but came up with nothing very useful. Although everyone knew of the L-1011

incidents, there was the continued hesitancy to talk about them. I made an abortive pub-crawling canvass, to see if I could pick up any scuttlebutt in and around the favorite haunts of Eastern crews in Miami Springs. In all of them, the rock music was so loud that the bartender could barely hear your order for a drink. It was useless.

An important follow-up was Emily Palmer, the Eastern flight attendant I had on my trip on Flight 401 in March. She was in and out on trips so much that it was difficult to contact her. I finally reached her by phone, and we made the arrangement for her and her husband to have dinner with me when she returned from her next trip. By that time, she would have her notes on the L-1011 incidents organized. She also told me about some of her friends who flew for Eastern, each of whom had had some sort of experience with the phenomenon on the L-1011. They included Denise Woodruff* and Ginny Packard,* both flight attendants. She was sure they would talk to me, as well as the TWA pilot who had some information about the L-1011s that TWA leased from Eastern during the season when Florida traffic was light.

I was able to reach Ginny Packard by phone right away. I told her briefly about the story I was researching.

"Have you gone through Eastern public relations on this yet?" was the first question Ginny asked me.

I told her I hadn't yet done so, but didn't expect to get much information from them. I had been in public relations myself at one time, and knew the arts and dodges employed in a situation like this. She was very hesitant to talk, but after I convinced Ginny that her name would not be used, she went on.

"Well," she said, "I know of another flight attendant who went through the same experience as I did, and she ended up being sent to the Eastern psychiatrist. I just don't want to put myself in that kind of position."

I told her I didn't blame her.

"I'm afraid this is going to sound weird as hell," she said.

I asked her not to worry. I had talked to flight crews who felt the same way

"Lord," she said. "This is so strange. You've got to understand I'm absolutely sane and normal."

129

I told her that Emily Palmer, had given me her name, but she was still reluctant to talk. I had to reassure her over and over that her identity would be kept confidential. Finally she began talking, but the story involved both Denise Woodruff and Doris Elliott, the stewardess who had had the strange premonition about the ill-fated Flight 401. I felt that if I could talk to the three of them at the same time, I could better piece the story together. Ginny agreed, and I asked her to see if the three of them could have lunch with me at my hotel. She said she thought the others were in Miami and would call me back if they were available.

Fortunately they were, and the four of us met the next day. They were high-spirited and good-natured. There seemed to be a spirit of camaraderie among them, a sense of defiance in that they were absolutely confident of what they experienced, and were damned if they cared whether anyone believed them or not. They were serious underneath, but took it in light good humor, too. As they began talking, I put my Sony TC-55 cassette tape recorder on the table to begin piecing the story together.

It was about three months after the accident, Ginny told me, in March 1973, that she was assigned to an L-1011 flight out of New York to Fort Lauderdale, along with her close friend Denise Woodruff. It was Plane #318. Both of them liked to work the spacious L-1011s either up in the cabins or down in the service galley, where over 200 meals could be heated in the glass-doored stainless steel ovens that rimmed both sides. It was a cozy, quiet area. There was soft illumination coming from lighting panels that spread across the entire ceiling. Some preferred to work down there, because they could be alone with their thoughts as they loaded the carts full of trays on the two skinny elevator platforms, and sent them up to the cabin crew above for serving. The elevators carried either the food carts or two cramped stewardesses. There was less hassle and more privacy down there, away from the incessant demands of the passengers.

The flight carrying Ginny and Denise was full, and the service demands were heavy. Denise squeezed into one of the tiny elevators and came down to the lower galley to give her

friend Ginny a hand in the galley. In the meantime, Ginny was on her way up to the passenger deck to see if she could help the girls up there. The two elevators passed each other. On the main deck, Ginny learned that Denise had gone down to the galley to help her.

It took only a couple of minutes for Ginny to get ready to return to the lower bay galley. Unknown to her, Denise was coming up the other elevator as Ginny went down. Ginny was a little surprised not to find Denise there. She thought nothing of it, however, except that she had a strong feeling that Denise was still down there. As she continued her work, the feeling grew. Denise *was* down there, she was sure. She could feel her presence; it was quite a pronounced feeling. She shrugged it off, and continued loading the meals from the ovens, on the carts. The feeling of a presence in the galley bay increased.

Then Ginny was convinced she knew the reason. Denise was never above a healthy practical joke and must be hiding from her. There were several cabinets in the galley. Perhaps Denise was idiot enough to squeeze into one of them for a big surprise sort of thing. Ginny decided to wait her out.

But now the feeling of the presence of someone else in the room grew until it became almost intolerable. Ginny *knew* someone was there in the galley with her, and it was an awkward, uncomfortable feeling. She was convinced that she was going to be tapped on her shoulder any minute. She couldn't stop herself from glancing back over her shoulder to avoid it. She laughed at herself and then tried to shrug the whole thing off.

It didn't work. Ginny finally gave up. She went over to the cabinets, opening the doors and shutting them again. Denise was nowhere to be seen. And as much as Ginny tried to dismiss it, the feeling of a definite presence was growing so strong now that she found herself backing against the wall to avoid anyone who might be behind her. She felt silly and ridiculous. Now the feeling of the presence was overbearingly intense. She had never felt anything like this before in her life. A genuine fear gripped her. She had to get to those elevators, and get away from the closed-in galley. She was

131

almost paralyzed with fear. She slid against the wall, against the row of ovens, toward the elevator. She couldn't believe the way she was acting.

Ginny reached the elevators, pressed the button, and waited with her back up against the wall beside the elevators. It seemed to take an endless time for the elevator to arrive. She leaped into it, white and shaking. The ride up seemed interminable. At the main cabin, she pushed open the door and almost knocked over Middy Darrow,* another flight attendant.

"Ginny," she said, "what on earth's the matter with you?"

"I can't talk about it," Ginny said. She felt foolish and ashamed of herself.

"Come with me," Middy told her.

She followed Middy to the back of the plane. Denise was there, and she, too, was visibly shaken.

"You're both more upset than I've ever seen you," Middy said. She turned to Ginny. "Did the same thing happen to you that happened to Denise?"

Ginny was beginning to get more command of herself. "What happened to Denise?" she asked.

Denise blurted her story out. When she had gone down in the elevator to the lower galley bay, Ginny must have been going up, because no one was there when she arrived. She was immediately hit with a cold, very clammy feeling, something she had never felt before. She had waited a few moments for Ginny to return. The feeling grew worse and seemed to completely overpower her. She had done the same thing Ginny did later: run for the elevator. Reaching the main deck, she told Middy Darrow about it and went to the back of the airplane to try to recover. She had no idea that Ginny was experiencing the identical feeling. They asked Middy not to say anything to anyone about the incident, and she agreed.

What puzzled both Ginny and Denise was that neither knew that the other was undergoing the strange encounter, yet both of their experiences were almost identical. They compared notes again. It was something that was inexplicable, and they forced themselves to put it out of their minds.

\*     \*     \*

132

It was only a few weeks after this that Doris Elliott was working the lower bay galley of Plane #318. It was the same plane on which Ginny and Denise had their experience, but Doris knew nothing about this. She had gotten over the shock of her premonition about Flight 401, but she would never forget it entirely. She still loved to work the L-1011s. She had no fear of them at all, nor did most of the crews, in spite of the crash. In fact, like many others, she felt more confident about the plane than ever because of the changes in equipment and procedure that would prevent a similar accident.

There were minor inconveniences, but these were the type of things that could happen on any airplane of any airline. There were no major problems, such as the one that the DC-10s or the 747s would be facing with their sealed doors, causing the tragedy where the cargo door blew out, the floor collapsed and the DC-10 plummeted to the earth. The L-1011 doors closed from the inside, where cabin pressure kept them pressed against the frame. There were some problems that developed with the three giant engines, but they were slowly overcome. In the interim, the huge craft could land safely with only one engine, even though it could not take off on one. The plane had the most advanced landing system in aviation, in spite of the fate of Flight 401. At times the passenger call buttons failed to work, the heating or air-conditioning system might be inadequate, the ovens might overheat, the baggage racks might not latch correctly—things of that nature.

Alone in the galley on Plane #318, Doris Elliott suddenly realized that she was experiencing one of those minor kinks when the galley became uncomfortably cold. She kept on working, stacking the freshly heated passenger trays neatly in the service carts. The cold persisted, a damp, penetrating cold. This was strange, because if anything, the opening and closings of the ovens often made the galley warmer.

She finally called the flight engineer down to see if he could correct the situation. When he arrived, he agreed the temperature was extraordinarily cold, and went to check the thermometer reading. It read 90° F. without question, but the cold was still persisting.

Although he was puzzled, he was sure that the situation

could be corrected by maintenance, and he would report the anomaly on landing. In the meanwhile, the rest of the flight would not take too long, and Doris planned to go to the passenger deck as soon as she finished serving.

Except for the distinct discomfort, neither the engineer nor Doris gave the incident further thought.


I studied the girls carefully as they pieced the story together. There was no question of the intensity of feeling about their experiences, that they believed them, and that they corroborated each other's stories without forcing the issue. We took a break from the story long enough to relax a little. In spite of thier experiences, they had great affection for the L-1011s and constantly bid for them.

"I'm an L-1011 freak," Denise said. "I love them. I could probably have a lot better line on the 727, but I'm so happy with the L-1011. The passengers like it, and they're in a better mood on it. They're so astounded by the size, and there's more for them to do."

The others agreed. They began filling me in on the background of the appearances. From what they had learned from other flight attendants, Second Officer Don Repo reappeared on the craft most frequently. Captain Loft had appeared, too; once very vividly, according to Ginny, but not as frequently as Don Repo. "Emily Palmer can probably fill you in on a lot of these," Ginny said. "She's kept a very complete record."

I said I was going to see her soon. Denise said, "Doris and I just missed a very dramatic incident with Captain Loft—at the Newark airport."

I was about to ask her to describe what happened when Ginny said, "I haven't told you yet about my most incredible experience. Would you like to hear it?"

I told her I would, but I'd like to get some more back ground information first. I wanted to know how the incidents had affected them. They were unanimous about wanting to keep the experiences quiet as far as Eastern was concerned. "This referral to the company shrink is no joke," Denise said. "It's the first step in getting laid off. Also, we could be just plain held up to ridicule. That's hard to take, too. We're

134

taking a big chance right now in trusting you not to identify us."

I reassured them again, and then turned to Ginny to ask her to go on with her story, and for the others to pick up the story where they came in.

After their experiences, Ginny and Denise continued on their normal routine, Ginny said, flying mostly L-1011s according to their line-bid assignments. Eastern had some 5,000 flight attendants. Once a month, each bid for whatever trips seemed to be most favorable, and hoped to get it. Ginny had been with Eastern for five years. Her trips would include Miami to Boston, to New York, to Tampa, and many other points on Eastern's vast labyrinth of routes. Some attendants liked the commuter-type turnarounds, where they would fly to New York on Flight 26, arrive there in the early evening, then fly back on 401 or 477 to Florida and be home about midnight. Others didn't mind the extended flights, with layovers in New York or Boston or Philadelphia, or elsewhere. There were also the choice trips, to Mexico, San Juan, or other parts of the Caribbean. The work was hard and demanding, but it had its compensations in free passes or reduced fares. The actual working days totaled only fifteen or sixteen per month.

Despite the strange experience she had shared with Denise, Ginny had no fear of the L-1011 galley. In fact, she still preferred that duty to the necessity of constantly responding to individual passenger demands. She was a pert, attractive blonde with a strong sense of independence and a lively enthusiasm. Several weeks after her first experience with Denise, she was flying routinely on Flight 401 from New York to Miami. She had noted that the craft for the flight was #318, the same one on which they had their experience before.

Down in the galley, she was waiting by the elevator doors, ready to send up some more food carts to the flight attendants above. In peak periods the elevators were often slow. They would not return down their narrow shaft until the doors on the passenger deck were firmly closed and latched. Ginny was growing a little impatient. She pushed the button several

times to summon the recalcitrant elevators , and waited. Then she leaned back against the starboard wall of the plane, and rested. To her left was the bulkhead that separated the galley from the section that carried the electrical equipment for the plane. It could be entered by a large, heavy bulkhead door with a small window, the size of a porthole.

Out of the corner of her eye, she became aware of hazy cloudlike formation, just in front of the bulkhead wall, above the door. Puzzled, she turned and looked at it. The galley was brightly lighted, and she had no trouble in examining it in detail. It was not condensation or steam or smoke; she knew that. It seemed to be about the size of a grapefruit, but it was getting bigger. It was also pulsating in a strange way, and the shape was much more substantive and articulate than smoke. If it had been smoke—or even condensation—she would have immediately notified the flight engineer. To make sure, she checked a nearby vent. There was no condensation anywhere near it.

She pushed the elevator button again, and then turned back to look. The cloud was now the size of a slightly elongated basketball, a few inches out from the wall, and was beginning to form into a thicker, much more solid shape. She was fascinated, transfixed by it. It was still growing larger. She pushed the elevator button harder and turned her face away. "Perhaps," she said to herself, "if I don't look at it, it might go away." She pushed the button again. The elevator still didn't come.

She wanted to look and not look at the same time. She could still see the shape out of the corner of her eye. It was more pronounced than ever. She looked again. There was no question about it now. It was clearly forming into a face, half-solid, half-misty. She heard the elevator door above slam, and the lift begin to come down. She pushed the button frantically, even though it was unnecessary now. It seemed to be taking an interminable time to reach her.

Just as the elevator reached lower galley level, she looked again. It was a complete, clear face now, with dark hair, gray at the sides, and steel-rimmed glasses now forming clearly on the three-dimensional image. There was no question it was a face, and no question that it was wearing glasses. They were now sharp and clear. This was the final touch. She had been

136

able to try to rationalize the beginnings of the formation by explaining to herself that it *had* to be condensation, even though she knew it wasn't. The steel-rimmed glasses and the clearly identifiable hair removed any uncertainty from her mind.

The elevator arrived. She jerked open the door and jumped into it. She was upset and shaking. At the passenger level, she went immediately to the biffy—the airline term for washroom—and tried to regain her composure. It was hard to get herself together. She would be afraid to tell anybody about this. It was too weird, too unbelievable. The first experience was difficult enough, but that was shared with Denise. Now she would be alone. She didn't even want to tell Denise. When she had seen the eyeglasses form on the already well-articulated face, she knew in her own mind that she was not creating an image of her own. She knew nothing about any other experiences, and didn't have the comfort of that as a support for her own experience. She felt terribly alone and was determined not to tell anyone at all about what she had seen.

Approximately one month later, Denise Woodruff and Doris Elliott arrived at Newark Airport on a routine L-1011 flight from Miami. They had a relatively short wait for their turn-around flight, and went into the flight attendant lounge. Here they encountered a scene of considerable consternation. Half a dozen flight attendants were discussing an incident that had happened earlier that day which, in view of the previous experiences of Denise and Doris, was startling.

Assigned to a Newark flight, they learned, Plane #318 was undergoing its normal preflight check before a turnaround flight back to Miami. The Second Officer had completed his walk-around; the Captain and First Officer were in their seats in the cockpit, running through the endless list of details designed to make sure that nothing was overlooked that could affect flight comfort or safety. In the cabins, the flight attendants were preparing the plane for boarding. The Marriott caterers had already finished loading the food containers in the lower galley, and all was set.

In a few moments, the passengers were boarded, directed to their seats, and prepared themselves for take off.

In the first-class section, Sis Patterson,* the senior stewardess for the flight, was making her routine head count. She found that the count was off by one passenger, and went back over the seats to double-check. It didn't take long to find the discrepancy. There was an Eastern captain in uniform in one of the seats, and obviously he would be one who was deadheading back after bringing another plane to Newark. This was a very common thing, and at times the deadhead captains would ride in the jump seat after sitting in first class for the first part of the trip. It was still necessary to confirm this, and Sis approached the captain with her list.

"Excuse me, captain," she said, "but are you jump-seat riding this trip? I don't have you on my list."

The captain did not respond. He stared straight ahead.

"I beg your pardon, captain," she repeated. "I've got to check you off either as a jump-seat or first-class pass rider. Could you help me?"

The captain still would not respond. He continued to stare ahead, acknowledging the flight attendant by neither voice nor gesture.

Sis was puzzled. Diane Boas,* the flight supervisor, joined her. She was equally puzzled. The man seemed perfectly normal in all respects, yet he seemed as if he were in a daze. It worried both of them. They were somewhat uncertain as to what to do. Finally Sis went forward toward the flight deck, and entered the door to the cockpit. Perhaps the flight captain would be able to get a response where she couldn't.

The flight captain was also perplexed. He got up from his seat in the cockpit and came out to the first-class compartment with Sis. There were about half a dozen regular passengers in the immediate vicinity of the recalcitrant deadhead captain, rather curious about what was going on. The flight captain approached the seat, anxious to get on with the flight. What puzzled him was that there was no record of another Eastern captain listed as a jump-seat occupant, and apparently the man had no pass for the flight.

With both the stewardess and flight supervisor beside him,

the flight captain leaned down to address the other captain. Then he froze. "My God, it's Bob Loft" he said. There was silence in the cabin. Then, something happened that no one in the vicinity could explain. The captain in the first-class seat simply wasn't there. He was there one moment—and not there the next.

The captain returned to operations office in the airport. There was a long delay. The plane was searched. The missing captain could not be found anywhere. Finally Plane #318 lumbered down the runway for takeoff, its passenger count now checked and balanced, but with a stunned and perplexed group of passengers and crew.

Within hours the story was spread across Eastern and half a dozen other airlines. When Ginny Packard and Denise Woodruff heard the story, in one sense they were greatly relieved. It verified their experiences and made them feel less lonely. It also made them very curious.

Ginny Packard was particularly wary of the situation because of her experience in the galley when the face had formed clearly and unmistakably beside her. It was a much greater shock than the first experience, where she and Denise had only sensed a presence, and had not seen anything.

Ginny was a sensible, practical girl. She was intelligent, witty, and not at all prone to flights of fancy. And she was also convinced of her own sanity and rational capacity for observation. She was popular and had many friends, all of whom regarded her with warmth and respect. She had reexamined the chilling incident in the galley in her mind, trying to rationalize it and to convince herself it was a product of her imagination. Each time she tried, she was forced to bring herself back to the conclusion that she *had* seen the face, the hair, the glasses form in graphic reality in front of her. She did not believe in ghosts and did not subscribe to any such stories.

She shared her concern with her husband Fred, a promising young executive with another airline. He fully reassured her of her sanity and helped her to laugh at the incident, whatever it was. He pointed out that he knew Ginny's strengths and weaknesses better than anyone, and that she was as much of a realist as he was. When he heard the report

of the Newark incident, which included as witnesses a senior airline captain, a stewardess, a flight supervisor, he pointed out to her that she was now off the hook and that she didn't need to worry anymore.

His confidence in her cheered her up considerably because she was scheduled for a Miami-New York turnaround the next day, flying up on Flight 26 and returning on 401 again. Ginny had no fear of the plane. In fact, she felt safer on it than on any other craft. Nor did she have any fear of another strange encounter. She was actually intrigued by it, now that the chill had worn off. Her fear was not a lack of confidence in herself; it was more that she was afraid of what others would think if she let them know what she had seen.

Fred drove her to Miami International Airport that afternoon. She had regained her old, lively spirit. She kissed him good-bye and went down the ramp to the plane. She peeked out the concourse window at the tail section, where the plane number was displayed. It read N318EA, the official designation for Eastern's L-1011 Plane #318.

"Good," Ginny said to herself. "I'm ready for anything."

Flight attendants Denise Woodruff and Doris Elliott found themselves in Newark three days after the startling incident in the first-class section of Plane #318. In defense of her own sanity from her previous experience with Ginny, Denise was determined to find out what had happened in the Newark incident in more detail. The details of the story that was circulating were amazingly consistent, but Denise wanted to know more. Doris joined her in this feeling. They were not dealing with a ghost story of old English castles or huge Victorian mansions. This was the modern jet age. The ambiance was stacked against the conventional stories of ghosts. And further, the Newark incident was not dealing with any transparent, gauzy image. It was dealing in a fully three-dimensional apparition that appeared completely solid—and then simply disappeared.

At Newark, Denise and Doris were pleased to notice that their return trip would be on Plane #318. This would give them a legitimate chance to check the plane's logbook, where every incident, minor or major, had to be recorded by FAA

regulation. These reports accumulated in the official logbook over an extended period of time and became a permanent part of the aircraft's record. The logbook remains on the aircraft until it is filled up—usually a period of two or three months. The pilots record the mechanical incidents on one side of the page; the flight attendants do the same on the opposite side.

At the end of each trip, the senior flight attendant will write up her CDR—short for Cabin Discrepancy Report—on gummed stickers. These in turn are pasted to the proper page in the logbook, to become part of the permanent record, side by side with the flight crew's technical report.

Before they boarded the plane for their assigned flight, Denise and Doris went to the crew scheduling office to talk to Hal Griffin,* a friend of theirs, to get more definite information about the uncanny story of the disappearing captain. As a crew scheduler, he would get his information firsthand. Hal confirmed the story in detail. The entire flight crew had left the plane, he told them, reported the incident, entered it in the log. The flight had been delayed for almost an hour. Eventually the flight did go out, and it was uneventful.

The confirmation by the crew scheduler was more than Doris and Denise expected. They had been sure that the details must have been exaggerated and distorted as they made the rounds of the flight-attendant lounges, the ticket counters, the baggage handlers, or the reservation desks. It seemed that everywhere they went, Eastern personnel were talking about it. It seemed so incredible. Their own experiences, along with Ginny Packard's, seemed pale in comparison. As they prepared to board Plane #318 for the return trip, the first thing they planned to do was to look at the logbook.

They found it and picked it up with considerable tension and expectation. When they opened it, they noticed something very strange. All the pages up to and including the date of the incident had been removed, contrary to general practice. Whatever comments recorded by the captain and crew of that unusual flight were completely missing.

Puzzled and somewhat miffed, Denise and Doris went about their jobs of preparing the plane for the return flight. It was strange that the old pages of the logbook had been removed. On the other hand, it was understandable. How

could a flight crew make a technical report on the appearance of an apparition? Or if they had recorded the incident, how would they describe it?

If the incident was as graphic and true as the evidence seemed to indicate, there were some important questions that could be asked. Was this an indication that an individual could survive after death and return in such a vivid form that a technically minded flight crew could be overwhelmed by it?

Like Ginny and Doris, Denise was no longer afraid after her own experience. Her curiosity was mounting, however. When she went down to work in the galley, she actually found herself hoping that she might encounter another incident. With over 200 meals to prepare, however, she had little time for dreaming. She began organizing her routine for the flight, her fears no longer with her, but her curiosity burning more intensely than ever. And yet, in spite of this, she found herself unconsciously hanging her garment bag over the oven of Right Bay 1, making sure that there would be no reflection.

"Was it utterly absurd to seek behind the ordering structures of this world a 'consciousness' whose 'intentions' were these very structures? . . .

"We sense that the meaning of 'consciousness' becomes wider and at the same time vaguer if we try to apply it outside the human realm.

"The positivists have a simple solution: the world must be divided into that which we can say clearly and the rest, which we had better pass over in silence.

"But can anyone conceive of a more pointless philosophy, seeing that what we can say clearly amounts to next to nothing?

"If we may no longer speak or even think about the wider connections, we are without a compass and hence in danger of losing our way."

—Werner Heisenberg,
*Physics and Beyond*

# Chapter VIII

The stories were pretty heady stuff, and hard to absorb. After she had recounted her part of the story, Denise said, "The strange part was the missing lobgbook pages. Every time we'd get our hands on #318's log, it would always be a new one. But the things that happened to us happened before any of the stories began circulating. We weren't influenced by them at all. All we wanted to do was to keep quiet about it as far as Eastern was concerned, and keep it among ourselves. Later, when many girls started refusing to go down into the lower galley, I used to say to them: 'Why are you so afraid of someone who has never done anything? He's always been helpful, as far as I've heard.'"

"All right," I said, "the most graphic appearance seems to be the one at Newark. How can I get more information on that? Who was the captain? Can you remember the date?"

"Now you come to the big problem," Denise said. "Emily Palmer, who's been keeping very thorough notes on the incidents, has a lot of trouble with this sort of thing. Have you talked with her yet?"

I told her I had talked briefly with her and was going to see her shortly.

"Good," Denise said. "She'll be very helpful, as long as you keep her name out of the papers. Anyway, the trouble she's found is that when you have an incident like the one at Newark, everybody is so freaked out about it, they forget to notice all the details they normally would. People talk much more freely then because of the excitement of the time. But the next day, they'll clam up and pretend to know nothing about it. They're running scared. Take me, for instance. I

144

never remember to write down dates or flight numbers—but I can remember the incidents very clearly. The cockpit crews don't like to talk about the incidents at all. It's just like the UFO situation. Pilots will admit confidentially they've seen them, but they've learned now never to report them or talk about them on the outside.''

I later learned more about the problem Denise was talking about. I was lucky that the flight attendants I was interviewing were willing to share whatever information they had with me. Others were not so cordial, perhaps because they were distrustful. In a way, I couldn't blame them. Most people are very reluctant to talk about experiences considered to be paranormal. The fear of ridicule seemed to be as strong as the fear of losing a job.

''You've got over five thousand flight attendants on Eastern and more than two thousand pilots and engineers. You can't get their home phone numbers. Even *we* can't get them from the office. And you don't know who to call if you did. I don't envy you your job.''

I was beginning to think she was right. It was frustrating. The story was elusive; the research seemed even more so.

The three flight attendants seemed unanimous in feeling that there were many more incidents with Second Officer Repo than with Captain Loft. There were no reports that anyone had heard regarding the reappearance of First Officer Stockstill.

''The problem is,'' Doris Elliott said, ''that I would love to have another experience, in a way. I honestly think it reflects the possibility of life after death, and I dig that.

''Sometimes when I'm down in the galley alone, I'll kid around and say, 'Repo, I don't mind talking to you, but I don't have time. Check me later, but I've got lots of people to feed.' The fact is, the reports have stopped completely now. I haven't even heard any for months.''

There was no question about the affection most crew members felt about Don Repo. ''He was a very virile-looking man,'' Ginny said. ''And very strong. But he was so soft-spoken I never heard him raise his voice once. And he was so much fun. He laughed with us all the time, and was constant-

ly pulling little gags or coming up with a new joke. His sense of humor was terrific. If you wanted to describe him, that's the first thing you'd think of."

Everybody who knew Repo described him in this way. He was competent and thorough in his job and lightened it with an infectious sense of humor. This was true, it seemed, of the trio who described him to me that day. The only thing to discount about their comments was their natural exuberance, which was high-spirited and might have led to some decoration of detail.

Then Ginny volunteered another incident that she couldn't explain, which still bothered her.

She was on cabin duty on Flight 26, Plane #318, heading for New York. She was determined that if she ran into any more strange incidents, she would make sure someone else was around, and that she would be the last to report it to anyone. Two experiences were enough. The flight was relatively smooth, except for some minor low-altitude turbulence. After they passed through it, the plane showed a tendency to roll slightly to the right, then straighten, and roll to the right again. This continued for a considerable time, until landing at Kennedy in New York. The plane was checked thoroughly there, with the hydraulic and electrical control systems carefully tested. No apparent reason for the roll was found. Minor adjustments were made, however, and Plane #318 took off again on schedule from Kennedy to Miami International, as Flight 401.

It wasn't long before the plane began the slight roll to the right again, followed by an equally slight recovery motion. It was somewhat annoying, but not really disturbing. Ginny went about serving the Beefeater martinis, the scotches, the Cokes from her beverage cart, a little annoyed at the slight yaw to the right, but not concerned about it. She was approaching the cabin section situated over the wing area, when a man sitting there called her down the aisle to him. He pointed out the window and said to her, "What is that over the wing?"

Ginny bent down and looked out. Out toward the wingtip was a luminous, hazy mass that was definitely not a cloud,

because its mass was opaque and it hovered over the wing, as it continued moving along with the plane. Ginny watched it with the passenger for some time. They noticed that the mass—about the size of a large piece of luggage—would rise up a few feet off the wing, and as it did, the plane would level out. Then the mass would settle down on the wing. As it did, the wing would distinctly dip. Then the process would repeat itself over again. After they had watched it for several minutes, the passenger suggested that Ginny might want to go up and notify the flight engineer.

She did so hesitantly. He came back from the cockpit with her and joined the passenger and Ginny to observe it. "It must be a cloud," the engineer said. "It'll go away."

The passenger protested. He told the engineer that they had been watching it for several minutes. The engineer stayed there for some time and was frankly baffled. His only theory was that it was condensation, but he thought it a weak theory. He assured them that the plane was perfectly safe in spite of the roll, and that he would have it checked when they landed in Miami.

About half an hour later, the plane began rolling to the left, continuing in a similar pattern as before. By now, Ginny had reached the point where she was more interested than concerned or worried. When a passenger sitting over the wing section on the left side called her across the aisle, she was almost able to take it as a matter of course. She joined the passenger in looking out. The luminescent mass was there again on the other wingtip, and the plane was not rolling as long as it was above the wing. But when it came down and sat on the wingtip, the plane would roll, and the controls could not correct it.

The plane landed safely at Miami International, and Ginny went home to tell Fred about another incident. At least, she was thinking, I didn't even look for anything unusual until two different passengers pointed it out to me.

The thing that bothered all three of the flight attendants most was the missing pages in the logbook of Plane #318. "It makes me mad," Denise said. "I think they've got them thoroughly hidden. We came on 318 another time, my room-

mate and I, after we heard another story of Repo's reappearance. By this time, I was in the habit of flipping through the log everytime I got on the plane. We dashed on the plane that day, but it was a brand-new book again.''

"The problem now," Doris Elliot said, "is that most of this happened over the months that followed the crash. That happened at the end of 1972. I think the stories reached a peak around June in 1973. Isn't that right, Denise?''

"Just about. They were hot and heavy for the first year, I'd say. Up until late spring in 1974, maybe June. I don't think I've learned of any new incidents since then, have you?''

"That's just about right," Doris said. "That's why it's hard to pick up any new information. The stories seemed to stop very suddenly, around March or April of 1974. Maybe a little longer. Emily Palmer might be able to pin it down a little better for you. If these things were still happening, we'd probably have a pile of stories for you, the way we used to get them.''

The pattern that the girls discerned during the first year after the accident emerged as we talked.

Each of them involved the sudden appearance in the L-1011s of either Captain Loft or the flight engineer, Second Officer Don Repo. They also involved the sudden disappearance. The apparitions were clear, solid, and identifiable. They would appear and disappear in front of pilots, flight engineers, or flight attendants completely unexpectedly, and usually in flight. Most of the stories centered on Plane #318, regardless of what route it was assigned to. But flight crews reported other L-1011 sister ships to be involved. The appearances of the dead crew members were unpredictable as to time or place. Some flight crews, both cabin and cockpit, expressed a strong desire to experience an encounter with the apparitions; others shied away from the idea. But there was no consistent pattern. Each time any of the trio was assigned to Plane #318, she would immediately look at the logbook. Nearly every time any of them did so, she would find that pages had been removed from the book, or a brand-new book had been supplied. This was not consistent with other sister ships of the L-1011 fleet, where the cumulative record over many weeks filled the logbooks, and only rarely was a new

logbook found, after the old book had served for many months.

"By the way," Ginny said. "There's one more person you might check. He's a flight engineer based in Boston. He's very interested in this subject. Name is Dick Manning*."

"Has he encountered either of the apparitions?" I asked.

"I'd better let him tell his own story," Ginny said. "I think you'll find it interesting."

I made a note of his name and the small town outside of Boston where he lived. She didn't have his phone number, but I hoped it might be in the book. Then Denise said, "I think you'll get a lot more general information when you talk with Emily Palmer. She's been keeping better tabs than we have. The three of us only know about our own experiences, even though we've kept tails on the others. Emily's got a better overall picture."

Denise's evaluation was correct. I met with Emily and her husband Don at the hotel for dinner. Don worked as a flight engineer for another airline and had heard many of the stories repeated among its flight crews.

"After talking with them and with Emily," he said, "I'm convinced this is a story that just can't be discounted. Yet it's still hard to pin down. I really don't believe in ghosts, but I'm broad-minded enough to think there's always that possibility."

"That's just about the way I feel," Emily said. "I haven't seen any of these apparitions myself, but I have no reason to doubt the crew members who told them to me. But there is still the problem of no one's wanting to be identified. They'll talk to me informally, but that's it. In some cases, they'll even withdraw the story the next day. They'll ask me to forget about what they told me only the day before."

I asked her, "Are all the stories centered on Plane #318?"

"The majority of them," she said. "But there are other L-1011s involved, too."

She brought out her notes, and we went over them carefully. "I'm not a reporter, remember," she said. "And these are all rather sketchy. I've been keeping them just for my own interest, and because I'm convinced that there's something to

them. These people are not idiots. The flight crews would not be flying if they were. So how do you explain it? If these things happened, then it's one of the damnedest stories you could run into. If they didn't happen, it's still the same. Why should sane people bring these things up? They have nothing to gain by it. I'm puzzled by it all, that's what I am."

The notes were very interesting and quite complete, considering she was just keeping them for her own interest:

JFK . . . L-1011 flight . . . Miami turnaround. Plane being fueled and checked . . . Eastern vice-president pre-boarded plane, prior to regular passengers. VP entered first-class section, which was empty except for an Eastern captain in uniform. VP stopped by the captain to say hello. . . . After the greeting, the VP suddenly realized he was talking to Bob Loft, the deceased captain. . . . Loft suddenly simply vanished, disappeared . . . VP went immediately out to ramp agent . . . complete search of plane and area was made . . . no sign of any captain found . . . no deadhead pilot was found on the passenger manifest list . . . told to me by JFK crew sked . . . would not reveal VP's name . . .

Capt. Loft . . . seen again in first-class section in New York (JFK) by flight captain and 2 flight attendants . . . they talked to him, and he disappeared . . . flight was canceled . . . told to me by captain involved . . . asked me to keep his name confidential . . .

Flight attendant—New York to Miami . . . does not want name mentioned . . . pulled back compartment door on overhead bin during preflight check first-class cabin . . . knew Capt. Loft . . . had flown with him on many flights before the crash . . . found herself looking directly into Capt. Loft's face in the compartment . . .

Aircraft involved seem to be more than one . . . reports coming in from #317, 308, others . . .

Flight attendant—Miami . . . reported to open door in galley oven compartment . . . saw face of 2nd officer Don Repo there clearly . . .

Denise W. tells me they were watching a crew of Mariott caterers boarding the food carriers with food trays on Plane #318 . . . she and another flight attendant saw a sudden commotion . . . the catering crew had left the plane and did not want to go back . . . because they said they saw a flight engineer standing in the galley, who instantly disappeared before their eyes . . . long delay before they could be persuaded to continue loading the plane . . . very excitable . . .

Plane #318 from New York over Everglades on approach pattern to Miami Intl . . . male voice came over PA system to announce customary seat-belt and no-smoking precaution to the passengers and crew . . . no one in plane's crew, either cockpit or cabin, claims to have made the announcement, and PA system was not in use at all during that time period . . .

L-1011    flight . . . Plane    #318 . . . Atlanta-Miami . . . Second Officer sitting at engineer's panel monitoring the flight of the ship . . . heard loud knocking coming from compartment below cockpit, down in the hell hole. . . . Engineer went to trap in floor . . . turned flashlight on and scanned whole area below . . . nothing unusual there . . . compartment empty . . . looked back at engineer's panel, and says he clearly saw the face of Repo, had known Repo well . . . entered incident on plane's log . . . asked me to keep name confidential . . .

L-1011—location not specified . . . flight engineer came to flight deck before doing "walk around" preflight inspection and engineering panel check . . . saw man in Eastern Second Officer's uniform sitting in his seat at the panel . . . the engineer quickly recognized him as Don Repo . . . the apparition of Repo said

something like: "You don't need to worry about the preflight, I've already done it" . . . almost immediately the three-dimensional image of Repo disappeared, vanished . . .

L-1011 stewardess in lower galley, preparing meals while in flight . . . discovered that Right Bay #1 oven indicated an overloaded circuit . . . a man in engineer's uniform appeared within a few moments . . . shortly after that, another flight engineer appeared, asked what was wrong with the oven . . . new arrival insisted he was only engineer on the plane. . . . Later, the flight attendant looked up Repo's picture, who she immediately identified as the man who first fixed the oven . . .

Newark crew sked tells me confidentially that captain came off San Juan flight, and told him of a direct encounter with Repo. Repo is supposed to have said, "There will never be another crash of an L-1011 . . . we will not let it happen. . . ."

One particular story that intrigued Emily Palmer involved a woman passenger in the first-class section of Plane #318 scheduled for a New York-to-Miami flight. The plane was still at the ramp, and the head count had not yet been taken by the flight attendant in the first-class section. The woman was seated next to an Eastern flight officer, in the uniform of a flight engineer. Something about the officer worried the woman. He looked sick and pale, and when she said something to him, he would not respond. She asked him if he was all right, and should she call the stewardess to help him? There was still no response. The woman became disturbed and called the stewardess who agreed that the flight officer seemed ill. She asked him if she could help. Several other passengers also noticed him. Then—in front of the group, as before—the flight engineer simply disappeared.

Everyone was disconcerted, but the woman became almost hysterical. When she arrived in Miami, she demanded

that she be shown pictures of the Eastern flight engineers to try to identify the man. According to the story, both she and the stewardess involved picked out a picture of Repo as the officer who had been in the first-class seat.

Emily tried for several weeks to track down the story to its source. She had learned of it from four independent sources at four different times. All were Eastern employees: a flight attendant, a Second Officer, a ramp agent, and a mechanic. All told the identical story almost down to the last detail. She could not trace the date or the flight number, nor could she locate the crew members involved. It was illustrative of the difficulty in tracking down the stories in an airline with so many employees and so many daily flights. There were the other reasons, of course: the fear of ridicule, the fear of being sent to a psychiatrist, and the general concern that anyone has when it comes to reporting such an elusive thing as a ghost.

But Emily kept her notes as accurately as she could. Some came directly from the crews involved, some came indirectly. She was lax on dates and times, but had assured herself, at least, of the validity of her associates she gathered the information from. She made her notes beginning in mid-1973, and continuing through the rest of that year and into the next. As she did so, she noticed a discernible trend that others confirmed: the stories about Bob Loft were fading out, and the stories about Don Repo were increasing in frequency. One thing that appeared evident to her was that all the events concerning Repo seemed to indicate that he was on board to help out whatever flight was involved. Unlike the classic ghost stories, there seemed to be nothing sinister about them. She counted about two dozen events concerning the apparitions. Most of them continued to center on Plane #318, although not exclusively.

Emily found herself wishing she could run into one of the apparitions directly. Although she flew L-1011s almost exclusively, including #318, she never had the luck to encounter either Repo or Loft. The reports were coming in so fast, that it was difficult for Emily to tabulate them. By her judgment, they were coming from sane and logical people who were not prone to exaggerate and who, for the most part,

were thoroughly experienced airline employees. They had flown in many kinds of planes, but never had encountered the phenomena in any planes except some of the L-1011s.

What was also difficult to understand was that the appearances seemed to involve full-bodied, three-dimensional figures of the former captain and Second Officer of the tragic flight, and that there was actual communication with them. It was quite easy to laugh the incidents off. Obviously many could be discounted. But many could not be told in full because of the reluctance of those who experienced the incidents to be identified. Flight crews, especially, are trained in observation and in the realities of flying and navigation, and have no desire to become involved in a series of events that are inexplicable in terms of engineering, physics, or mechanics. Yet the reports were persistently being made, and they circulated fast. Almost every airline crew member on any airline, including some foreign ones, knew of the stories by the end of 1973.

The series of events was beginning to have its effects on the flying crews. Most stewardesses whom Emily talked with were intensely interested and unafraid, but some simply could not get themselves to work down in the lower galleys of #318 or many of the other L-1011s. Others told her they were eager to work down there in the hope of finding some answer to the riddle. None was afraid of the plane itself, or any of the other L-1011s.

It was a long dinner. By the time the table was cleared, the waiters were glancing at us, obviously anxious to close the dining room. We apologized and went up to my room to continue our discussion.

"John's problem," Don told Emily, "is to get more direct information. Emily, you're flying in planes constantly. Even with that, it's like mining for gold. Let's say there've been two dozen incidents. If you multiply the number of people in the flight crews Eastern has by the number of passenger miles they fly every day, it's like hunting for a needle in a haystack."

"Another problem is that I hear the stories faded out about a year ago, last spring. In 1974. Is that right?" I said.

"That is right," Emily said. "I haven't run into any

recently at all.'' She thought a moment, and then added, ''Did Denise and Ginny tell you about the incident at Newark, where the apparition of Captain Loft was in first class, and the flight captain came out of the cockpit and identified him before he disappeared?''

I said that she did.

''I know that captain fairly well,'' Emily said. ''He told me the story directly. There was no nonsense about it. If he gives me permission to let you know his name, I'll give it to you and you can call him yourself.''

I talked to Emily on the phone about a week later. The captain's name was George Fischer,* and he told her that he'd talk to me if I called. I put in a call immediately and he answered. I told him I was interested in the strange event that happened at Newark, and that Emily Palmer had said it would be all right to call him.

There was a moment of silence on the other end of the phone, and then Captain Fischer said, ''Yes, I did tell Emily that, but I've been thinking about it ever since. You'll have to forgive me, but I just don't feel I should talk about it. Thanks for calling, anyway.''

He was polite but firm. There was no way I could get him to talk, nothing else to do but end the conversation. It was one more of the frustrating things that seemed to be blocking the research constantly. I began to wonder if there was any way at all of cracking the story open. Just on principle, I hated to quit. Somehow I felt that the story was more important than just a ghost story. I knew I was going to continue if only out of stubbornness, but I also knew there wouldn't be any pat answer as to how to get around the obstacles.

"Physical science has limited its scope so as to leave a background which we are at liberty to, or even invited to, fill with a reality of spiritual import."

—Sir Arthur Stanley Eddington, *The Nature of the Physical World*

# Chapter IX

There was a picture shaping up, but it was a jumbled mosaic. There was a lot to follow up on. The flight engineer in Boston that Ginny had told me about. The pilots who were mediums. The FAA supervisor who also, incredibly, was a medium. The New York mechanic. And I particularly wanted to try to track down the story of the Mexico City incident that had been written up in the Flight Safety Foundation Bulletin. The sources were scattered; I knew the job would continue to be frustrating.

From what I had gathered from the four flight attendants, the new L-1011 series had continued to gain in popularity with both cockpit and cabin crews, in spite of the crash and the stories about the apparitions. Passengers continued to like it for its spaciousness and quiet. Not many passengers knew of the phenomenon, but Emily had mentioned that she had run into some who sought out the L-1011 to learn more about it, or in the hope of experiencing it. There was general agreement that in spite of the long series of events that were being reported, there was nothing dangerous or harmful about the incidents. The stories involving Don Repo, for instance, seemed to point to his wanting to help with the airplane, whatever L-1011 flight was involved. If this was a ghost, it was a good ghost.

During this time, the minor troubles with the L-1011 fleet were being ironed out successfully. Other flight attendants, like Denise Woodruff, described themselves as L-1011 freaks and preferred not to work on any other plane. More of the giant jets were coming on line, each one costing close to $20,000,000 dollars, for an eventual total of 49 of the craft. But the planes were capable of producing up to $75,000

worth of revenue a day, and the investment was worth it. Like other airlines, Eastern was having its troubles with both inflation and recession. The big new jumbo jets could help them get back in the running.

But the events could be startling. As the anniversary of the tragedy passed and 1974 came in, one Eastern captain told a reporter that he would wring the reporter's neck if his name was mentioned, but that he was warned by a flight engineer riding in the jump seat of his L-1011 that there was going to be an electrical failure. Without even thinking about it, the captain called for a recheck, and a circuit was discovered to be faulty. Later, after a double-take, the rest of the cockpit crew identified the intruding Second Officer sitting on the jump seat as Don Repo.

I decided to attack the Mexico City incident first. I asked Rachelle to dig into the Miami FAA records to see what she could find there. A check with the Flight Safety Foundation revealed that the story had come into them from several pilot sources at Eastern, but that they were not at liberty to reveal any names.

Rachelle returned from the FAA office with several documents available through the Freedom of Information Act, which fortunately gives journalists access to government material not listed as secret or confidential. We tracked down the flight numbers, the route of Plane #318 at the time, and the official reports of the mechanical problem with the engines, known as the MRR reports. We could not get hold of the Eastern logbooks, because they were sealed in the company vaults and, as private files, were not available under the Freedom of Information Act. This would be the only record of the alleged appearance of Second Officer Repo's apparition, and it was impossible to obtain. If what Denise Woodruff and Doris Elliott had said was true, the logbook would have been immediately whisked off the plane, and a new one substituted. We were able to locate one Eastern technician who could check the files, and he brought back word that the reports for that time period—February 1974—were no longer in the files.

This particular story was so well known that I had gathered several versions of it from Eastern flight attendants on several

of my trips over the previous few months. The stories were amazingly consistent, but this may have been because of the Flight Safety Bulletin report.

Also missing were the names of the Eastern crew members involved, both cockpit and cabin. These, too, would be recorded only in the unavailable logs. This was a weak point, and I knew it, but there was nothing to be done about it. I decided to make one stab at Eastern officialdom, knowing that it would be futile.

I called Eastern public relations, and was put in touch with Jim Ashlock of that office. I told him that I was interested in the persistent stories of the apparitions, and wondered what Eastern's point of view was on the matter. He summed it up rather succinctly.

"Well," he said in a pleasant Southern drawl, "we think it's a bunch of crap. That's all it is."

I asked him if he had done any checking on it.

"I guess I did the most extensive checking on it that anybody ever did," he said. "I checked all through the logs. There's nothing in them at all."

"Have you talked to any of the Eastern people who have reported the stories?" I asked.

"Nobody's ever reported it," he said. "There's no track to anybody having reported it. I think it's entirely an insight into the phenomenon of rumor. Of course ghost stories relative to modes of transportation go back as far as you want to go. The *Flying Dutchman*. The ghost ships on the sea. The Rod Serling series played a lot on it. The only thing I could figure out was that it was an outgrowth of the somewhat extensive publicity around the 1011. The first wide-body accident, stuff like that."

His response was just about what I had been led to suspect. I couldn't help wonder why I had been able to get quite a few people to talk while he seemed unable to. In fact, earlier in the day, I had talked with a friend of mine who was an Eastern pilot, who had confidentially tried to dig up some information for me. He was unable to get any specific information over his previous trip, but he did say that some of his fellow crew members had seen some of the logbook reports of Plane

#318, and they were "really wild—unbelievable." This of course was in conflict with Jim Ashlock's statement.

As expected, my request to look at some of Plane #318's logbooks was rejected, and I went back over the material Rachelle had assembled, along with my notes scrawled out on various flights in the past few months to see what could be put together as a composite story about the Mexico City incident. Another mosaic formed, and it was intriguing, even if inconclusive:

By February 1974, Plane #318 was making several trips on the Mexico City run. Early in that month, #318 was proceeding on its endless round of routine flights, all under one of the various flight numbers to which it was assigned. It flew routinely from Palm Beach to Kennedy in New York as Flight 191, then proceeded on a turnaround back to Palm Beach as Flight 196. All was uneventful. The problems were simple and easy to cope with. The coffee maker was stubborn, and refused to work right. The mushroom on the floor of the cabin, a device that locks and clamps the food and beverage carts securely to the floor, was troublesome and failed to lock the cart securely.

As Flight 191 again, Plane #318 went back to Kennedy, where it was assigned to Flight 903, a New York-to-Mexico City run. On 903 the lower-galley flight attendant was going through the usual routine of preparing the food carts on the trip. Like every other stewardess, Eastern or other, she was aware of the stories about the continual appearances of Second Officer Repo, as was the flight-deck crew on her flight. In fact, she had known Don Repo and was well aware of what he looked like.

Like every flight attendant who now worked in the L-1011 galleys, she also knew the reports of what had happened with the oven doors on many flights. The reflection theory had been widely circulated as the answer to the enigma, but as a theory it could not hold up if the numerous other nongalley incidents were reliably reported, as many insisted they were.

What happened on #318's flight to Mexico City came quickly and unexpectedly. The stewardess looked at the window of one of the ovens and clearly saw the face of Don

Repo looking out at her. She immediately ran to the elevator, the only exit to the passenger cabin except for an emergency panel in the ceiling. On the main deck, she grabbed the first stewardess she could find. Together they went down to the galley and crossed to the oven. The second stewardess clearly saw the same image, and there was no question of its not being a reflection. They called the flight deck and gave the story to the flight engineer there. He came down immediately.

Repo's face was now clearly formed, and the engineer recognized him. In addition to that, he spoke audibly to the engineer. "Watch out for fire on this airplane," he said. Then he disappeared, completely.

The plane landed without incident in Mexico City. The event was reported by an aviation safety insurance newsletter to be entered in the craft's log. But when the engines were turned over for the continuation of the flight to Acapulco, the number 3 engine on the starboard wing would not start.

The repair job was apparently a major one and required a full engine replacement that had to be done at the Miami base. A ferry crew was dispatched from Miami to handle the job of bringing the craft back from Mexico City on two engines. Since the L-1011s are designed with plenty of reserve power, they could both take off and land easily with two engines. With a single engine they could only land, but not take off.

In Mexico City's high altitude, care would have to be taken. The thin air reduced the lift considerably, at the 6,000-foot altitude of the airport. In many high-altitude airports, such as the one at Mexico City, planes are permitted to land only early in the morning or after sunset, because the high temperatures of a tropical day can combine with the rarefied air to reduce the lift so critically that the plane never leaves the ground and ends up crashing at the end of the runway.

The temperature was not a problem here, but the altitude was. Even with all three engines, a takeoff needed careful attention. Plane #318's ferry trip was assigned the flight number 7200, and the ferry crew warmed up the engines at

idle speed for about four minutes, then taxied the empty plane down toward the end of the runway.

Cleared for takeoff, the captain pushed the throttles of the two operating engines forward and began the takeoff. They reached the three stages of the takeoff at the expected marks: V-1, where the plane was approaching takeoff speed, but could be aborted if necessary; V-R, where the steering column was pulled back to lift the plane in the process known as rotation; and V-2, where the plane was definitely committed to takeoff and could not be turned back under any conditions at all.

At the altitude of 50 feet, barely off the ground in the thin air where lift was minimal, engine #1 stalled and then rapidly backfired several times. It had to be shut off immediately, leaving only engine #2 operating. The plane was forced to climb to an altitude safe enough for the plane to circle and get back to the runway. The captain quickly discharged the carbon dioxide fire agent preventing the engine from bursting into flames.

Then the plane climbed on its single engine slowly to 400 feet, enough to circle the airport and get back to the runway. It was a masterful job of plane handling. Some considered it miraculous that the plane was able to continue climbing and be brought back safely on one engine. under these conditions and at the high airport altitude.

New engines were shipped down to Mexico City. Engines 10109 and 10211 were replaced on the number 1 and number 3 positions. Cockpit voice recorder—the CVR—number 14236 was replaced by number 16993 by Eastern maintenance. Again, Plane #318 was well and healthy and back in service. But one thing was noteworthy: an entire disassembly of number 1 engine showed no reason whatever for the engine to stall and backfire.

I was a little puzzled why the cockpit voice recorder was replaced. Certainly it had nothing to do with the faulty engines. Could this have anything to do with the vague rumors that parts were being taken off #318 because they seemed to be connected with the appearances of the apparitions? It was a wild idea, and I tabled it. I couldn't help feeling that

whether the stories were real or apochryphal, they were in one way or another affecting the operation of one of the largest airlines in the country—without endangering lives, but creating major mystification among a large segment of Eastern's thirty thousand employees.

Reports kept coming in from Elizabeth Manzione. Her travels with Northwest Orient airlines took her to Eastern airline bases all over the East and Midwest. Many of them were repeats of the various incidents, but they all had a remarkable consistency about them. It seemed that there was practically no one in Eastern—or in most of the airlines— who didn't know about the incidents. She had tracked down several direct sources and wanted to know if she should interview them. Since she had time off in between regular trips, I asked her if she wanted work on a regular fee basis during these times. She was so interested in the story by now that she agreed. She had an uncanny ability for making friends with people she interviewed, and being a flight attendant herself, she could relate to them well.

Meanwhile I received a call from Rachelle while I was still in New York. While I was trying to assess and analyze my long discussion with the Eastern pilots, she and J.R. had been continuing to dig in the Miami area with some interesting results. "I learned more about the FAA executive who is interested in parapsychology," she said. "You going to stop in Atlanta to see him?"

"I plan to," I said.

She went on to tell me some of the details of his work, and said, "I've learned that he's highly interested in the psychic field. Not just superficially. Just wanted to make sure you weren't going to miss him."

"Nope," I said. "I'm going to head down there in a couple of days. Anything else new?"

"We've got a lot of supportive material. I'll tell you all about it when you get down here."

She described some of it. It would be very helpful. The sources would have to be protected, and I would have to be careful in the way I used it. I was encouraged by this material because it added a considerable amount of solidity to the base of this tantalizing and perplexing story.

"One other thing," Rachelle said. "Believe it or not, J.R. has found another medium who works for Eastern. She's based in New York and works in ticketing. She has a lot of friends down here and comes down to visit them often. He feels sure she'll be able to help. She's very interested in the case. Her name is Laura Britebarth."*

I still couldn't get over my long interview with the pilots, and the fact that there were so many full-blooded mediums around. Those connected with the airline business were especially interesting. They would be able to evaluate the situation from both the aviation and the psychic aspects. This seemed to me to be an unusual combination, and one that I certainly never expected to find.

I finally reached Bill Damroth,* the FAA supervisor from the Atlanta area, by phone. He agreed to talk with me when I got down there. I met him and his wife at their pleasant, modest suburban home. He was a quiet, thoughtful man in his fifties, soft-spoken and serious. I was curious about how he got interested in the psychic field, and he said, "I always used to be a hard and fast skeptic. I thought it was strictly for kooks. My background is technical, and so is my career.

"This whole thing started for me when I visited some close friends of ours in the Midwest. The husband is an executive with American Airlines, and you've never met anyone more sane and sober. He was very active with a psychic group, and I went with him to some of the meetings. I didn't pay much attention to it at first. Then I talked to several mediums, and they came out with information about me that there was no way for them to know. It threw me. So did a couple of séances they held. Then I did a little digging into the background and found that it wasn't as illogical as I thought. I found a spiritualist church, and they held classes. Then I discovered I had some ability along this field myself. You know, the problem is that people are afraid of this sort of thing. They can't tell you why, they just are. My theory is they don't know enough about it. We tend to be afraid of the unknown."

I discovered that Bill Damroth was very interested in psychic healing and had been concentrating on that. He had not become involved in the Eastern incidents, but was in-

trigued by them. He promised to see what he could find out about the story and would get back to me. "I think you're going to find," he told me as I was leaving, "there's a lot more truth to this than you've ever realized. As a matter of fact—have you thought of trying to contact Repo through a medium?"

I told him about the same suggestion from others, but that the whole thing was so foreign to me personally I didn't know what to think.

"Think about it," he said.

Before I left Miami for Atlanta, I put in a long-distance call to the TWA pilot whom Emily Palmer had told me about. I wanted to climb down away from this rarefied atmosphere of the psychic, and talk to someone purely on the technical side. I reached Captain Al Morgan* by phone.

As in all the contacts I made on the story, I always felt a little sheepish in approaching someone about it because it was such a strange story. I felt awkward and even embarrassed. It wasn't like an ordinary journalistic interview, where you went after facts that anyone would be familiar with. Self-consciously, I didn't want the person on the other end of the phone to think *I* was a kook. Conversely, I wanted to reassure whomever I was calling that I didn't think *he* was a kook. I think these were the hardest interviews I had yet run across.

After he was assured I would not use his real name, Captain Morgan did much to relieve my feelings about this. "All I can tell you is hearsay," he said, "because it has not happened to me directly. I don't fly the L-1011s. But I've heard from many people I respect, that a hostess went down to the galley below on one of the L-1011s we lease from Eastern, and heard noises unlike those she had ever heard on an airplane before. She called the flight engineer and he came down. But he couldn't identify the noises, either. They were completely foreign to anything in an aircraft. So the girls just refused to go down to the galley anymore.

"But in addition to that, we went into Phoenix one night. There was an L-1011 parked there with police cars all around it with their beacon lights rotating. We wondered what was happening."

Then Captain Morgan went on to describe the incident at Phoenix in detail:

In the off-season, during the hot summer months, Eastern made a practice of leasing some of their L-1011s to TWA, since the light Florida traffic during that season could not fill them. Captain Morgan pulled his plane up to the ramp in Phoenix, Arizona at 1:00 A.M. on a trip he was flying in a Boeing 727. There was one of the L-1011s leased from Eastern at the ramp next to his. His attention was attracted by several police cars surrounding the L-1011, their rotating lights whirling around in the domes on top of their cars.

Captain Morgan and his cockpit crew had a forty-five-minute wait before their 727 flight continued. They deplaned and went over to the scene to find out what was going on. They discovered that the L-1011 was on a continuing, through-flight with several stops en route. A woman in the coach section had been perfectly quiet and undisturbed through the flight up until the time the plane approached Phoenix. Quite suddenly she began screaming and said that a man had suddenly appeared in a seat near her. She had been looking directly at the seat. The man had not walked up to it, she claimed. He had just suddenly come into being there. Then he had disappeared the minute she started screaming.

The cabin crew could not quiet her down and finally had to call the police. She became so hysterical that they had to take her off in a straitjacket. The incident piqued TWA Captain Morgan's curiosity. Later he began making inquiries among other TWA pilots and maintenance men who flew and serviced the L-1011s leased from Eastern. He did not believe in apparitions, but he had an open mind.

A TWA pilot and copilot, told him that they had been going through a preflight check on an L-1011 leased from Eastern. They didn't recall the plane number, so they weren't sure that #318 was involved. One of them noticed another man in the cockpit jump seat. He, too, disappeared in front of their eyes. They called the flight attendants in the cabin to ask who had entered the cockpit. The attendants swore that no one had gone in or out from the time they had boarded the plane with the pilot and copilot. There were several other

TWA reports, similar to the Eastern incidents in both the galley and flight deck.

Along with these incidents, Captain Morgan learned more about the salvaged-parts theory from TWA maintenance. The maintenance men had heard from their counterparts at Eastern that all the events, that had taken place since the first had been reported, seemed to center on those L-1011s which had been equipped with nonstructural parts salvaged from the wrecked plane in the Everglades. These were said to include radios and other electronic and avionic instruments that had been carefully checked and rebuilt, so that they were perfectly operative and in sound condition. There was nothing wrong in this process as long as the equipment met rigorous tests. The rationale for the use of the rebuilt equipment was not hard to understand. The electronic and avionic equipment for each plane runs into thousands and thousands of dollars. If the parts are salvageable, and can meet the strict testing procedure, there is no reason why they should not be used.

Another rationale for using any possible salvageable equipment was that the L-1011s were behind schedule in coming off the line from Lockheed. Delays were encountered because critical parts were slow in delivery, holding up a plane that was otherwise ready for service. Many parts were simply not there when they were needed. It would not then be just a question of economics, but of time schedule.

Captain Morgan learned of another story that was emanating from Eastern operations. Certain parts of the galley equipment, such as elevators and the stainless steel ovens from the wrecked L-1011 had been in good enough condition to be used in some of the sister ships coming off the line at that time. Again, this would be a perfectly safe practice since the equipment had to be thoroughly tested before it was put to use. The parts were not part of the basic structure of the plane, so that no hidden stress problems would be involved. All this led to the question: why was the phenomenon alleged to take place only on those planes that utilized some of the parts and equipment from the ill-fated Flight 401?

"These things are very, very strange to me," Captain Morgan said. "I don't believe in apparitions. But I also have

an open mind, and you wonder if there is something to it. I have heard that this takes place only on L-1011s that are equipped with some galley equipment from the wrecked plane. Now there's one thing. There's a service area on the plane for hydraulics. And there's a light switch they throw on so they can service this area. And they can't understand why the light in this one particular airplane will not stay illuminated. There always seems to be something that will keep that light out. So the mechanics won't go up and service that part of the airplane after dark. But on the other hand, the fellows I know who fly the 1011 think it's the best plane ever. They think it's far superior to the 747.''

This was a consistent report I was getting from Eastern flight crew members, and it spoke well for the plane. The series of incidents did nothing to diminish this confidence. If anything, they reinforced it because of the apparent benevolent attitude reflected in the appearances. The uneasiness, reflected by some, had nothing to do with the performance of the plane.

"Now I have heard," Captain Morgan continued, "that there have been sane and sober cockpit members from Eastern that simultaneously spotted a fourth crew member in the cockpit. Have you heard that?''

I told him that I had, from several different sources, and that I was getting more details. He was interested. He said that if he had any more information, he would let me know.

The interview with Captain Morgan was successful, but again frustrating. I didn't have any idea of where I stood on the story, but I knew it was growing more intriguing. It was also becoming a minor obsession. There was a lot of smoke; it seemed that there just had to be some fire somewhere. What still nagged at me was that if the stories were simply vague and wispy rumors, they would be bound to shift base, if only to a 727 or a DC-10 or a 747. But they stuck and stuck hard—both to the L-1011s and to Eastern. The only time they moved away from Eastern was when some of the planes were leased to TWA. What's more, the reports were coming from responsible professionals. They were still too vague to be conclusive, but it was just as strange that they had been so persistent as it was strange to believe them.

When the TWA captain mentioned the rumor that parts of Plane #318 had been removed for apparently no reason, I thought of contacting Garry Lewis,* the New York mechanic J.R. and Rachelle had learned about in New York. Since he had worked temporarily in Miami during the time when the apparition stories had reached flood tide, I was hoping he could shed some light on the matter.

I had to go to New York for several days, and I called him at his Suffolk County home on Long Island. "Well, there's no question that there's a lot of funny stuff going on about the ghosts," he said. "Both in the air and on the ground. I think you've got to believe some of it."

I persuaded him to let me come out to his house for a few moments, and drove out to Long Island the next morning, since he was on the late shift. With him in the living room was another Eastern mechanic, Frank Heller.* Both were salty, down-to-earth men, and they seemed to have a no-nonsense approach to the story.

"I asked Heller over here," Garry Lewis said, "because what he has to say will sort of back me up. You don't like to feel lonely in this business. Matter of fact, Frank's had a real experience—I've just been watching from the sidelines. Why don't you tell the story, Frank?"

Both the mechanics went through practically the same procedure as the other Eastern employees I talked with: they had to be guaranteed that their names would not be used.

I was perfectly willing to guarantee this, and I told them so. "It's not only that I don't want to look like a damn fool," Heller said, "and get the pants kidded off of me, but I'm sure you've heard all the stories about people being sent to the shrink because of this. But anyway, what happened is, I was working down in the galley—the lower galley—where a lot of this stuff is supposed to have happened. They were filling the fuel tanks, and all the power in the plane was shut off. All of it. Strict procedure. Friend of mine was down there with me, and we had a few minor things to adjust. Remember, there was no power on that plane at all. But all of a sudden, the galley fan came on. You never seen two guys get the hell out of that place faster. We checked the electrical foreman

right away. He agreed with us. There was no way it could have come on, even with a short circuit."

"Heller's not the only one who's run into strange things on 318," Garry said. "Jack Derr* works with us on our shift. About a year ago, he was down in the lower bay. He couldn't find his screwdriver. He put his hands out to the sides, palms up, the way you do when you can't find something you're looking for. All of a sudden, he felt something as if it was slapped in his hand. It was the missing screwdriver. No one else was anywhere near him on the plane. He told us he had to run off the plane and get himself under control."

These stories came direct to Garry, but we talked about how hard it was to nail down the others, especially since they had died down over a year before.

"You're going to have a hard job doing this," he said, echoing the others, "but let me tell you what I've run into. It's a very curious thing, and I'm really puzzled by it."

He continued with his story:

Like nearly everybody else at Eastern, Garry was aware of the dozens of stories, and was struck by the consistency and the reliability of those who reported them. As a New York-based mechanic for Eastern, working temporarily at Miami, he knew the workings of the 727s and L-1011s intimately. He had been working on 727s recently, however, and did not have direct knowledge of what was happening on the L-1011s.

Later his interest in the long series of events still high, Garry found himself back working on L-1011 maintenance after a long stint on the 727s. Working in another part of the plane, he happened to notice part of the crew removing one of the elevators that had carried the stewardesses down to the lower galley. There had been minor bugs in the early planes of the L-1011 series; nothing serious, but often annoying. One of the bugs involved the elevators, and some of them had to be changed when the often-delayed delivery of new ones arrived.

As Lewis passed the crew removing the old elevator and replacing it with a new one, he said, "That damn thing crap out again?"

"Nope," one of the mechanics told him. "This one works fine."

"Well how come you're changing it?" Lewis asked.

"You won't believe it," the mechanic said, "but this is one of the parts that came from the crack-up of Flight 401. There's a work order to remove it."

Lewis asked why they were removing it when it was perfectly good. The mechanic told him that the word going around was that the reappearances of the ghost images seemed to be directly connected with those L-1011s using salvaged parts from the Flight 401 plane.

"How'd you find that out?" Lewis asked.

"Ask 'em over in stock. That's where we found out."

Later, on his lunch break, Lewis went over to the stock department. Here all the costly electronic equipment was stored and cataloged by serial number, after it had been checked, overhauled, tested and inspected in the shops. It was expensive stuff. A small piece of equipment could cost thousands of dollars.

The stock records indicated the serial numbers of each part and also a record of what plane it was on or is on. From the stockmen, Garry Lewis learned that they were going through all the records to find out which of the L-1011s were utilizing the salvaged radio parts from the plane that had crashed in the Everglades. They were checking all the equipment, taking down the serial numbers, and matching them up with the records of the L-1011 that had crashed. The radio men, Lewis was told, would then remove any part that had been salvaged from that plane, even though it was in perfect working order.

It just didn't add up. Could it be possible that all this labor was being done because of the strange series of ghostlike appearances on the planes? It was hard to believe. It was also hard for Lewis to learn any more than what he had heard from the mechanics and stockmen. There were two things that were fully confirmable, however. One was that the computers from the Avionic Flight Control System (the AFCS) of the wrecked plane—except for the roll computers—were installed in another L-1011 for testing, indicating that they

172

were operational after the crash and demonstrating that parts from the wreckage could be used. In addition, there was no question that the CVR—the cockpit voice recorder—number 14236 from Plane #318 was removed after the Mexico City incident.

# Chapter X

When I returned to Miami, I called Denise Woodruff. She said she had been trying to recall other things that had happened, and there was one that had attracted her interest: Right Bay 1 oven on Plane #318, she now remembered, had been removed from the lower galley about one year before, although none of the flight attendants had been aware of a problem with the oven. When I told her about what I had learned from Garry Lewis up in New York, she wondered if the two procedures were related.

I had learned from J. R. Worden and Rachelle that students of the psychic and the paranormal claimed that there was a direct relationship between an inanimate object and its attraction to the spirit world. They called it psychometry. It was said to involve several facets. A medium would hold an object belonging to a person and receive from it information that could come from no traceable or conventional source. Peter Hurkos, the famous Dutch medium, would use this technique. Although he had notable failures in helping police solve crimes and locate missing persons, he also had striking successes. He helped Scotland Yard find the stolen Stone of Scone, revered by the British, and he accurately described the murderer of a Miami taxi driver in 1958.

Another aspect of psychometry was the theory that the spirits of the deceased who felt they hadn't fulfilled their goals would remain near objects and places they were familiar with, in a different dimension, but able at certain times to briefly and to fleetingly recreate themselves by crossing over from one energy form to another, causing a clear but temporary manifestation that could be seen and sensed by people in the vicinity. The question was whether authorities at Eastern

could possibly believe in this theory enough to order the removal and replacement of the Right Bay 1 oven? If so, no one was saying anything about it, and Denise was unable to trace the reason for the actual replacement of the oven.

Whether the salvaged parts had anything to do with it or not, there were many reports that some crews had refused to fly Plane #318. In contrast, there were an equal number of crews who *wanted* to fly it. These included some who felt that in spite of the events that seemed to center on that particular plane, the plane would actually be protected by the benevolent apparitions that indicated they wanted to help.

There was no question that some of the stewardesses continually begged off duty in the lower galley. One senior stewardess told me she asked a junior girl to get an extra meal from the galley. She wouldn't do it until she got another flight attendant to go down there with her. Others remained steadfast in not going down to the galley at all, and took assignments only on the passenger deck. Again, however, there was an ample number of stewardesses who wanted galley duty on Plane #318 and found nothing disturbing about working there.

If there was one thing consistent about the stories, it was that whatever the images appearing were, they were not harmful. They were frequently impassive, sometimes mischievous, but in no sense a threat, except to the jangled nerves of some who were faced with an encounter. In fact, if the compendium of the stories about the appearances of Don Repo could be believed, he was concerned with the safety and operation of the L-1011s and wanted desperately to help out.

In one instance on an L-1011 that mechanic Garry Lewis told me he learned of, Repo had encountered the plane's flight engineer and conducted him directly to a trouble spot in the hydraulic system. It was only after Repo instantly disappeared that the engineer was shocked into realizing that he had not been talking to a man, but to an apparition.

There was no question, however, that the incident did have a measurable effect on the airline's operation.

Eastern authorities still were concerned, whether the stories were real or not. From the point of view of what was

considered reality in the modern jet age, it was impossible to accept them.

Later, a reporter from *The New York Times* looked into the stories and was told that an Eastern Air Lines executive spent several hours poring over the flight logs, but couldn't find any reports of a ghost. It is doubtful, of course, that if the executive found any information that he would release it to the *Times* or any other paper. The *Times* reporter went on to say about the executive: "His effort, however, reflected the extent to which Eastern has gone to track down an elusive rumor that has been hounding the air line for several months."

The *Times* story continued: "But there has been no documentation whatsoever as to the existence of ghosts, the company spokesman insisted. Yet the reports of the ghost are continuing to circulate."

This was the same kind of response I had received from Eastern. What was puzzling about what the spokesman told the *Times* reporter was that the executive admitted to spending only "several hours" trying to track down the story. If the executive had taken the time to hop on any L-1011 flight and talk to the flight crews and flight attendants, he would have come up with a dozen or more leads that could have been traced back to the original sources. The press handout sort of interview demonstrated either that Eastern was making no effort at all to get at the base of the matter, or that it was not about to tell all that was known. In either case, the information given *The New York Times* was as inconclusive as my interview with Eastern had been.

For several days I concentrated on the routine interviews regarding the crash itself, but that process was simple, ordinary journalism. The imponderables were of a different sort. Both J.R. and Rachelle were convinced that it was possible to get direct information through the psychic mediums they knew through both Spiritual Frontiers and the Arthur Ford Academy in Miami.

I was wary of this because I did not want to get involved directly with a group organized for that purpose. It might be too biased. I wanted to keep at a respectful arm's length, although J. R. Worden and Rachelle had convinced me that

both the Spiritual Frontier group and the Arthur Ford Academy were sound institutions made up of intelligent and perceptive people who had found that the modern medium was an effective channel in helping others with their problems. Its membership included everybody from bankers, pilots, brokers, and professors to almost any part of the career spectrum. In addition to helping the development of mediumship, the group fostered psychic healing through those mediums who demonstrated that capacity.

I knew about the late Arthur Ford only through hearsay. J.R. had a Spiritual Frontiers newsletter at hand, and I glanced through it. In it was a quotation from Arthur Ford's book *A Force or A Farce* that gave a little insight into his outlook:

I always resent it when people speak of spiritualists in a sort of sneering and unpleasant manner. Every man in the world is a spiritualist if he is not a materialist. It is a perfectly good philosophical term. I am a spiritualist because I believe in the spirit. No matter what name you wear, whether you are a Methodist or a Catholic or a Buddhist, if you have any conception of God or a spiritual quality that doesn't perish at death, you are in a true sense a spiritualist. The alternative is to be a materialist and depend only on the things that you can see and hear and touch.

We talk so much about keeping the screwballs out. Every church in Christendom started as a heresy, and every man who has ever been of any value to the kingdom of God has been a heretic.

Apparently Arthur Ford was testy and robust about his beliefs. When I finally visited the academy with J.R. and Rachelle, it hardly suggested anything that had to do with the conventional concept of a medium. It consisted of an attractive suite of rooms in a modern office building in southwest Miami. It was brightly and tastefully decorated with comfortable modern furniture and subdued wall-to-wall carpeting.

I was introduced here to Patricia and Bud Hayes, founders

of the academy, who looked much more like a young couple out of the pages of an Abercrombie catalog than the mediums they are. Bud Hayes was a successful advertising executive with his own agency. They had married quite young and now had five children. After they had their third child, Patricia had stumbled across a volume of Emanuel Swedenborg, the great Swedish scientist and mystic, who had predicted Einstein's theory of relativity back in the 1700s, and who had written volumes on his spiritual experiences concerning life after death. The study of his works catapulted the Hayeses into their dual activity in the Spiritual Frontier movement and in secular accomplishment. Their enthusiasm for their work in the psychic field was exuberant and persuasive.

They believed intensely that everyone had within him the capacity of being a medium and needed only development. A small publication of the academy stated:

> The spiritual development of a medium is not necessarily embellished with any significant act of birth or heritage. It is something every person has the ability to develop, and to use to one degree or another. We are not mystics. Most have never been blessed with great visions of past or future events. We certainly do not discount the fact that many people are born with a sensitivity far beyond the normal range. For the most part, we have studied under capable leadership, and concerned ourselves foremost with the love of fellow man, and a sincere desire to help each person who comes to us.

I have always been confused about the whole concept of mediums, and cautious of their validity. The vibrance and enthusiasm that both the Hayeses reflected confused me even more. Their sincerity and conviction were self-evident. Their confidence in the validity of the psychic was total. "Most people who question the things that happen in the psychic field simply have never studied the evidence," Patricia Hayes told me. "The medium acts as a channel through suspending the conscious personality, and allowing higher spiritual forces to come in. Simply because these forces are in

a different dimension from ours does not mean that they are less real. There has been so much hard, real evidence transmitted this way in the history of mediumship, that even the most obdurate skeptic would change his mind if he *honestly* studied the history. The problem is to get them to study and weigh the evidence."

The Hayeses generously offered all the facilities of the academy, including mediums, in an attempt to probe into the L-1011 story. "There is a chance," Patricia Hayes said, "that contact might be made with Repo or Loft through a medium, and that enough evidential facts might come through to confirm it. I know that evidence is what you're after, since you're a journalist."

Although I was willing to try anything, I had great doubts in my mind whether such a contact would clearly indicate any real evidence, or if it did, how anyone, including myself, would believe it.

"There's another thing we could try," she added. "If you could get hold of any fragments of the plane, we could have some of the mediums try psychometry with them." Even some scientists were taking psychometry seriously, in the wake of the solving of many missing persons and crimes through the method. It was similar, in a sense, to exposing a hound to a piece of clothing of a victim or criminal, to lead them on the trail. The University of Virginia Medical School had conducted many controlled laboratory tests on this technique, with rather startling statistical results. In fact, one experiment there dealt directly with the question of life after death. Under the direction of Dr. Ian Stevenson of the Department of Psychiatry, the experiment is labeled the "combination lock test." Researchers in parapsychology had ruled out chance or hoax in their tests on mediums, but they were not certain whether the precise and accurate information seemingly coming from deceased persons was not the result of ESP coming from living persons.

Dr. Stevenson planned to distribute strong, reliable combination locks to volunteer subjects, who would set their own combinations. The locks would be sent to mediums, who would attempt to open them while the volunteer subject was still alive. After the death of the subject, the mediums would

continue to try to open the locks (six-digit combinations with a random chance of 125,000 to 1 to open). If the combination of the lock spontaneously came to a medium after death, but not during the lifetime of the volunteer, there would be evidence of posthumous communication. It was a complicated test, but it demonstrated how seriously a leading university was taking the subject.

I felt that I would like to investigate the down-to-earth leads J.R. and Rachelle had unearthed before even thinking about the possibility of trying to reach Repo or Loft through mediums. After J.R. had told me that the two Eastern pilots he had met were both mediums, and had utilized their capacity in their "soul rescue" effort. I was extremely curious about this unique device, which I had never heard of before. I was also interested in meeting pilots who were also mediums. It was an unusual combination.

I made plans to return to New York, and arranged to meet pilots Rich Craig and Stan Chambers and their wives at the Chambers home in Rockland County. On the phone, Stan Chambers was cordial and receptive to the idea because he felt that the story would illuminate a field that many people shied away from because they had little knowledge of it. He further felt that the evidence showed that the "soul rescue" mission had worked. The reappearances had not been reported for several months now, as far as he knew, where before the reports were coming in every few days from startled Eastern crews. Further, he felt that if the story were honestly presented, it would do much to reassure Eastern passengers about the basic soundness of the L-1011, which he felt was among the best planes in the air.

I know that after the preliminary research on the story, I agreed with him about the plane. I took it whenever I could, because of its comfort and stability. I took the L-1011 Flight 26 back to New York, making plans also to stop over in Atlanta on my return to Miami to interview Bill Damroth, the FAA executive who was also a medium.

On the flight back, I reflected on the unusual fact that there seemed to be mediums under every rock, even in the technical field of aviation. I had always thought of mediums as rather a mystical group who shunned the mechanical or

technical, or the everyday world for that matter. Instead, I was running into them in advertising, piloting, electronics, (J.R. Worden worked as a technician in an electronics firm), and engineering (FAA's Bill Damroth had a degree in mechanical engineering). Not one of them seemed the least bit mysterious or occult, or fit the stereotyped concept.

But they were unanimously serious about the subject. When I arrived a few evenings later at the Chambers home in suburban New York, I was immediately impressed by the way both the Chambers and the Craigs took the subject as calmly as if the wives were discussing a political campaign, or the pilots were talking about the spoilers and flaps on a 727. Craig was a husky Down-Easter with a New England twang and over 18,000 flying hours. He spoke with the quiet deliberate tone of a certified public accountant. You would find prototypes of either of the wives working on a suburban hospital drive, or at the train station meeting the regular commuter run. Chambers, a rangy Californian with a pleasing smile, could pass for a line-backer on the Baltimore Colts. The group couldn't be more down-to-earth.

I began to dig in to find out how the four of them had become interested in the paranormal. Eleanor Craig had begun to notice she had capabilities before she was ten. The others had had slight indications of psychic awareness off and on for years. When the two couples discovered their mutual interest, they began a serious joint study of the subject. They began to develop enough psychic awareness to indicate that they had capabilities of acting as mediums, as a channel for psychic forces. Both pilots had a highly technical background, and for most of their lives had been interested in mechanical things, but their interest in parapsychology grew over the years.

The two couples met an experienced medium who had been a protégée of the well-known deceased medium, Arthur Ford. She worked with them for a considerable period of time. The pilots and their wives began to discover that they could not only summon up specific, evidential information from forces outside themselves, but that they could put it to good use in helping others in counseling them on their problems. As mediums, they could ''see into'' another dimension

beyond our own. Further, Rich and Eleanor Craig became interested in psychic healing. They had considerable success with this among their friends, and broadened their work, never charging for whatever they were able to accomplish.

Both the Craigs and Stan and Carol Chambers were able to put themselves in an altered state of consciousness, where they were able to feel that they directly contacted those who were dead, and to recognize spiritual forces that were beyond themselves. They could do this with or without psychometry.

Pilots Rich Craig and Stan Chambers continued their studies and sessions in the mediumship field, as they continued their regular schedule as pilots for Eastern. All of the four members of the group were deeply religious, and had joined a New York branch of Spiritual Frontiers.

The stories about the apparitions of Second Officer Repo and Captain Loft circulated in a rather spotty pattern. Both Craig and Chambers were slow in hearing about the stories. Rich Craig, piloting a 727 layover flight to Cleveland, got talking to his Second Officer, who had just been on a flight to San Juan where Repo had appeared in the cockpit to warn of a possible malfunction coming up. He then, as usual, vanished. The captain of the San Juan L-1011 had turned the plane back from the taxiway, where the minor malfunction was verified. The flight crew was pretty well shaken up emotionally.

At the time that Rich Craig was flying to Cleveland, Stan Chambers was working a flight to San Juan. When he arrived there, he found that there was quite a bit of consternation there about the semi-aborted flight. No one could believe it, yet it apparently had happened with a seasoned flying crew aboard.

When both Craig and Chambers returned to their home base in New York, they compared notes. As mediums, they had a cautious belief in the reality of the deceased engineer's ghost. Their studies into the paranormal had led them to the belief in the survival of the individual personality after death. The studies had included the records of both the American and British Society for Psychical Research, where scholars and scientists like William James, Oliver Lodge, and Sir William Crookes had taken the well-documented appear-

ances of ghosts and apparitions as a matter of course. The two Eastern pilots decided to learn more about the L-1011 incidents, and to check back with each other at intervals.

Their chief concern grew out of studies made by members of the British and American psychic research societies. Ghosts and apparitions were, according to various scholarly papers on the subject, the result of tortured or agonized souls who either were not aware that they had died, or did not know how to go on to their further spiritual development after death. According to classic theory, if any of the crew members had died with heavy feelings of guilt, it could cause them to cling to their former surroundings to try to assuage the guilt feeling and to try perhaps to repair the damage they might feel they had done.

Regardless of what the situation was, pilots Craig and Chambers went about gathering all the information they could, determining to find a way to help both Eastern Air Lines in their enigma about the situation, and to aid the souls of Repo and Loft in their apparent distress.

The Craigs and the Chambers got together one evening in New York in March 1974 and went over the accumulated notes they had collected. There were many, and they were unusually consistent. Many came from unimpeachable pilots, engineers, and flight attendants. Nearly all of the accounts suggested to them that Second Officer Repo appeared most persistently. The reports concerning Captain Loft seemed to have faded out over the months, indicating to them that he had moved on to his own spiritual development, and away from what was considered to be "earthbound."

In their work as mediums, the pilots and their wives were familiar with the process known as "soul rescue." It was a method used by mediums over the years, in cases where an apparition or a manifestation of a deceased person seemed to not realize he was dead. This, it was said, most frequently happened when someone had died through a sudden or unexpected event.

A hard-headed British physicist and mathematician from the University of London, G.N.M. Tyrrell had made an intensive study of the best documented cases of apparitions

over a fifty-year period. He gradually phased out his professional work in wireless telegraphy with Marconi in order to study the phenomenon in depth: he became fully occupied in an attempt to fuse modern science with parapsychology. In analyzing what he called "crisis apparitions," Tyrrell noted two things about them. One was that they were so like human beings as to be frequently mistaken for them, until they vanished. The other was that they do not occur when people are expecting them, or because people are worried or anxious about them.

If Tyrrell's theories were true, there was little question that the manifestations on the L-1011s fitted into the crisis-apparition category. He pointed out in his research that those in this classification look like full-rounded human beings, although they most often behave in a somnambulistic manner. In spite of that, there were many records of actual vocal communication between the crisis apparition and living people. In addition, there were reports of some rare instances of physical touching of the person perceiving the image.

Tyrrell's theories were published in 1953, as a result of the studies he made when he was president of the British Society for Psychical Research. This was the cautious and erudite organization that spent as much time exposing fraudulent mediums and psychics, as it did exploring the field of parapsychology. Tyrrell's theories published back in the 1950s, however, had a strong bearing on what was happening in the 1970s aboard the Eastern L-1011 jets.

His observations from the hundreds of cases he studied led him to analyze a characteristic of apparitions that intrigued him greatly: their remarkable imitation of normal perception.

"Apparitions behave as if they were aware of their surroundings," he wrote. "They may come in at the door. They nearly always move around a room with normal respect for the position of the furniture. If they wander about the house, they make normal use of doors, passages, and staircases."

Tyrrell was also intrigued by the way apparitions as a rule consistently behaved with regard to the lighting of the scene, the distance from the recipient, and the presence of intervening objects, exactly as a material person would do. "This again," he wrote, "may not seem surprising at first sight.

But it is very significant in view of the fact that the apparition has no physical basis, and no need to pay any attention to physical lighting.''

He had other observations, all of which had bearing on the question in the minds of the Eastern flight crew, who wondered how such apparently solid forms could appear and disappear before them with such vivid reality. Except for a few accounts aboard the L-1011s, there was nothing misty or ghost-like about the appearances in the galleys, the flight decks, the passenger cabins. Most of the reports indicated full and complete lighting.

Tyrrell noted that when a person looking at an apparition shut his eyes, the figure would disappear. If the apparition was nonphysical, why wouldn't it stay with the perceiver, like an afterimage or a dream image? He also traced cases where the image had shown up clearly in a mirror, indicating its capacity to reflect light waves.

The collective sightings intrigued Tyrrell the most. Why should two or more people see exactly the same image, as many flight deck crews and others had reported? This was a burning question and seemed to rule out hallucination as an explanation for the phenomena.

One other observation of Tyrrell had direct application to the L-1011 cases. ''Another characteristic of apparitions,'' he wrote, ''not invariable but fairly frequent, is that the percipients experience a feeling of cold. One can see no reason for these cold feelings; they are just an empirical fact. He quoted a long list of statements made in the cases he studied: ''I felt myself grow perfectly cold . . .''

''A cold shivering feeling came over me . . .''

''I felt an icy wind blowing . . .''

''We felt a cold wind rushing by us . . .''

Tyrrell felt these impressions might have been subjective and not physical, yet there had been cases where there seemed to be strong physical evidence, too.

Whatever the case, it was practically certain that few, if any, of the crews and passengers in the L-1011 encounters knew anything about Tyrrell's theories and studies. Both Rich Craig and Stan Chambers were familiar with them, along with their wives, but only because of their intensive studies in the field. Even with this knowledge and back-

ground, neither of the pilots had encountered the apparitions.

With Tyrrell's theories in mind, the two pilots and their wives came to the conclusion that a "soul rescue" mission was clearly indicated in the L-1011 phenomenon, especially in the case of Second Officer Repo, whose appearances were continuing to be reported. They agreed that they would plan to do this after serious meditation during the week.

They met at the Chambers house in Rockland County, New York, on March 18, 1974. Like most mediums, each of the four had his spiritual guide that they could count on to try to bring Don Repo into their circle, so that they in turn could guide him out of the limbo state and on to his spiritual development.

The theory of a "soul rescue" differed from that of an exorcism. According to theory, exorcism is designed to get rid of a negative entity or influence thought to be possessing a person by taking over his body and mind. A soul rescue mission was designed to help a soul who for one reason or another is thought to be earthbound, to help him on to his spiritual progress and development. They reasoned that in this case, a soul could be confused. He might still think he was in the physical realm. He might find it hard to face the fact that he was in spirit. A sudden death out of normal time span could create a state of turmoil. The soul rescue process was used most often by mediums in cases of a sudden or unexpected death to help the deceased to realize that they are no longer in the body, but in spirit. This would be the first step.

The second step, again according to the theories extant, was to get the deceased to open up his eyes spiritually, to see the light that could lead him out of his confusion. "It's like you're looking through a big, long tunnel, and you see a little spot of light at the other end. It's pitch-black up to that point, but there are guides and conductors there," was the way Carol Chambers explained it. "This is their sole job—to take a new spirit and guide him toward this light. They have their hands there, and the deceased simply has to take their hands and be guided. Once they get into this light, then they can start expanding. It's just like a newborn baby. They're just reorienting themselves to a new existence."

Carol Chambers, who had been psychic since she was a child, had no doubts at all that these theories were correct. The others in the group were convinced because of their more recent experiences as mediums, and from their intense studies with the Spiritual Frontier group.

They would begin the session sitting in the Craigs' comfortable living room, Rich Craig in an armchair, Eleanor Craig on the sofa beside Carol Chambers. Stan Chambers was in another chair. At about nine in the evening, they began meditating. Then Rich Craig directed them in deep, slow breathing that would intensify their meditation and slowly move them toward an altered state of higher consciousness.

They had a tape recorder, and I listened to the cassette later. Rich Craig spoke softly in it to say: "The purpose for this sitting this evening is to contact Don Repo for any information and to help him in any way."

The meditation lasted for several minutes. It was a procedure that, from past experience, would create a picture or communication in the nonconscious mind that would channel through one or more of the mediums at the session. They would, according to the theory, actually see the subject in the mind's eye, and experience his emotions. The meditation might or might not produce contact with the deceased. If it did, the image of the deceased being sought might appear in the mind of one of the mediums, and other verbal communication might come through the voices of one or more of them.

It was hard to tell what might happen at any given session because each was spontaneous. Any conscious thoughts were intentionally blocked to let whatever spiritual channels there were come through.

They would be looking for any evidential facts that might come through the nonconscious channels, or any duplicate images that might arise in the nonconscious minds of more than one of them, thus providing a cross-check. None in the group, for instance, had known Don Repo or had any idea what he looked like. Neither of the wives knew any details about the operation of the aircraft. If any scenes of this nature could be re-created, there would be some evidence that the session was getting through.

At the end of the lengthy silence, Stan Chambers, the

L-1011 pilot, began speaking. His voice was low and somnambulistic.

"I get a clear picture of a man," Chambers said.

Eleanor Craig cut in at this point. "I get dark hair . . . a little gray . . ."

"Dark hair, yes," Chambers agreed. "Some gray. His uniform is very clear . . ."

He went on to describe other details. The sideburns were slightly heavier than his. His hair was full in the back, but not sloppy. There was not enough detail for the description to be fully evidential, but it did fit fairly well with Repo's description. Enough, they felt, to continue on with their soul rescue mission. There were several interchanges, that they learned later fit in with the physical description of Repo.

Then Rich Craig spoke. His voice was low. "We welcome him here and ask that if he wishes to communicate, he do so."

A long silence followed. Stan Chambers, who seemed to be getting a very clear picture said, "He seems to be a little bit shocked."

There was another silence. Then Eleanor said, "I get the impression I'm feeling pressure around the top of the head. Especially around the temple. This might possibly have something to do with the way he passed? There must have been head injuries." [The final medical report showed that Repo had suffered a blunt impact injury to the head with fracture of the skull and cerebral contusions.]

Stan Chambers commented, "If you're in the forward section, your head's exposed, of course."

Rich Craig added, "This could be verified." Then Eleanor, apparently now getting very clear pictures of the entity they were trying to help, said, "He said he doesn't quite know what to do. Let's ask our guides in spirit to help him." There was a pause, then: "I feel stronger in the vibration waves."

Part of the soul rescue process was designed to counteract the bewilderment and shock of an entity who suddenly found himself no longer living. Rich spoke up, saying, "You need not be afraid of those who are around us, for they are here to help us. They will help you in your effort to communicate

with us in any way they can. This is why they are here.'' He was referring to the spirit guides that the session was designed to summon.

Stan Chambers was now getting more impressions. ''He is saying something about a small door. Could he be trapped there?'' Mediums say that in a sitting of this sort, the images are created in the mind, almost as if a film is being projected on a screen in the mind's eye. They also say that they experience the emotions of the subject at hand, often intensely. Eleanor Craig later reported that she felt excruciating head pain during the session.

Rich Craig, who was not receiving any clear impressions at this point, was acting as a moderator for the session. He responded to Stan's last comment by saying, ''That would not be the galley, from the way the L-1011 is designed.'' Both pilots had intentionally refrained from studying the full details beyond the mechanical and technical aspects of the Flight 401 crash, in order not to confuse the impression they might receive through the nonconscious channel used in the soul rescue effort. Stan Chambers, for some reason, had thought that Repo had been in the galley at the time of the crash. He asked Craig ''Is this what he's showing you?''

''Yes,'' Stan said. ''I see a porthole, like a round window. Now I see a strut. It's a landing-gear strut. The retract lugs are straight. Everything looks normal. It's forward of the galley. Not the galley.''

''We thank him for this information,'' Rich said.

''It's black out there,'' Stan continued in his flat, sleeplike tone. ''He's got a light. A small light. It's cold down there. Is there a passageway? I see his flashlight.''

Rich Craig and Carol Chambers had now assumed a passive role in the sitting. In contrast, Eleanor Craig and Stan Chambers were reporting very vivid scenes and reactions. This seemed to be a common thing in group sittings. Some received sharper images than others. Eleanor said, ''I'm looking down the shaft to a wheel.''

Stan said, ''Nose-gear strut looks quite far away right now.'' Their images seemed to be coinciding.

Eleanor asked, ''Is that what you call it? A strut?'' Then she added, ''It looks like a bump on the shaft. Like a locking

mechanism. . . . I get the impression of moonlight shining down on the wheel. Also see light shimmer on something below. Looks like water." (What the lighting situation was at the time of the crash was never determined. The CVR had revealed that Second Officer Repo mentioned throwing on "the little light." Several passengers noted they saw landing lights or other lights reflecting on the wings.) Eleanor continued, "I feel a rush of water coming up to the plane. It's coming up fast. I feel fear. Terrible fear. He realizes what is happening." Eleanor showed signs of great distress.

Stan said, "He's trapped down in this hole and can't get up. He sees or feels the nose strut starting to buckle and spray coming up."

The voices of both Stan and Eleanor were now intense and trembling, almost agonized. Rich Craig interrupted them.

"Okay, thank you," he said. Then, to Stan and Eleanor: "You need no longer have this fear or emotion, because he has left us behind."

Eleanor's voice became lower and calmer, almost inaudible. "Very heavy," she said. "Feel as if my body . . . very heavy. I feel the weight of the . . ."

Stan spoke. "The physical has ceased to exist."

Rich Craig said, "Ask him to look around, for there are many here. Included in those who are here, are those who will help him." He was referring to the theory that there are spirit guides who meet the deceased at the time of death.

Eleanor received another impression. "The top of his skull is very badly damaged." Then she seemed to address herself to the image she saw. "You are in spirit now," she said. "And you know that you should develop and find your way in the light, that your love will be for those you still love who are here, that you will be able to communicate. You no longer need to remain here. As you walk into the light, there will be many who will help you." She added, speaking to the others in the room, "I get the impression that he doesn't want to accept it."

All through the session, the eyes of all four remained closed. The voices were soft, except for a few moments of rather tense emotion. Stan was speaking again now, his eyes still closed.

"The light first appears to you as a dim light. There are those there who will guide and help you. Ask for their help They will be there. Go toward the bright, clear light. A spiritual entity will take your hand. Go with them. Don't be afraid. Be humble as a child. Go with the bright, clear light. Go now."

Rich asked, "Do you pick up anything clearly now?"

Eleanor said, "I see that he's very reluctant. I am asking spirit to please guide him and to help him. I get a clear impression that he's very attached to the earth plane, and he just had so much love here for his wife and family, you know. He just doesn't want to leave her."

His eyes still closed, as in prayer, Rich Craig said: "Let us project to him that his love will grow more as he goes toward the light."

Stan said, "Don, you've got to go. There's more to be learned. Don't hang on to the earth. Go now. Accept what's happened."

Eleanor added, "Don, let spirit direct you and help you. Your presence back here on the earth is not needed. You have more things to do on the other side. We ask that you look for the light. You are surrounded by help."

Stan spoke. "He's moving away from us."

Rich said, "Yes. This will take time. But he's moving toward the light. I can see him." The flat, disembodied tone of both their voices continued.

Then Eleanor added, "Don is leaving. He's moving toward the light. He's being helped. Don, go."

There was a moment of silence. All four, the two pilots and their wives sat with their eyes closed, breathing slowly. Finally Rich Craig spoke again.

"We thank him for this information he has given us."

The soul rescue session was at an end. As the group returned from the altered state of consciousness to the normal state, they opened their eyes again and looked around them. Eleanor Craig and Stan Chambers felt drained. They vividly recalled the emotions they had felt, as if they had been on the plane itself. The pictures they had seen in their altered state remained clearly in their minds.

Eleanor got up with a pencil and paper and asked Stan to

draw what he had seen. She would do the same, in the dining room. They did so. Both pictures showed the nose gear from the same perspective, and were almost identical. Eleanor Craig had known nothing about the design of the strut beforehand.

The procedure I heard on the tape was strange to my ears, difficult to comprehend. Here were two pilots, fellow flightcrew members of Don Repo, moving from the technical world of the jet plane which they knew so intimately, and into the unknown world of spirit. They were convinced, though, that they knew how to navigate in that obscure area as surely as they could make an instrument landing at Kennedy Airport. They seemed confident that they had helped and guided a troubled, puzzled confrere who, except for the grace of God, could have been either of them.

I had a lot of questions to ask as a follow-up, and they were very cooperative in trying to answer them.

"After the soul rescue session," Rich Craig told me, "Repo came back to us once more. It must have been about a month ago. This was with several other people who had no knowledge of the phenomenon. They gave us a pretty good description of what they were seeing. It matched very closely what we experienced in our session. Since then, neither Stan nor I have heard any reports and haven't been able to gather any."

I was trying to get some kind of concept as to how they went about conducting this strange ritual, and I asked them.

"The process is quite interesting," Stan Chambers said in a matter-of-fact voice. "The four of us went into meditation, and it seemed that Eleanor Craig and I began picking up the same picture of Repo in the hell hole of the plane. It is not unusual in a session like this to pick up a subject quickly. We both identified the guy by the situation he was in and by descriptions we had heard about him. The one purpose was to see if we could bring Repo in and see if we could end the strange incidents that were happening on so many L-1011 flights."

Rich Craig added, "We wanted to help him get on to his own spiritual growth. To move on to his growth."

"This is very hard on someone who has just died suddenly," Carol Chambers said.

"Eleanor and I seemed to be tapped in to the same thing at the session," Stan Chambers continued. "There was a lot that we didn't say out loud during it. But we saw it clearly. It was as if we were on that plane, in Repo's position."

"I felt all the emotions he went through," Eleanor said. "I felt his frustration of not being able to do anything in the last moments. When we drew the sketches of what we had seen, we did it to verify the incident. They were strikingly close. It appeared that we saw and received the same impressions."

"I could feel how disturbed Repo was," Eleanor continued. "Especially as far as his ability to tell where he was, and the fact that he didn't want to be where he was. He didn't want to be in spirit. It seemed that he wanted to re-create for us what had happened at the time of the crash, to let us know he was disturbed and shocked."

"He seemed to be so upset that he was actually bound to the airplane," Stan said. "We got the impression that he really liked the airplane, and this seemed to be holding him into this earth state."

"What we did for the poor fellow," Eleanor said, "was that we explained to him what had happened, and where he was. Then we told him, gave him direction as to what he should do from that point on—to turn around and look for the light." The theory was that, in the shock of sudden death, the victim didn't realize he was dead.

"How did you know how to conduct this session?" I asked.

Carol Chambers said, "We've all done a lot of study in the psychic field and talked with many serious, experienced mediums. We've even gone out to help with exorcisms of various houses. Lots of times, people who have died in a sudden accident have no idea they are dead. Sometimes they try to attach themselves to the medium involved. We got the feeling that Don was trying to attach himself to Rich, here. I was feeling the attachment he was trying to make and felt a little uneasy. So we just told him to look for the light and develop himself. This often happens. You have to be sure to guide them on further."

"You sort of have to block out this emotion that comes up in this kind of situation. We felt really sorry for the guy. He was an airman, just as we are," Stan said.

"Since that time, we got one more unconfirmed report that Repo had showed up on an L-1011," Rich Craig added. "But we could never pin it down—who saw it, what plane number it was, or anything like that. Since then we've heard no more. What we did was apparently successful."

Stan went on to describe their later session when they felt they received a distinct confirmation that the "soul rescue" had worked: "He came through to us later in an entirely different vein. Far more relaxed."

"This was at a Spiritualist Church," Eleanor said. "None of the others there knew anything. Yet they brought him in to the séance. They were puzzled about it but we weren't. We recognized who they were talking about. And it was in the vein of 'Thank you for what you've done.' We felt and were sure that he had moved into the new area. He was no longer earthbound."

"I think at this point," Carol said, "that there could be communication with him through a medium. He's developed enough; he's calm enough now so that I think he could come through very evidentially."

It was very difficult for me, as an outsider, to absorb both the atmosphere and the matter-of-factness of the subject, so strange and alien to my comprehension. There was calmness and assurance in the voices of the pilots and their wives, and utter confidence in the validity of their experience. The subject was mystical, but there was nothing mystical about the way they approached or discussed the matter. It was as if the pilots were talking to the approach control tower, or the wives discussing the planning of a family budget. There was no question about the intelligence and capabilities and stability of the four people at the discussion. All of these qualities were impressive.

I wanted to know more about how they had decided to tackle the "soul rescue" project, so I asked them that question.

"After we confirmed several of the stories about Repo," Rich Craig said, "we began discussing several different

aspects about what we could do. Such as to arrange to go to the airport when the airplane was in New York overnight. We could actually sit in the airplane that he was most commonly seen on. Plane 318 was the most common, and 325, and 304—or it was 308, rather. These were the three predominant ones on which Repo would appear, that we knew about at least. Then we discussed who we should talk to at Eastern to set this up. But we finally decided not to do it there, because there would be too much red tape involved. It's not exactly an easy thing to explain to someone who knows nothing about this kind of thing. We felt we could do just as good a job here in Rockland County, away from the airport.''

I asked, ''Did you have confidence that you could make a contact with Repo when you tried this?''

''We figured this way,'' Stan Chambers said. ''That with these numerous appearances on Plane 318 and others, Repo was apparently trying to make contact with somebody that he could talk to. Instead, he found a lot of crew members who didn't know anything about this kind of phenomenon. Some of them even were panicky. It seemed as if he wanted to get through and show us that the nose wheel was actually down and locked.''

''We got the distinct impression,'' Rich Craig said, ''that he really did like the airplane. He knew that it wasn't a mechanical failure of the airplane. He seemed to be giving a quite strong indication about that. That it wasn't the airplane. His emotional position, whether he thought he was alive or dead, seemed to be that he wanted to talk to crew members about this, but nobody would sit and listen to him.''

''There didn't seem to be any pointing and putting the blame anywhere,'' Rich said, ''other than he just wanted to show that there was just nothing wrong with the airplane.''

''And then he was in this emotional state,'' Stan added, ''and we felt that if the motivation is sincere, that a good medium can make contact with anyone that wanted to make contact.''

''Especially in a state like this,'' Rich said. ''In a state that he's obviously trying to communicate.''

''And we were very pleased,'' Stan said, ''that there seemed to be a response from him.''

"Now we'll go one step further," Rich continued. "None of us knew the man personally. We hadn't even seen his picture before the session. But we wanted to go at this, on our part, not only for what it could do to the airplane, or psychologically to the passengers, but for Eastern, as a company. It was a concern on our part that we had to do something. And we knew that we had the capability of doing it, between the four of us, this psychic business is a strange business. We get just as amazed about some of the things that happen as anybody else. But we decided we ought to do something about this, because the situation was actually getting out of hand. You can't believe how fast the stories were accumulating. But after the session, we got nothing further firsthand."

"But from the quality of the reports, and the crew members we talked to before that, there was no question in our minds that this was the real thing," Stan said.

I was interested in the mechanics of their "soul rescue" process, and I asked, "When you decided to do this, tell me how you went about it. Did you go into a trance state, or what did you do?"

"Well," said Eleanor Craig, "we do what we usually do—we put ourselves into an altered state of consciousness. It's not really a trance state. There's no vocal communication as there sometimes is in a full trance state. There is more thought transmission, but there is some visualization, too."

"What manifestation did you get that indicated to you that Repo was disturbed?" I asked.

"It's as if their energy field joins with yours," Eleanor said. "You feel all the emotions. I was seeing the impressions as they were coming, and so was Stan. Almost simultaneously. We could see the nose wheel as it seemed to be coming up to the water in the Everglades. And saw the wheel hit, impact in the water. And then blackness. Oblivion. In other words, this is the way he was showing it to us. It was after the session that both Stan and I drew the picture that he showed us."

"Now, of course, Eleanor isn't technically oriented," Rich said. But both pictures, drawn by Stan and her, were almost identical. The correlation was amazing.

"What amazed me," Eleanor said, "is that usually when an entity or a discarnate person comes through, he will come through one person. But Repo was so strong that he was coming not only through me, but through Stan also. We were also ready, if we heard further reports on the L-1011, to go back and repeat the process. Sometimes once is not enough. And you have to watch out for possession. This is a very real thing. You guard against this in a session by keeping at least one person in the group in almost a conscious state. Then if there's any indication of the discarnate person becoming too strong, this person can control the entity."

"It was interesting," Rich said. "We personally know of only one appearance of Captain Loft, and none of the First Officer. The vice-president who sat next to him in the first-class section suddenly realized he was sitting right by Loft. He rushed out to get the ramp agent, and by the time he came back, Loft was gone."

"What about the rumors that 318 was sold, or had its number changed?" I asked.

"There's nothing to that at all," Rich Craig said. "It's still around and in good shape. Fact, we rode on it recently."

"What about the Flight Safety Foundation Bulletin report that Repo's apparition actually spoke to the flight engineer in the Mexico City incident?" I asked. "Is that possible in psychic theory?"

"This would be what is called 'clairaudience,' " Rich said. "It's been reported in one of several forms. There's the individual observer, who is the only one to hear what is alleged to be said. Sometimes it's only a voice inside the ear, sometimes outside, but the observer is the only one who hears it. There's also what is called 'direct voice' clairaudience, where everybody in the area can hear it."

"What amazes me about the whole incident was that Repo was able to manifest, able to make himself actually seen by others. Very few people who die are able to do this. Second, that he was able to be clairaudient. Third, he was able to come through two mediums at the same time," Eleanor Craig said.

Rich added, "There seemed to be a very strong need to do so. He was concerned. It seemed very evident that he liked the airplane, that he didn't want it to get a bad name."

"I got the feeling that he wanted to be back in the flight line, and that he wanted to be back with his wife. I felt certain about this," Stan Chambers said.

All through the discussion, I was trying to sort things out in my mind. If it weren't for the solid credentials of the two couples, I would be listening to what they were saying with a large grain of salt. Somehow they made it sound believable. They were exploring in a strange world—but then again, so was I. At the end of the evening, I at least knew one thing was certain: I was going to continue on my odyssey in search of the truth about the L-1011.

"As for a future life, every man must judge for himself between conflicting vague probabilities."

—Charles Darwin

# Chapter XI

Just where to continue was not exactly clear. There were a lot of blind alleys, and the failure to get many crew members to talk continued to be frustrating. I knew I needed something clear and evidential, and I wasn't getting it. I had not yet followed up the lead that Ginny Packard had given me about Dick Manning, the flight engineer from the Boston area. I decided to try to phone him from New York, not having too much faith that the call would be productive.

I reached Manning after several tries, and explained a little bit about what I was encountering in my research. Like most of the other interviews, it was a little difficult to break the ice.

"In what respect are you writing the story?" he asked.

I told him I had been digging for material in the FAA records and among the Eastern crews, and that I was finding some very unusual things. In all these interviews, I found it best to go about them cautiously. In many cases, the crew members refused to talk, even though they had confided their experiences to their friends. I told Manning that I had run into his name through Ginny Packard.

He knew her, he said, and then added, "You're working at this about the supernatural aspect of the 1972 accident?"

I told him yes. I would be writing the story in a very low key. He said this was important, then said, "Yes, I've done some background research on the phenomenon." He continued to speak cautiously. I asked him if he had heard about Stan Chambers and Rich Craig, the two pilots who had carried out some research, too, and had actually conducted a "soul rescue" project.

"Let me get a pencil and paper," he said. "I'd like to get

your name and address." When he came back to the phone, he said, "There's been a lot of talk going on about this, especially since the Pan Am people picked it up."

I pointed out that I'd heard the story on almost every airline you could think of, foreign as well as domestic.

"Well," he said, "several crew members have talked to me about it and related their experiences to me in detail. And I have to admit that practically all of those who have talked to me are very well-balanced people. They're not given to a lot of emotion. I had studied parapsychology for some time at one period—very extensively, as a matter of fact—but I've got completely out of it now.

"So I knew a little about it. And I discovered that none of those who brought their stories to me had had any kind of psychic experience before. I checked this the first thing, to see if they might be predisposed to this kind of thing. But they weren't. They weren't conditioned to expect, or even to recognize, phenomena like this."

"I've noticed that, too," I said.

"Of course," he said, "you know, people are so interested in the supernatural, which is something that the company management couldn't quite get through their heads."

I said that I was finding that out.

"A lot of times," he continued, "the phenomenon showed up in the lower galley. Some of them in the ovens—but the girls are convinced they are not reflections. And also, at times, it showed up in the crew compartments. And a few captains have walked out into first class to see the apparition of Captain Loft sitting in a seat there. There've been five pilots I know of who have been involved in this, and they're very closed-mouthed about it. I understand that Ginny was offered psychological help.

"Now I've also looked at this thing from a scriptural standpoint. I found the Bible has quite a few experiences of this sort recorded. Now tell me this—have you had any contact with anyone who has had any experiences like this recently?"

I told him no. He asked me a long series of questions about

what I had found out, and I answered them. I told him I would have to be in the Boston area, and that I would like to arrange to see him.

"Fine," he said. "I might have something interesting to tell you."

He did. Elizabeth, who was flying a Boston layover for Northwest Orient, and I met with him and his wife at the Boston Sheraton. He was a rangy, athletic, dark-haired man in his mid-thirties. His wife was a pleasant, attractive woman about the same age. He filled us in on all his research among the Eastern crews. Then he told us a series of events that led to a surprising climax.

At just about the same time that Stan Chambers and Rich Craig had learned of the phenomenon, in early spring of 1974, Dick Manning was flying routinely on the L-1011s, on various flights. He considered the craft "the greatest plane ever made," joining in with the feeling of most flight crews that flew them.

His admiration was not diminished by a couple of incidents he underwent in flight, which were inexplicable to him. One of them involved the electrical circuits on an L-1011 flight from Orlando to Atlanta. For some inexplicable reason, the entire electrical power system on the plane went off, but just as inexplicably, it came back again. The plane was checked on arrival at Atlanta, but no reason could be found for the incident. As a flight engineer with a highly technical background, Manning was puzzled by this and couldn't figure out a logical reason for it.

As he was pondering over this event, he began to hear the first stories about the reappearance of both Captain Loft and Second Officer Repo. After he had heard several, he began to notice one common thing: the crew members involved with the incidents were prone to be very unemotional and level-headed. None of them had any inclination to believe in ghost stories, and many of them had been total skeptics before their encounters.

Because of this appraisal of those who brought their stories about the apparitions to him, he was inclined to take them at their word. In a sense, this disturbed him, because in his Bible studies he had absorbed the theological view that ghosts

did not exist and were contrary to conventional theological thought.

Like several others at Eastern, he dug into the cases that had come up, and probed widely to get at the bottom of the mystery. Yet the more he did this, the more he was inclined to believe that these crew members were convinced what they were saying was the truth, especially those who had been completely skeptical before.

Manning had known Repo and Loft, but did not know either Eastern pilots Rich Craig or Stan Chambers in New York. He knew nothing about their parallel concern. But his thoughts were running parallel to theirs, in almost identical pattern. He was disturbed about what he felt was the "earthbound" condition reflected by the reappearances, and also because he was concerned about Eastern and the L-1011 getting a bad name. He wanted to do something constructive, but he wasn't sure how he could go about it.

Manning began by reassuring those who had experienced one of the incidents that they did not need to be upset by them. Their main reason for being upset was that they were frustrated about not being able to tell anyone about the experience. He had flown one trip with Ginny Packard shortly after her encounter in the galley alone. She confided in him the distress she felt in not wanting to tell anyone about it. With his wife, he consoled her at the airport, and she felt greatly relieved just to get it off her chest.

Manning channeled his Bible studies into a search for some kind of theological justification for apparitions. He was a brilliant student of the Bible and could quote chapter and verse at length. Without quite being a fundamentalist, he took the Bible literally. He didn't go along at all with the psychic or the paranormal and was in contrast to Craig and Chambers on that point. He did, however, believe in the "laying on of hands" for healing either physically or emotionally because it was scriptural, and thus, by his code, acceptable. But he had rejected anything psychic because it ran contrary to biblical Christianity.

In his tracing of both the Bible and religious literature, Manning finally came to the conclusion that ghosts or apparitions were scripturally correct, as he put it, and passed this

information along to those he talked to about the phenomenon. He found passages related to demonic spirits that continue in existence until they are freed, and scriptural texts indicating Christ's recognition of ghosts.

This led him along the line of thinking that he possibly *could* do something about it. As he continued his flights and his Bible studies during the early months of 1974, he noted that he wasn't receiving as many reports of incidents as he had had over the previous year. One of them involved two stewardesses on a Miami-Newark flight on Plane #318 again. In mid-June, they told him, a full-scale apparition of Second Officer Repo appeared in front of them in the galley. He had said nothing, merely stared ahead. Then he disappeared as quickly as he had appeared.

The two girls were terribly shaken. When they arrived at Miami International, they went to the flight attendant's lounge to try to regain their composure. By this time—a year and a half after the accident—it was not very politic to report such happenings because there would be the inevitable suggestion from the Eastern supervisor to visit the company psychiatrist. One girl had been put on sick leave for a considerable time because she made such a report. A flight crew was said to have been grounded for a while. For those who felt they had gone through such a trauma, it was difficult to repress their instinct to get it off their chests.

There was more than an hour's layover in Miami before their L-1011 was scheduled to take off for a return trip to Newark. Second Officer Dick Manning arrived at the ramp ahead of schedule for a deadhead back-flight, en route to Boston. Both girls were back on the plane alone, still trying to shake off the trauma of their experience in the galley. Manning asked them what was wrong. They didn't want to talk about it. He sensed their distress. Since they knew Manning from several other flights and were aware of his interest in religion, they finally confided in him sheepishly. Both girls had been skeptics before.

He listened sympathetically. Then he told them of the many other reports he had correlated. He also told them of his belief in the biblical validity of apparitions, and that he believed in their story. Their chief concern was being sent to

the company psychiatrist if the story got out. He reassured them that he would keep their report confidential and that they didn't need to see a psychiatrist. He read them a few verses from the small Bible that he carried with him, which he kept with the technical manuals of the L-1011. This seemed to calm them down.

At this point, he finally decided to carry out the idea that had been growing in him over the past few weeks. Manning had done considerable probing into the theory of possession and of exorcism. Exorcism had been generally considered as a Catholic rite, but Manning felt that anyone baptized in the Holy Spirit could conduct it. He did, however, prefer to think of the process as deliverance, more in line with his Protestant studies. It was also more in line with the L-1011 situation to think of the deliverance of Second Officer Repo from his anguish, rather than a situation of possession, of which there was no evidence.

The idea, however, of exorcising a plane was without historical precedent. Manning knew nothing of the efforts of pilots Craig and Chambers in their soul rescue attempt. Coincidentally, he was taking a parallel course with the same objective: to help a fellow flight officer in an unprecedented series of events that, apparently without any negative intent, were disrupting the operations of a major airline.

He told the two girls to remain on the passenger deck while he went below in the galley. He explained that, in a sense, he was going to exorcise the aircraft and at the same time deliver the former Second Officer from the desire to cling to this life after he had passed along. He hoped he could put him to rest. Manning was an impressive and erudite speaker, and carried great conviction.

He went down to the galley alone and brought with him a cup of water. Describing it later, he said, "The moment I got down there, the lights started flickering on and off. I sanctified the galley with a cup of water, which was symbolic of the blood of Christ, and I sprinkled it around and around the area. As I did, a wind started blowing down there, all over the place. It was like a thirty-knot wind.

"It grew cold. It grew so cold that it was like standing inside a deep freezer. I sensed a presence in the room. Then a

207

shape began to form. It kept fading in and out. It formed articulately enough for me to recognize the features of Repo. There was no question about it. I said to him, 'Don't you know you are dead? You are dead. You have lost your life. Your spirit remains here, but you have not been taken to your rightful place, where you belong.'

"I didn't say anything about his present condition in limbo, because I am not a judge. You do not judge unless you want to be judged yourself. I am just an instrument of the Lord, nothing else. So I said, 'In the name of Jesus, by his blood, you are begone from here. I am calling an angel of light, and he shall take you to the place that you belong. This is scriptural.'

"Then, where the shape of Don Repo was standing, there was a light. A very bright luminescence. It was so bright, I had to turn my face away. Then everything was gone. He was no longer there."

The two stewardesses met Manning when he reached the passenger deck. They were concerned because the lights had been going on and off for several moments after he went below. Manning reassured them that they need no longer be troubled. He was convinced that there would be no more incidents on the L-1011, and there never had been any concern about it mechanically. "It's the most dynamically stable aircraft that has ever been built," he told them.

It was said that Repo felt that way, and that might have been the reason for his clinging to the craft that he loved. Whatever it was, the reports of any more incidents in the galley or cockpit or cabins suddenly stopped short. None of the flight crews or maintenance personnel who had followed the long trail of stories over many months, learned of any new experiences.

Second Officer Dick Manning was also confident that Repo was comforted and sanctified. He learned, however, that the story of the exorcism had spread across the airline, among the flight crews. Eventually his supervisor called Manning into his office to talk to him about it. He was disturbed by the story going around and wanted to get the details on it. Manning explained to him that what he did was fully within scriptural propriety, and that he did it not only for

the sake of Don Repo's peace and comfort, but for the sake of Eastern Airlines, and an aircraft that was one of the best in the air.

The supervisor said to Manning, "If I believed—if I really thought—that you believed in that, I'd send you down for a psychiatric examination."

Manning looked at him directly and said, "I believe it. I dare you."

He never was sent to the psychiatrist.

When Manning finished telling us the story, we told him about the "soul rescue" in New York. He seemed pleased. Elizabeth and I were more bewildered than ever about the story. Here was another "exorcism" by a technically minded crew member who dealt constantly with the engineering complexities of the new superjet, and yet was delving back into medieval practices as an antidote. It was a fascinating mixture. Whether Manning or any of the others involved should be censured by Eastern depended on one's point of view.

In the modern world, there seemed to be a parapsychological revolution breaking out. People who once would never even admit the possibility of a paranormal experience were now discussing that possibility freely, across the dinner tables of the most sophisticated and elite circles. Bookstores were stocking special sections on unexplained phenomena, and trade was brisk. The acceptance of parapsychology by the American Association for the Advancement of Science marked a milestone of the renewed interest in a highly controversial field. Mining exploration companies increasingly hired dowsers to explore for hidden water or mineral deposits. One dowser located a water supply running 175 gallons a minute for a new Bristol-Meyers Company plant in New Jersey, a fair return for his $2,500 fee. Dupont and RCA successfully used dowsers, along with many oil and mineral companies, but understandably kept their dowsing results hidden.

There was so much smoke here, so much baffling detail, the story was hard to ignore; yet it was elusive to pin down. I thought maybe the Eastern public relations man was right—it was all a bunch of crap. Then I thought that with many details

emerging, inconclusive as they were, the whole thing couldn't be invented. And what about these "exorcisms"? The flight-crew members had been fully motivated to take the time and trouble to carry them out. There had to be motivation for this. But if exorcisms worked, how would anyone know? I asked Manning this in the lobby of the Boston-Sheraton as we were saying good night.

He said, "I had checked the whole phenomenon out very closely myself, and talked to people who had been flying Plane 318 for months and months. After the ritual on the plane, I did the same thing again. As far as I could learn, the reports had stopped. Perhaps what the other two pilots did—and what I did—worked. There's no way of being absolutely certain, of course."

At dinner that night, Elizabeth and I pondered the whole thing. Three qualified flight-deck crew members had found the situation alarming enough to take these unusual steps for the purpose of helping both a flying colleague and Eastern Airlines. The juxtaposition of the modern, technical world with ancient cabalistic practices was utterly fascinating and unreal.

"The more I learn about this psychic business, the more I wonder," Elizabeth said. "There's just too much here to ignore."

We took a pencil and paper and tried to sum up the evidence that was emerging, to condense it into some kind of form that would bring the strange story into focus. The facts seemed to boil down to these:

1. There was massive, believable evidence from theoretical studies that apparitions could exist.

2. They often coincided with sudden, unexpected death, and continued after that.

3. The apparitions could appear in solid form, in broad daylight, and could appear to intelligent, rational, and competent observers as actually being in the area, just as any other human being.

4. There could, in rare cases, be vocal communication.

5. There was voluminous testimony that deceased

crew members of Flight 401, especially Don Repo, had appeared in this way on a considerable number of sister ships of the ill-fated plane.

6. This testimony had come from sane, competent observers, many with technical backgrounds.

7. Whatever the apparitions were, they were not harmful or destructive; in fact, the reports indicated the opposite was true.

8. In spite of this, some refused to work in the lower galleys of the L-1011s, while others liked the assignment.

9. The L-1011 planes were exceptionally safe and reliable. Crews and passengers preferred them, sought them out.

10. Two different forms of "exorcisms" had been independently carried out, by two pilots on one hand, and a flight engineer on the other. Both were on behalf of Don Repo, since reports on Loft had practically disappeared.

11. Since that time, no further serious reports of the incidents could be tracked down.


"Well," Elizabeth said, "that ties the whole thing up in a package. Where do you want to go from here?"

"I'm not sure," I said. "Half the time I believe it, and half the time I don't."

"That's more than you were at the start," she said.

"How about you?" I said. "You've checked around enough now to get a reading. What do you think?"

"Just like you," she said. "I bounce back and forth on it. Logically, it couldn't happen. Logically it *has* to have happened. Not all these people are insane. Or if they are, I'm going to quit flying."

"What about the mediums? And the Arthur Ford Academy?"

"What about them?"

"They suggest I try to get direct evidential stuff through some of their mediums."

"I like the Hayeses," Elizabeth said. "They are honest and direct. They have nothing to gain by it."

She was commenting on the fact that the Hayeses had volunteered to conduct some experiments.

"They asked if we could get some parts of the plane that crashed. They could try psychometry with them."

"But that's impossible, isn't it?" Elizabeth asked.

"I don't know," I said. "Maybe we could get an airboat and go out to the site. J.R. and Rachelle have a friend who has a boat and knows the Everglades backward."

"What are we waiting for, then?" she asked.

I wasn't sure. I was hesitant. I still didn't have the confidence in psychic experimentation to attempt anything like this. If it turned out to be a complete flop, I would be disappointed. If it turned out to be inconclusive, it would be just as bad. In spite of this, we decided to bring the question up again to Pat and Bud Hayes of the Arthur Ford Academy, as well as with the pilots and their wives. What was to follow would change the whole course of the story.

"But here the thing is. It did not exist before as a formulated whole, either in our minds or in any of our reading: it came—and is coming—in the manner set down. Those are the facts. They may be explained as you will, but they exist."

—Stewart Edward White,
*The Unobstructed Universe*

# Chapter XII

There were many other leads to track down. It was a laborious job and not very fruitful. Elizabeth became more and more important, however, through her interviews during her days off from flying for Northwest, especially because of her capacity to relate to other airlines personnel. Her interest and enthusiasm were increasing. She wanted to learn more, not only about the L-1011 incidents, but about the whole psychic field itself. She began digging up a great deal of background material in the library, matching it up with the details of what had been happening with Eastern. She was also a good sounding board.

We both tried to analyze and compare the thoughts and ideas of Rich Craig and Stan Chambers and those of Dick Manning. There were two schools of thoughts involved that seemed diametrically opposed. Manning had employed a biblical concept, and felt the psychic approach was wrong. The pilots from New York believed that the modern-day medium was a highly ethical person who used his ability to become a conscious spiritual and psychic channel. In this way, the medium would pick up feelings that brought information and impressions from spiritual sources higher than himself, without any prior knowledge of a person's background or problems. This, in turn, according to the theory, could be put to use in helping a person with problems by bringing him to an understanding of his own emotional and spiritual needs. Further, this guidance was designed to help another person resolve his conflicts and fulfill his best potential. In a sense, an ethical medium acted as a spiritual supplement to a psychiatrist.

The two pilots and others in their Spiritual Frontier group

saw no conflict between this and the principles of Christianity. In fact, they believed that it was simply an additional way of serving God. They also saw no conflict between modern mediumship and the modern-day technical world. More than that, they felt that the demands and pressures of a materialistic society highlighted the need for spiritual development and psychic awareness. Their own work as pilots demanded exacting technical realism. Their work as mediums fulfilled their own desires to grow spiritually and help others to do so.

The crash in the Everglades had dramatized the fragility of physical life. The events that had followed it suggested there was concrete evidence that there was a continuation of an individual's existence after death, infinitely more permanent. If this was accepted as being so, wouldn't it have a forceful impact and bearing on the way people conducted their lives in the fragile and fleeting physical world? If it were clearly evident that the physical body was an idea that continued on after death, that nothing could really destroy it or imprison it, could this demonstrate the futility of wars, violence, oppression?

To the two pilots in New York and the flight engineer in Boston the entire scene went far beyond the tragic accident of Flight 401, without any knowing of the others' concern with the phenomenon. It encompassed all of mankind, as a symbol of physical life versus the timeless existence of the individual consciousness. The New York pilots and the Boston flight engineer represented two different points of view, two different aspects of the same thing: one from the purely biblical, the other from the mystic consciousness that led to God. But both points of view coincided in one area: the need to free the spiritual distress of an airman who kept reappearing on the L-1011s and to remove any stigma attached to the aircraft they respected and admired.

I was still having trouble picturing an apparition that was solid and clearly observable. I still clung to the old concept that if there were such a thing as a ghost, it would certainly be something vague and misty, and on the steps in a Victorian hallway. I couldn't picture an L-1011 flight deck with a solid form sitting in the cockpit jump seat. I could see now that if I

were going to keep after the story, I would have to learn more about the background and history of psychic research on the subject, specifically apparitions. Just how much material there was on this, I didn't know. But I did know that whatever material Elizabeth and I gathered would have to be from the most reliable, scientific, and credible sources possible. The subject matter was much too controversial from the start to entertain specious or conjectural sources. What we unearthed about the subject surprised us.

Most serious books on the subject of apparitions were extremely erudite, but rather dull and repetitious. G.N.M. Tyrrell's *Apparitions* was most perceptive and thorough, however, and his theory on apparitions provocative. He threw a sharp lance at science for dismissing apparitions as distortion of sense perceptions. "Whatever doubts infect sense-perception," he wrote, "must also infect the whole body of experimental science, which ultimately rests on sense perception. Scientists no doubt discover a great deal by the use of instruments; but it must be remembered that these are aids to the senses, not substitutes for them."

As a leading physicist and mathematician himself, Tyrrell could appraise both worlds with one foot in each. He defined the perfect apparition as "a material thing without a physical occupant." All the sense-data of normal perception is present, except that there is no physically occupied region. But there is visual, auditory, and even tactual perception in many cases where apparitions have appeared. He also points out that in the majority of cases, the figure obscures the background, thus making it opaque rather than ghostlike. Some, however, were conventionally transparent.

But generally, in the most vivid cases such as those that had been reported on the L-1011s, an apparition was, according to Tyrrell "a motion picture in three dimensions, and its creator has access to unlimited stage property." The fact that apparitions are seen by more than one person is of extreme importance to Tyrrell, as it was to the pilots and flight attendants of Eastern. In the cases studied by the British Society of Psychical Research, there were 130 collective experiences. "This is too large a number to be dismissed out of hand," Tyrrell says in his book. He does not ascribe these

collective cases to mass hallucination, but to the imprint of a telepathic communication in the form of an "idea pattern" on the minds of several people to produce them. In the case of an apparition of a living person, the transmitter is the living agent. In the case of a dead person's appearing before several people, he theorizes that the telepathy would have to come from the dead person. He dismisses the idea that a subjective hallucination could spread to others.

This, of course, assumes the reality of the survival of an individual's consciousness after death. It also assumes that mind is independent of the brain. To get at this question, Tyrrell suggests that we suspend common sense in favor of *un*common sense. "The common-sense view of time must be utterly inadequate," he writes. "Modern science agrees with that, and the best of modern science deals with un-common sense."

But if individual consciousness does survive after death, what possible form would it take? If the individual consciousness merely merged into a homogeneous tank-car full of milk, there would be no significance to life after death. The floating about on clouds with trumpets and angel wings was obviously an illogical absurdity. There would certainly have to be more cogent postulates than those to even consider the question.

I had run across a very interesting theory on this several years ago. It had made me wonder for the first time whether there couldn't be a rational potential for survival. I felt this way because the proposal suggested a clear theory as to how consciousness *could* exist apart from the body mechanism. The source was several papers and tracts* by Professor H. H. Price, emeritus professor of logic at Oxford, who had been a visiting professor at Princeton in 1948, and at the University of California in 1962.

Professor Price believed that it was ridiculous to study evidence of life after death unless we could form a clear idea of what it might be like. It could not be physiological, because the body was useless after death. The only portion

*H. H. Prince, "What Kind of Next World?" in Eileen J. Garrett, "Does Man Survive Death?" (New York: Helix Press Books, 1964).

that could survive was the individual consciousness. What kind of geography could this ephemeral thing float around in to make any sense at all?

Professor Price suggested that the body would be supplanted by what he called a "higher form of matter," which would substitute for the physical body. The only thing remaining at the death of an individual would be the nonmaterial soul or spirit. Although part of the individual dies at death, this part would remain. It was not dependent on the human brain. In fact, it had motivated the brain.

But where would this geography that could house the soul or spirit be? Certainly not out in conventional space. He explains it in this way:

We have no reason for assuming that physical space with which we are now familiar is the *only* space there is. The Next World, and all that is in it, might just be in a space of its own, different from space of the physical universe. Moreover, it might be a different *sort* of space as well. And the causal laws there must differ from the laws of physics if such phrases as "higher body" and "higher kind of matter" are to have any meaning.

Then Professor Price asks the question: "If the after-death personality is something completely immaterial, can there be any sort of other world at all?"

Here he points out that our own dreams are a perfect analogy for a space-geography that doesn't take up any room, that no real estate agent can sell or buy, no armies can fight over, and are limitless in boundary. What's more, this kind of "space" could easily furnish the background for something as wispy and nonmaterial as a spirit, and still allow it to have a very well-shaped form. "To sleep, perchance to dream," expressed Hamlet's great fear of death, for he was aware that such stuff that dreams are made of can be terrifyingly real.

A sleeping person often believes in the total reality of a dream, until he wakes up. "Both for good or for ill," Professor Price says, "our dream experiences may be as vividly felt as any of our waking ones, or more so." He points out that the imagery of dreams takes place in what appears to be real

space. The street scenes are real to the senses, the houses, the trees, the fields, the cars, the clothing.

It would of course be a psychological world and not a physical one. It might indeed seem to be physical for those who experience it. The image-objects which compose it might appear very like physical objects, as dream objects often do now; so much so that we might find it difficult at first to realize that we are dead.

Under this concept, the life and awareness of the individual would continue in image form. But it would be no less real. There would be communication, just as there is in dreams. The communication would probably be telepathic, and since we have strong evidence of telepathy in our current lives and dreams, there would be no reason to exclude from this concept, perhaps in a stronger or more articulate form.

The theories of Professor William Ernest Hocking, Alford Professor of Philosophy at Harvard from 1920 to 1923, fit in closely with those of Professor Price's. Writing in his book *The Meaning of Immortality* (New York: Harper and Brothers, 1957), he said:

Without a body of some sort, there can be no personal living. Existence for a person implies awareness of events in time—a continuity of particulars, not an absorption of universals or The One. What has perished (at death) is the livingness of structure and function, the organic and personal integration of persisting elements. Our question relates to *this* perishing, whether it is absolute, cutting through its every strand of personal being—most vulnerable through its very marvel of unified complexity; and whether it, too, may be relative, leaving a germinal strand of self-hood intact. The "how" of survival is a matter far less attended to by philosophical discussion, one might fairly say neglected, and yet essential to our own inquiry.

Hocking states that man is both part of nature and also outside of it. Man has demonstrated that he can often change

the course of nature. Like Price, Hocking feels that it is wrong to assume that there is only one kind of space. And also like Price, he finds a partial answer in the dream:

> The dream world is not somewhere in the waking world. There is no road or passage, nor any astronomical line of distance and direction. . . . The passage between them is as swift as the change of direction of thought. I raise the question whether we have not here something, not identical with, but more literally than the journey image, akin to a believable "hinge of transition" between this world and another.

Along with Price, Hocking finds that dreams can have a three-dimensional reality that could allow for a space geography beyond our own. Dreams went far beyond memory in imagery and a sense of reality. He dramatizes the fact that space experienced in dreams and our space can't be measured in the same terms, by an interesting example. A person dreams he is in a canoe, headed toward a waterfall. He wakes up suddenly. How far is it from the bow of the canoe to the foot of the bed? There's no way of measuring it, of course. If you have a picture of a mountain on your wall, you could measure the distance from the peak to the floor with a tape measure, but it would be a meaningless figure. He asks how much space do you need for a soul? Or a thought? How much does a dream weigh? Or the consciousness, that part of a person that even scientists are beginning to feel is apart from the brain or bodily mechanics?

"The event of death," Hocking writes, "involving the body of the self belonging to one nature system, does not necessarily involve the death of the self. . . . Death may thus be relative, not absolute. And the transition in death, a mental transition, devoid of distance."

These three erudite and reputable gentlemen opened up my mind at least to the possibility of the L-1011 incidents having the validity that the testimony seemed to indicate. All through checking the story, I was still swinging back and forth on the pendulum: the incidents could never possibly have hap-

pened; the incidents *must* have happened because of the persistence of the reports from credible people who would have nothing to gain and a lot to lose by reporting them. The stories had not yet reached the stage where they were embellished by legend.

On the other hand, I didn't like getting the material secondhand. The suggestion that I try getting evidential facts through a medium still bothered me, even though I realized it might be a device for making direct communication. Even if strong evidence did turn up, it would be difficult to crosscheck or get across. Meanwhile I continued trying to probe the rational theories behind the phenomenon.

British theorist W. Whately Smith had independently come up with a postulate that fit neatly into those of Price and Hocking. He felt, with them, that if consciousness persists after death, it must do so in some state of embodiment, since the idea of pure essence is inconceivable. He looked for the answer in the temporary absences of self-awareness an individual encounters during his life: in sleep, in anesthesia, in unconscious states. He contended that there is a fourth dimension that our self-awareness goes into that is not part of our three-dimensional world, and that dreams were the best example of it.

I realized that what I was doing was trying to find a theory that would match the L-1011 evidence that was turned up. This was necessary because of my doubts, which were considerable. It was also comforting to find rational and intelligent minds that had explored the subject. One of the most articulate of these was the late Professor James H. Hyslop, a former professor of ethics and logic at Columbia University. His book *Science and a Future Life* was applicable to the L-1011 story, even though it had been published in the early 1900s.

Professor Hyslop regretted that, in his time, millions were being spent to explore the North Pole and the stars, for deep-sea dredging, and for studies of protoplasm, all of which searched for the origin of man, while none was being spent for man's ultimate *destiny*. Yet wasn't this the question that really counted? He felt that the psychic field could serve

as a bridge between religion and science. He was certain that the contempt of the skeptic for studying apparitions, for instance, was the result of failing to examine the evidence. At the same time, he acknowledged the reasons for their contempt. Some apparitions were the result of hallucinations. Some could start an irrational craze for the subject. Caution was important, but should not serve as an excuse for not investigating the serious reports. These should be studied either from the point of view of psychiatry or for establishing the evidence of the survival of man after death.

Professor Hyslop also felt that the evidence of apparitions appearing simultaneously with death or injury of the person were too frequent and well documented to be coincidence. He also felt that this evidence discredited subjective hallucination as an explanation. He questioned why, as the atom became scientifcally known as being closer to energy than matter, and therefore more occult, it was less respectable to examine the possibilities of spirit and life after death. He also wondered why some scientists considered it wrong to consider that consciousness was not a function of the brain, but apart from it.

With all this in mind, Hyslop went on to examine what evidence there was to satisfy the skeptic. He stipulated two things: first, it would have to be shown that an individual consciousness could be separated from its organism to prove an independent existence; second, it must be established that communication with such an entity was possible:

The first class of phenomena that claims to represent evidence of departed spirits is that of apparitions of the dead. If we could assure ourselves that these incidents were plentiful enough and verifiable in any such form as would attest their real existence beyond the imagination of the percipient of them, science might be more strongly impressed than it is with them.

He realized, in his analysis of the problem, that knowledge from beyond the senses must be shown by fact. He also

realized that these facts must illustrate and prove personal identity of the deceased:

> The facts must prove that the source of the phenomena is what it claims to be, and this personal identity of the discarnate means that the deceased person shall tell facts of personal knowledge in his earthly life and tell them in such quantity and with such a quality that we should not doubt his existence any more than we would if we received the same incidents over a telegraph wire or through a telephone. In this way alone can we show that the intelligence involved is outside the medium through which the facts come.

Professor Hyslop saw no reason why telepathy should be substituted as a theory for communication with the dead, because there was no reason to assume that the dead couldn't communicate by the same method, especially with a reliable and serious medium.

He defined a medium as someone who claimed to communicate with the dead, whether it was through trance or conscious state, automatic writing, table tipping, or the Ouija board. He went on to examine some of the classic cases that fulfilled his strict criteria in great detail.

Ironically enough, after Hyslop's death in 1920, his secretarial assistant documented dozens of séances with mediums which brought almost unassailable evidence that Professor Hyslop himself was communicating through the medium and providing information that met his criteria for authenticity. In some of the most impressive of these sessions, the medium utilized the Ouija board.

I was intrigued by this because of the Ouija board experience with the Elinor Wylie incident at the MacDowell Colony in New Hampshire. I also discovered that Stewart Edward White, the famous naturalist and author who wrote *The Unobstructed Universe* and over forty other books, had gone deeply into psychic research after discovering that the Ouija board could bring out startling articulate messages from a personality who showed evidence of being from "the other

side," as psychics refer to this ultimate state of man's condition.

White's books on everything from Africa to the history of the American West were solidly realistic. I was surprised to discover he had delved into the psychic as deeply as he did. It began as a lark. A friend persuaded him and his wife Betty to play around with a Ouija board. "The occasion was derisive and gay," he wrote, "and pretty muddled. It did not impress me much, but I agreed to try my turn provided my opposite would agree not to fake."

They used a small, inverted whisky glass because the indicator that came with the board seemed too clumsy, and White went on to say:

> The little glass moved, and without the slightest conscious volition on my part. That much I could determine. How much was unconscious muscular action, I could not for the moment decide. After a time, whenever the glass moved away from me, I let my fingers go limp and allowed the mechanism to pull them after it. It did so, and once or twice dragged the glass from under them. This was interesting. The force that moved that glass away from me was either an outside force, or my partner. It certainly was not myself.
>
> Here was peculiar unanalyzable movement of an inanimate object beneath our fingers. The fact that it spelled out simple sentences of whose purport we none of us had any conscious inkling, was an entirely secondary consideration. For my part my main attention was concentrated on the feel of the thing under my fingers. It had, it seemed to me, a peculiar thrill of vitality; but I fully acknowledged to myself that such an effect might well have been imaginative, following a strained attention. It also seemed to me that its movements preceded rather than followed even the slight unconscious muscular pressures; but that too could not be certain.
>
> I am setting down the details minutely, not because they were unusual—for I suspect them of being about the average—nor because of any serious experimental value, but merely to convey a sense of background for

what later developed, and to indicate our own mental attitude.

What did later develop was that White's wife Betty graduated quickly from the Ouija board to automatic writing —the capacity to act as a channel for an outside force that creates articulate messages that has nothing to do with the conscious mind of the writer. The pencil moves without conscious volition over the paper, often with the subject blindfolded or in trance. In Brazil, this strange phenomenon has produced some of the country's best classic literature. It is best evidenced in the work of the mystic Chico Xavier, highly praised by Brazilian critics.

Stewart Edward White called the entities that communicated through his wife Betty, "The Invisibles." She went on to record three books full of spiritual insight, revealing what White called the unobstructed universe. Her messages were reflected in capsule form in one particular statement: "Listen! There is only one universe. Consciousness is the one reality. . . . Thoughts are things!"

White's exploration of the psychic field appealed to me because he had approached the subject as a journalist with the same point of view I had, one of tentative exploration. White also reinforced the view that the mediums I had talked with insisted was possible: the direct contacting of Don Repo through psychic channels.

I was still half-resisting this idea. No matter what information I might receive, I would have trouble believing. It would have to be strong, articulate, sharp evidence without any chance of the material being consciously known to the medium or channel involved. Perhaps I was afraid of being disappointed. I preferred to explore the direct experiences of the crew members or other technical people themselves. I kept reaching for the views of the more technical minded as a means of assurance. They would be less likely to buy anything spurious or specious in such an incredible story.

As I was probing into the background and theory of the whole psychic field in connection with apparitions, I received an interesting letter from the FAA's Bill Damroth. He pointed out that care would have to be taken because often

plane numbers and specific incidents would be confused by crew members; and that while the incident might be correct, the data associated with it might not:

> I am not discounting any of the materialization experiences, because I know they can happen. Especially after sudden and catastrophic accidents. It is believed—and reported—that those making such an unexpected transition to the spirit world (so-called death) find it difficult to accept the fact that they are no longer of the physical world that they expend great effort and energy to communicate with those left behind. And many times succeed—to the disbelief of those who can see and hear the materialization.
>
> It would be interesting to talk to the pilots involved with the L-1011 materializations, by mediumship. I plan to see my friend from American Airlines this summer. Perhaps Don Repo might communicate. If he does, I'll let you know.

I again couldn't help reflecting how strange this was, to encounter an aviation technical expert and two pilots who were mediums. I wanted to get back to more of the straight technical side, but seemed to be reaching a dead end.

There didn't seem to be much choice left, and on a strange story like this it was probably necessary to touch all the bases, including this one. I had postponed it long enough. It was not that I had anything against mediums—it was just that it seemed too other-worldly, and certainly not a general custom in journalistic practice. I reluctantly made the decision to try to contact Don Repo through some of the mediums in the Miami area who had generously offered their help. There were some definite surprises in store.

"Discussing the creation of the universe in terms of time and space is like trying to discover the artist and the action of painting by going to the edge of the picture. This brings us very near to those philosophical systems which regard the universe as a thought in the mind of its Creator, thereby reducing all discussion of material creation to futility."

—Sir James Jeans,
*The Universe Around Us*

# Chapter XIII

I read through Tyrrell again to try to absorb more of the theory advanced by the serious scientific researchers. "The most widely known group of physical phenomena is that relating to the Mediumistic Trance," Tyrrell wrote, "since it is through this that communications are received which ostensibly proceed from the dead."

He went on to describe three main conditions where such communications were said to be obtained. One was where the medium goes into a trance, and some kind of entity takes over the motor and sensory mechanism of the body. Such an entity was supposed to come through in one of several ways—through voice or what was called "automatic writing" or the Ouija board. It didn't matter what form it took, as long as the messages were articulate and able to be examined and checked for evidence. When this alleged entity comes through repeatedly, it is called the medium's "control." The control had the function of passing on messages from the dead indirectly. A second condition was that in which the deceased entity communicated directly when the medium was in a trance. A third was where the medium remained conscious, but passed on the communication directly.

In any of these, voice or automatic writing was considered the most reliable. The Ouija board* was considered slow and

*NOTE: Serious students of parapsychology *emphatically* warn against the use of the Ouija board for any prolonged time, or for frivolous attempts at communicating with purported "spirits." The phenomenon of possession, they say, is not to be taken lightly, and, beyond that, the inclination to utilize the device as a crutch or support for decisions that should be made by the individual's free will, could

awkward, a beginner's tool. It was not a toy, and it should be used with care. It could, however, offer strong evidential material if used carefully.

One problem with the Ouija board was supposed to be that there could be frequent interference, much like static on a radio. Correct information could be flowing in, when suddenly either gibberish or a false message could come through. This was attributed to the fact that other entities could easily take over and garble the message or deliberately give false information through some unknown motive. In this way, strong evidence of communication could be received and checked out to be accurate: specific names and places unknown to the operators on the board which were found to be correct, or personal information that could be checked through a third party involved the operators could not possibly know. But false information could also come through without warning. The good would have to be sorted out from the bad.

Because of this, only information that checked out could be accepted. Other information, regardless of its apparent validity, was not to be accepted. In addition to static, there apparently could be a weak signal, or a signal that broke up just as in a ship-to-shore radio communication. In this way, letters could be scrambled at times in the middle of an otherwise articulate message. If this were allowed for, however, and weighted with other valid information, there was supposed to be no need for concern.

Tyrrell considered psychometry, where a medium holds an object belonging to someone, as another interesting tool. Its function, he reports, seemed to be to act as a link for putting the medium *en rapport* with the subject. "All we can say," Tyrrell writes, "is that it points strongly towards the view that there must be a vast amount of *something behind* the physical object as it appears to our senses."

grow to a point where serious psychological damage could result. As a device for guidance and forecasting of the future, it can be totally unreliable. Specific case histories show that some people, just as in alcoholism, form a psychological dependency, and can be particularly vulnerable to the device.

I felt at this point that I was getting into a wilderness as swampy and trackless as the Everglades. On the other hand, Pat and Bud Hayes of the Arthur Ford Academy were reassuring because of their successful grasp and submersion into the realities of life, as well as their capacities as mediums. The same was true of the two New York pilots and their wives. None of them qualified for the spook-and-kook image in any way at all.

J. R. Worden, along with Betsy Wilkes, and Rachelle, volunteered to arrange for an informal "sitting" of several mediums in the Miami area. They would be asked to try to communicate or contact a deceased entity whose identity would be revealed to them later. They were to be told nothing of the fact that I was researching the L-1011 case. "Don't forget," J.R. told me, "there's no guarantee. We're all of us fallible. Any information you get must be double-checked against factual evidence. You might have to try several times."

The meeting was arranged at the home of Norman and Mimi Cooperman. They were a relaxed and energetic couple, with a tasteful apartment in Miami. Norman Cooperman was a scientist with degrees in biology, psychology, and chemistry who spent practically all his off-hour time in researching the psychological aspects of parapsychology in conjunction with a local university. He had demonstrated considerable capacity for psychic healing. He was not content to leave this medically undocumented. As a result, he was working closely with several doctors, so that the effectiveness of his treatments could be checked and certified clinically. The results had been uncommonly successful.

The group had already assembled when I reached the Cooperman apartment. There were eight, altogether, including the Coopermans. They were sitting casually around the living room, as in any after-dinner social gathering. They were a varied group. A tall, pale young woman. A young, dynamic girl in jeans. A sensitive-looking black man, with handsomely sculptured features. A distinguished gentleman with a shock of white hair, and his wife, plump and middle-

aged. Later Laura Britebarth joined the group. She was the Eastern ticketing agent who had flown down from New York to visit the Coopermans. I learned that she was considered to be a particularly sensitive medium. She was a trim, attractive brunette in her twenties.

Cooperman began the session by explaining that he was not going to give out much information. The session was to be an experiment to try to "bring in" someone no longer living, who may or may not respond. "I won't cue you on anything specific," he said to the group. "We'd like to see what can come out of free meditation. I hope you'll be free to say whatever comes through your head, whether it seems to make any sense or not. If you'll close your eyes now, take a deep breath for a count of seven again. Relax. Continue this breathing; open your minds up. If anything forms in your mind, let it come out."

The group followed his instructions, relaxing in a silent circle. There was silence for over a minute, then Charles, the man with the white hair, spoke.

"For some reason," he said, "I seem to see a beautiful Oriental rug."

"What does that mean to you?" Cooperman asked.

"I'm not sure," Charles responded, "but I seem to associate it with flying."

"All right," Cooperman said, "let anything come out. Follow it up."

"Another oddball thought comes up. The number 900. This also seems to be connected with flying carpets. Doesn't make any sense to me."

There was more silence. The group breathing, eyes closed, except for Norman Cooperman, who surveyed them watchfully. After several moments, Jan, the tall girl, spoke so softly she could hardly be heard.

"I am getting a physical feeling that is not mine," she said. "It's a very heavy pounding of the heart. There seems to be help needed, but help is not there."

"Can you identify who it is?" Cooperman asked.

"It's not I," Jan responded.

"Go deeper into yourself," Cooperman said. "Count and breathe deeply. Speak as that person."

"I have the feeling of speed. There is speed. Air is rushing at me."

"There is a mirror in front of you. You are looking at yourself as this entity. Can you describe yourself?" Cooperman asked.

"Tall. Salt and pepper hair, kind of falling over forehead. A moustache comes and goes. Broad shoulders, athletic. Nervous energy."

"Do you have the name?"

Jan took several more breaths, then said, "I do. But this is known through Jan's conscious mind. I have sensed what the situation is. I don't want to mislead you."

"Tell us the name anyway," Cooperman said. I learned later that a legitimate medium will clarify any thoughts that come through the conscious level, in contrast to those thoughts which he or she believes come through as a telepathic channel, or a communication from the deceased.

Again there was a long pause, then Jan said, "Don."

"You are here," Cooperman asked.

"I'm here," Jan said.

Cooperman had told the group that I might ask some questions, as an observer of the session, so I spoke up. "Do you associate any occupation or action with 'Don'?" I asked.

"Janice knows the occupation from her conscious mind," Jan said, her eyes still closed, her breathing deep and slow. "So I'm not sure of the validity. But I'm sure it's flight engineer."

If this information had come purely from the unconscious channel, it would have been rather startling evidence of communication. But since Jan was honest enough to reveal that she was imparting information from her own consciousness, it would make other information questionable, regardless of how well-meaning Jan was.

"Can you visualize what is happening?" I asked.

"There are people yelling and grabbing at things."

"Do you identify what situation this is," I asked.

"It is difficult for me to disassociate the conscious knowledge," Jan said. "But it is the Everglades."

She went on in the low, soft voice. She revealed a great deal of correct information about the crash. Several others in

the group identified with the anguish and pain of the accident, as if they were experiencing it themselves.

But the problem was that no direct evidence that was unknown to either me or the group was revealed that could be checked and verified later. Things like the names of members of Repo's family, exact circumstances of his past, sharp technical questions involving the L-1011, personality traits that could be checked with friends, characteristic phrases, and especially, actual names of crew members he had allegedly appeared before on the various flights of 318.

Unfortunately, none of that sort of material turned up. The material that did come through was essentially correct, but it was muddied and revealed nothing clearly new. I was pleased, however, that no one pretended that conscious information was coming in as a form of communication. Each person in the group stated frankly whenever conscious thoughts and knowledge came through. This gave me confidence in the validity of the group. They were not pretending or attempting to sensationalize.

After the meeting, I spoke with Laura Britebarth, who more or less disqualified herself from the session because, as an Eastern employee, she knew many details consciously. ''You're not going to believe what I'm going to tell you,'' she said, ''but I'm going to tell you anyway. Just before going to sleep last night, I felt I had a very definite communication with Don Repo. He 'came through' as we say, clear and absolutely definite. This was not a fantasy. And the message was that he wants to work with you in making the story clear and accurate.''

I laughed and said, ''Come on, now. You really don't expect me to *believe* that, do you Laura?''

''I most certainly do,'' she said. ''He seemed very adamant about wanting the story to get out. He's pleased about it. He'll even work with you.''

''Laura,'' I said, ''everybody says you're a very intelligent and honest person. You appear that way to me. But don't spoil that image.''

I was chuckling, and she laughed, too. ''All right,'' she said. ''Don't believe me. You'll find out.''

"*All* of this is so impossible to believe," I said. "I don't know how I ever got myself into this."

She smiled again. "All of this is part of your education. You're learning. But it's going to take a long time. And I also heard from Bill Damroth, from the FAA. Did you know I knew him?"

I shook my head.

"Have you talked to him in the last few days?"

"No."

"You have a lot of respect for him I understand," she said, and she was being almost mischievous. "He's got an excellent technical background. Knows the aviation industry backward. He wouldn't be inclined to buy just anything in the psychic field, do you think?"

Again I said no, and wondered what she was driving at.

"Bill Damroth told me that Repo came through at a session he was attending. Seriously. I'm not pulling your leg."

The whole thing was too bizarre, too incredible. I was convinced that there was honest self-deception going on. It seemed too far-out, regardless of all the serious study that had gone on in psychic research. But I could accept that better than I could a direct contact with Don Repo, if only because the latter would be too fortuitous, too much of a coincidence even if there was evidence of it happening. The evidence would have to be strong and unassailable, and able to be crosschecked, for me to be convinced.

"Well," I told Laura. "Whether you're pulling my leg or not, I'll contact Bill Damroth in Atlanta and find out just what the story is."

I reached Bill on the phone the following evening. "Well," he said on the phone, "you're not going to believe this, and that's why I haven't called you sooner. I was trying to figure out a way so that it wouldn't sound so ridiculous. My friend from American Airlines and I were in a group session, and decided to try to reach Repo. They were using the old-fashioned method called 'table tipping,' believe it or not. There were four of us."

The information that the yes-and-no answers provided was interesting, but again too vague. The purported communication seemed to indicate that Repo was partway out of the hell

234

hole of the plane when the crash occurred, that he didn't feel Eastern was giving out the full story, that there was bias to it. But these and other answers could not be checked clearly, and yes-and-no answers provided by the table were subject to misinterpretation. Damroth felt that efforts should be continued to try to get evidential information, using whatever method was best, whether it was the Ouija board or psychometry with the wrecked plane parts, or other techniques.

I was still halfhearted about the whole idea, and the story had still not shaped up clearly enough to satisfy me. On the basis of trying anything once, I made arrangements with Glenn Cookerly, a tall, agile electronics expert who spent many weekends hunting in the Everglades on his airboat to go out to the wreckage site. Perhaps we could find some fragments of the wreck still there, that could be used in a psychometry experiment.

Elizabeth Manzione, still collecting more material, arrived on a Miami layover from Northwest. She joined me, and we met Glenn at a small Indian restaurant about twenty miles out of Miami on the Tamiami Trail. Cookerly had his fourteen-foot airboat on a trailer outside the restaurant, and after a quick lunch we followed him down to an earthern ramp just off the Tamiami Trail. It took him less than ten minutes to launch it in the swampy water by the ramp.

I climbed on the top of the wire housing that caged the engine and propeller, and sat as if I were on a saddle on the back of a camel, and as high off the ground. The only thing to hold on to was a metal handle. Glenn sat in front of me at the controls, on a platform halfway up the ten-foot-high caging. Elizabeth sat in front of him on a small jump seat. An airboat is not built for comfort.

The sound of the engine and propeller was deafening. After cautiously moving over a fourteen-foot-deep canal, Glenn gunned the engine. We started skimming over the sawgrass and water, as if we were moving over a thick, enormous bowl of watercress soup.

By the time the ramp behind us had faded in the distance, we were moving at some fifty miles an hour, unable to talk or even yell at each other. We would approach what looked like

a solid island, and suddenly the sawgrass would part, the boat would be cutting through the middle of it. It was literally breathtaking. I dug my heels into the sides of the cage, inches away from the propeller, and tried to fuse my hands into the metal brace. A small deer bounced ahead of us, veering sharply to the side before it disappeared.

Glenn seemed to move through the swamp by instinct. There was no observable trail most of the time. Nearly half an hour went by until Glenn throttled back the engine and he began circling slowly. Suddenly I saw a piece of silvery metal, a rectangle about a foot long, from my perch high above the surface of the Everglades. I did a double-take when I realized what it was: apparently a spoiler from the wing of the crashed plane. But Glenn did not stop. He moved the boat along slowly, then began a tightening circle. Soon there was scattered debris all around us, much of it visible through the brownish water, some of it on the muddy surface or in the sawgrass. Then he cut the motor.

The silence was almost a shock. We reached down in the water and began pulling out parts. Much of it was unidentifiable. There was an eight-inch piece of a green honeycomb material. A shaft of metal about the same length. There was a section of a duct, a jagged piece of small girder, a white enamel metal triangle. From almost under the mud, we dragged up an intact arm-section of a passenger seat. The call buttons for the cabin lighting, for music, for lights, for seat position, for service, were still readable, all intact and reflective of the luxury of the airliner. There was a soaked leatherette magazine cover and an intact plastic portion of someone's wallet for holding credit cards. It was empty. There was still an odor of jet fuel.

In the silence of the bright sun, it seemed almost irreverent to disturb the area. We selected about a dozen of the pieces and put them in the bottom of the boat without saying much. It was too easy to visualize what had happened on that night nearly three years before. How anyone could have survived in that swampy wilderness was incredible.

On the basis of an experiment to check for strict evidential material, Pat and Bud Hayes arranged to try out the pieces of

the wreckage as psychometric devices among their students in the psychic awareness classes at the Arthur Ford Academy. The pilots and their wives would do the same with their group in the New York area. J. R. Worden would also set up an experiment. None of them expected a miracle, but felt it was possible for some information to come through that might have a bearing on the story. About a dozen pieces were sealed inside thick paper envelopes. In two of them, decoy objects were placed. One was an old wallet of Elizabeth's; the other a hose clamp from a boat. The remainder of the envelopes contained pieces from the plane.

The students selected by Pat and Bud Hayes were those who had shown considerable sensitivity in psychic awareness. Some were children, in the ten-to-twelve age bracket. The instructions were simple. Each was to hold one of the numbered envelopes and go into meditation until he felt he was in an altered state of consciousness. He or she was then to let whatever phrases flowed from the unconscious mind, regardless of what the words were, or whether they seemed to make any sense or not. The purpose was to see if any direct evidential information came through regarding the crash or the reappearances of the flight crew that had followed it.

The results were strange—and mixed. Frankly, I didn't know what to make of them. Some were interesting and surprisingly close. Others were not. I made sure to lean over backward to avoid reading too much symbolism into the material that came through.

One student came out with the following.

PINK—SPLASHED ALL OVER

WARMTH AND LOVE ENDED ABRUPTLY

COLDER

PAIN—ALL OVER

WHOLE BODY DIZZY AND SWINGING ALL OVER

MAN—DRESSED IN BLACK—SMALL EYE MASK—THOUGHT

TO BE GUILTY BUT REALLY INNOCENT

SCENES RELATED TO PASSING—WIFE AND 2 CHILDREN (ONE BOY, ONE GIRL)

SOME SORT OF ACCIDENT AT NIGHT
FAMILY MAY OR MAY NOT HAVE BEEN WITH HIM

There was much material here that could be related to the incident in the Everglades on the night of the crash. The same could be said of another "reading" by one of the Arthur Ford Academy group:

BURIED IN WATER
SULFUR, STRONG ODOR
FILTH, MUD, RIVER
INCREDIBLE AUDACITY
SUFFERING—EXTREME
CALLOUS
INVESTIGATION
EVIDENCE

But some could only apply with a great stretch of imagination, or by resorting to symbolism, as this one:

STETHESCOPE
ONE INCH OR 116 VEGETABLE
DETECTOR
DARING DETECTIVE
MAINTENANCE
POLICE ASSOCIATED WITH GLASS DOOR
#831
BOX UNFOLDING INTO QUILT
BLACK WITH ROSES IN THEM
SHAPE LIKE BOX
GOLD TOP WITH EMBROIDERED ROSE

The reading that impressed me most was done by a thirty-year-old mother. She held the envelope and reported the following:

AN AIRPLANE THAT LANDS IN WATER
A MISSING PERSON

FEEL AS IF I AM CLOSE TO THE AIRPORT,
CLOSE TO A CANAL

I SEE LIGHTS, LIKE THOSE OF AN AIRPORT,
THEN I DON'T SEE THEM ANYMORE

FEEL A PAIN IN THE FOREHEAD AND EYES

THERE IS A VERY RESTLESS SPIRIT AT THE
CRASH SITE AND WILL NOT REST UNTIL HIS
MOTHER KNOW THAT HE BELIEVES SPIRIT,
GOD. THE MOTHER KNOWS ABOUT SPIRITUAL
THINGS AND TOLD HIM BUT HE DIDN'T BE-
LIEVE HER. NOW HE DOES

I SEE LIGHTS AS IF I AM NEAR AN AIRPORT.
THEN I DON'T SEE THEM

I FEEL A PAIN IN THE FACE, A SICK FEELING
TWO PLANES AT NIGHT, ONE FOLLOWING
ANOTHER

MALE VOICE SAYING MY MOTHER TOLD ME
ABOUT THIS BUT I DIDN'T BELIEVE HER. SHE
MUST STOP WORKING SO HARD AND SHE
MUST STOP WORRYING SO MUCH. . . .
I HAVE SEEN THE LIGHT . . . NOW I BELIEVE.
SOMEBODY MUST TELL HER

PLEASE TELL HER NOT TO CRY. I BELIEVE.

One other reading had remarkable application:

INTENSE HEAT, FIRE, CHILLS, DRY, BILLOWS OF SMOKE, GOGGLES—LIKE FLYING GOGGLES, UNIFORMS, KHAKI OR GREEN UNIFORMS, WATER, MUDDY WATER: JUST THE WORD "HELP," PEOPLE AS THOUGH ON THE OTHER SIDE:

LIKE SORT OF SWAMPY WITH BRUSH, NIGHT, TWO MEN, DEATH, STARS, COUNTRYSIDE—NOT COUNTRYSIDE—VAST EXPANSE OF LAND

A MAN WITH A MOUSTACHE, A DARK-HAIRED MAN AND A LIGHT-HAIRED MAN AND AFTER THAT MANY MANY PEOPLE—BLACK LIKE CHARRED, WINGS, WHITE LIGHT, PEACE.

The problem I had with all of this type of material was that it was again too vague. If there had been specific names, places, facts to check that could not be interpreted except in clear, traceable terms, the readings would have been of direct value in tracing credibility. As interesting as it was, the information did not go far enough. What it boiled down to was that the material that came through could have applied to one or more people and one or more incidents, as remarkable as the results were. There was also the question that the airplane parts were not personal objects, and because of that would provide only impersonal clues.

I didn't know enough about psychometry to assess it in very clear terms. Further, much of the material was being supplied by students, and did not match the sessions done by the experienced mediums, such as the Hayeses or the two pilots and their wives. I noticed that when Pat Hayes joined the group in a postscript session, her experience seemed to lend more specific information. Elizabeth was invited to join in, to see if further, more specific information emerged. I declined the invitation because I wanted to remain as an observer. Further, I had never had any psychic experiences of any kind, and doubted if I ever could.

Elizabeth sat in with the group of eight of the students, along with Pat Hayes. Sessions like this seem to go at a painfully slow pace, and this was no exception. They sat in a circle and held hands around it, eyes closed. Pat Hayes instructed the group: "Breathe deeply and begin to move into an altered state of consciousness. You will feel yourself lifting as you breathe deeply. Let your thoughts flow through you, like a radio. Let them flow from your spiritual society, from part of your higher entity, from your highest being." She continued for a few more moments in this vein, and then silence followed.

After several more moments, various persons in the circle began to speak. More information came through, in the nature of the psychometry experiment. One student came through with a message: "The baby lives." Just after he said this, Elizabeth spoke up with a very strange and trancelike voice. She said: "Her name is Christina. I get this name very clearly. There is also a Mrs. Jackson. A Mrs. E. Jackson." She paused for a few moments more, and then in the same voice added, "I also get the name Jacobs."

I was startled when she came out with this because she is very reticent to speak up in a group of strangers, and very seldom had she spoken with such firmness and authority. It seemed completely out of character. Her eyes were closed. The tone of her voice was flat and expressionless, markedly different from her normal tone. I had no research material to check the names she mentioned with me, and at this point neither of us had studied the passenger list issued after the accident.

After the meeting, Elizabeth mentioned to me that she was interested in learning more about the whole psychic field. She wasn't sure what she had felt during the session, but she felt *something* which was extremely different from any experience she had had before. I laughed and said that maybe she'd better wait until I had a chance to check the passenger list. It was possible the names might have just come in from left field, and were meaningless. Maybe it would be a good idea not to go overboard.

"It's not just this alone," she said. "In studying the background of this for the research, I've been getting more

and more curious about it. I'm serious."

"Well," I said. "What you do is up to you. How did those names come to you?"

"I don't know how. I really don't," she said. "But I know we're going to find them correct."

I said, "You're pulling my leg."

"Honestly I'm not. The names were just as clear as if I had written them down in front of me."

"Then you've studied the passenger list," I said. "You're pulling a gag."

"May I never speak another word," she said. "I never even saw the passenger list. You'd better believe me, or I'll be furious."

She was serious. I could tell. In all her research, she had been a no-nonsense person. She liked to kid around often, but you knew when she was and when she wasn't.

"Besides," she added, "I think there are *two* infants named Christina."

"Tell you what," I told her. "If there's even one child named Christina—and anybody named Jackson, or Jacobs, man or woman—I might even begin to believe you and this whole strange business."

Later we dug out the passenger list and went through it. The version we had was from *The New York Times*. Of the 176 persons on the "Known survivors" and "Presumed Dead" lists, only a few of the passenger names were familiar to me. None were the ones Elizabeth mentioned. Elizabeth assured me she had not looked at the list at all. "What point would there be in self-deception?" she asked.

We looked down the survivor list. There, in the small type, Christina Castado, age two months. Elizabeth was as surprised as I was. "I swear to God," she said. "I never saw this list or any list." I believed her.

By the time we got halfway through the alphabet on the same list, Elizabeth caught her breath again. She pointed. "There's another Christina," she said. "Christina Ochoe. One year old."

"Even if I believe you," I said, "and I do—how are we sure you didn't accidentally see the list? Unconsciously?"

"They're nearly two-hundred persons on both lists," she said. "I could never in a million years remember two names out of it even if I had seen it. Which I didn't."

"We've got to allow for that possibility," I said. "We can't just buy anything that comes down the pike."

"Have it your way," she said. "I don't blame you for being skeptical. But I know in my own heart, and that's what counts. I'm not trying to sell myself anything. Or you. There would be absolutely no point to it."

I agreed. We continued searching the list. Almost halfway down the deceased list, we saw it: Mrs. E. Jackson. Neither of us said much. Then Elizabeth said, "I'm trying to charge it off to coincidence, but I'm having a hard time doing it."

"So am I," I said, as we continued searching the list for the name "Jacobs." There was none on the passenger list. For some reason, I pulled out some newsclips of the crash, and scanned those. All of a sudden, I ran across the name Jacobs. It was a newsman who had covered part of the crash story.

I handed Elizabeth the clipping, and said, "I don't know whether that counts or not."

Elizabeth looked at it. "I don't either," she said. "But I'm actually shaking. Can four names—or three, if you just want to count the passengers—could they be a coincidence?"

I said that they could, but that it was unlikely. Another alternative could be that she had seen just a flash of the passenger list and forgotten it.

"If this were in a court of law," Elizabeth said, "I guess this could be called evidence, but not proof."

"Just about," I said.

"I think I'll take that course in psychic awareness," she said suddenly. "It might be interesting."

"If you feel that way, you should," I said.

She said, "It's worth a try. This whole business has got me bugged."

By the time Elizabeth finished an eleven-day trip to Tokyo, she was back in Miami and eager to go. There was a three-day intensive "total immersion" course at the Arthur Ford Academy coming up on the weekend, and she enrolled in it.

Meanwhile she had several long discussions with Pat and Bud Hayes, during which they had felt that she showed considerable promsie of psychic sensitivity. Although she might stumble into some evidence for the story as a result of the training, we certainly weren't counting on it.

The course was demanding. It would run from 8:00 A.M. until nearly midnight for three straight days. During that time, Elizabeth would be instructed in deep meditation, breathing exercises, and various techniques to reach an altered state of consciousness—which turned out to be similar in effect to a light trance state. Control of the consciousness, however, was always maintained. There were seven others in the class, ranging in occupation from an electrical engineer to a minister to a cosmopolitan socialite to a registered nurse.

I learned the details from Elizabeth later. On the theory that almost anyone has the capacity to develop psychic awareness in greater or lesser degree, the training emphasized the technique to lose the conscious thinking as much as possible, and allow higher spiritual forces to channel through the personality. The ultimate aim was to use the forces thus released for the ultimate benefit of others. Since the academy was allied with the Spiritual Frontier Fellowship, it was slightly oriented toward nondenominational religious ends, in a nontheological way.

If a student showed perception and talent in experimental readings, he or she was urged to develop it further. On the last half of the third day, volunteers were brought in from outside for experimental readings. The volunteer subjects were asked later to grade the ability of the student on his or her capacity to analyze any problems constructively and the capacity to come up with strong evidential information that could not be known in any other way except psychic sensitivity.

Elizabeth gave five readings, with unusually high scores. "I'm surprised myself what came out during the readings," she said. "It sounds ridiculous, I know. It wasn't *I* doing the talking. My conscious mind, I mean. Some of the people were actually startled at some of the factual details I came up with. I don't know what it is, but I know there's something to

244

this. I think I can help people. I really do. Maybe even on the research of the story.''

I told her that the only thing I could believe was if she, or anyone, came up with hard facts that could be checked against the record. "You're being very negative," she said.

"Just careful," I said.

"Are you willing to try some ways of trying to get hard facts?" she asked.

"At this stage, I'll try anything," I said.

"How about the beginner's tool?" she said. "You could get into the act yourself with a Ouija board."

I thought about that for a moment, about what I had read concerning the use of it. I also had doubts that I could act as any kind of a channel. My psychic abilities were grossly weak.

"Willing to invest in a Ouija board?" Elizabeth asked.

I was. But when we went to a department store to get it, I suddenly felt ridiculous. I made an excuse to go to another part of the store, while Elizabeth went to get it. When I met her at the store exit, I noticed that the bag didn't cover up the prominent name on the edge of the box. I covered it with a newspaper and smuggled it out of the store. This was all getting a bit thick.

But Elizabeth felt right at home with it. "Remember," she said, "you don't need to be psychic for this to work, they say. But I hear some psychics can use it alone."

We put our hands on the indicator that was supposed to glide along the letters of the alphabet, prominently printed on the board, along with a YES and a NO, and a series of numbers from 1 to 9, and a zero. The indicator was supposed to stop when the correct letter was reached. I felt foolish.

"If anybody ever looked in the window and saw us, they'd think we'd flipped out," I said.

Elizabeth laughed. "I promise I won't tell any of your friends," she said.

We had been told that questions should be asked out loud, and then you waited for the indicator to move. The letters were to be read through the round glass opening at the top of

the indicator. Since there was no one to write down the letters for us, we turned on a tape recorder.

After a minute or so, the indicator did begin moving, very weakly, slowly. There was no question that I was not moving it, but that it was either moving under its own force, or Elizabeth's.

"You're moving it," I said.

"Swear to God I'm not," she said.

"I'm certainly not," I told her. The indicator was moving in slow, irregular circles, sliding on the felt tips of its three inch-high legs.

"Is anybody here on the board?" Elizabeth asked.

The indicator continued to circle, then very slowly made its way up to the corner where the word YES was printed. As it moved, I studied Elizabeth's fingers. They were resting lightly on the indicator, barely touching it, as mine were.

"You're sure you're not moving it?" I asked.

"Not even the least," she said.

The indicator reached the word YES, made three or four small circles around it, and then came to rest clearly over the word.

"Do you have a message for us?" Elizabeth asked.

The indicator moved slowly down toward the letters of the alphabet now. It seemed to be gaining speed and strength. Then it began moving with a very positive firmness, sweeping over the alphabet, and stopping at a series of letters. It was a very eerie feeling. Now it was Elizabeth's turn.

"*You're* moving it," she said.

"My fingers are hardly touching," I told her.

This was true.

The letters were now being run off in a series, one after the other. But the problem was, they made no sense at all. We were calling out the letters on a tape recorder, and then played them back. They read.

TGRATWEBYSWGRSNW

"We're not reading you," Elizabeth said. "Will you try again?" Our instructions were to call out the questions vocally.

TWA URVPTMITNXNY

It made no sense whatever. There was no use of even trying to separate the letters. It was total gibberish.

"We're not going to give up yet," Elizabeth said. "Keep going, whoever you are."

If the letters were meaningless, the movement of the indicator was still building up strength. It would swirl in a wide circle, as if it was generating energy, then move to the letters and stop very clearly and deliberately at each one.

TNGRDIOIOIO

Still nothing discernable. My back was tired and I was ready to quit. "Keep going, please," Elizabeth said to the board. Then, suddenly, the letters began to say something:

TWAKNOWREPO

We stopped the tape, listened to the letters again, wrote them down, and separated them:

TWA KNOW REPO

I wondered immediately if this could be a random selection of letters. Julian Huxley had once postulated that if six monkeys sat at six typewriters, and banged away at random until infinity, they would eventually write all the classics of literature in correct order. Our letters could be a complete coincidence.

"Who is here with us?" Elizabeth asked. "Spell the last name, please."

There was more unintelligible gibberish, which reinforced my theory that the one sequence that did make sense, was a random shot in the dark.

Then Elizabeth asked: "You mentioned 'Repo.' Is that correct?" The indicator swept up to YES and stopped. Then it went back to the letters and continued to spell. At each series, we would stop the tape recorder, write down the letters, and try to separate them into words.

GPNE TO TO UN POSNTN

It was not making sense again. "Is this a place?" Elizabeth asked. The indicator slid quickly to YES again.

"On this earth?" Elizabeth said. Now the indicator shot to NO.

"Where?" she asked.

INFUTE INFINITE

It was getting more interesting. "What else can you tell us?" Elizabeth asked.

TWA 727 CHICAGO

Then the questions and answers came thick and fast:

"Are you a TWA crew member?"

YES

"Are you deceased?"

YES

"Were you killed in a crash?"

YES KNOW REPO

"What is your name?"

REPO

"What is your first name?"

DON

"Are we talking directly?"

NO

"Who are we talking through?"

TWA

"Do you have a message?"

YES

"Who is the message for?"

VN JOHN

"Last name, please."

FULLER

I was beginning to feel uncomfortable. All through this, I was watching Elizabeth's hands. Her fingers were still touching the indicator with the lightest of touches. I knew for certain I wasn't moving the indicator. I could constantly feel it pull away from me, so that I had to move my fingers to catch up with it at times. Elizabeth wanted to get on with the questioning. "What is the message?" she asked the board.

TO STOP WORRY

"Stop worrying about what?"

NAMES

In planning the writing of the book, I was constantly worried about the names of the people who had given me so much information. The last thing in the world I wanted was to put anybody in danger with his or her employer. Much of the material had been given to me in confidence. This was a real concern. But how did the inanimate Ouija board know this—

or if it were Repo, how would he know it? And how would he know to come to the board, directly or indirectly? There would have to be a lot more confirmation for me to even begin to believe this.

"Is this really Don Repo on the board?" I asked.

YES

"Spell out your name, please."

DON REPO

"What kind of plane were you on in the crash?" I continued

1011

This was interesting. I knew that the cabin crews referred to the plane as the L-1011, and that the cockpit crews used only the short form: 1011. I was determined to bear down hard.

"What was the plane number of the L-1011 that crashed?" I asked.

310

"Flight number?"

401

All this was correct. I was convinced by this time that neither Elizabeth nor I were *consciously* moving the indicator, that the instrument was spelling out articulate words that purported to be coming from Don Repo, and that much of the information was accurate. Just who the TWA crew member was, we would have to explore later. Further, I would have to get information that neither Elizabeth nor I knew anything whatever about, if we were to rule out our unconscious minds as the motivator of the messages on the board. Right at the moment, I wanted to get as much information as I could, as long as the letters were flowing so freely.

"Can you name the others in the cockpit crew on the night of the crash?" I asked.

BOB AND STOCKSTILL

"What airline?"

EAL

This was the official designation for Eastern. The crew member names were correct, except that he used Loft's first name and the copilot's last.

"Who was in the jump seat in the cockpit?"

DONADEAO

There was a slight mispelling here, but there was no question of whom he meant, and he was correct.

It was now time to get down to facts that the entity who identified himself as Repo would know, but which neither Elizabeth nor I did. At least the information we were getting was clear and correct. How we were getting it was a different matter. It seemed totally absurd that a toy could come up with information that could penetrate a wall between the known and the unknown. I was fully aware of how ridiculous this might appear in print, and torn about continuing with the device.

I recalled the words I had read of Professor Hyslop:

> *The facts must prove that the source of the phenomena is what it claims to be, and this personal identity of the discarnate means that the deceased person shall tell facts of such quantity and with such a quality that we should not doubt his existence any more than we would if we received the same incidents over a telegraph wire or through a telephone. In this way alone can we show that the intelligence involved is outside the medium through which the facts come.*

We had not reached that point yet, by any means. But it was impossible to resist going on.

"The fact is that there are huge tracts of experience to which scientific methods cannot be applied. . . . we know we ourselves have feelings, and that they are different from, but quite as real a part of ourselves as our intellectual processes. A precisely similar argument should apply to those who tell us they have had certain mystical experiences."

—Raynor C. Johnson,
*The Imprisoned Splendor*

# Chapter XIV

My decision to go ahead with more experiments on the Ouija board was made reluctantly. Whatever ribbing I would get from my friends—and I knew there would be a lot of it—I would have to put up with. The objective was clear. Any information that came across would have to meet Professor Hyslop's rigid and unyielding terms. Facts that were as strong as those that might come over the telephone or telegraph wires. Facts that could be verified. This would not be easy with the doubts I had.

Before Elizabeth and I went ahead, I called New York to talk with Rich Craig and his wife for more details of what could be expected. He reemphasized that while a great deal of accurate information could come over, a lot of false material could frequently confuse the issue. Therefore the sorting-out process was very important. The static interference, he theorized, could come from entities who wanted to masquerade as legitimate sources, and who were very skillful at doing so. The only way to tell which from which would be by constant cross-checking. He also suggested that perhaps Elizabeth might be able to work the board alone, in view of her marked psychic sensitivity.

Regardless of the perils, we went ahead—being careful to close the curtains so that a caller or a passerby wouldn't think we had gone round the bend. In the next session, we asked the alleged Don Repo if he was willing to communicate. We got an affirmative answer. After asking him to spell his name as a confirmation, we continued. The indicator moved fast and firmly, sweeping over the letters of the alphabet, then making small circles over the chosen letter or number, then coming to a complete stop.

"What was the basic cause of the crash?" I asked.

NOSE GEAR

"What were the basic National Transport Safety Board finding?"

CAP NU STRUT PILOT ERROR

The last part was garbled, but seemed to be on the track. The first answer concerning the nose gear was basically correct. But of course this was information I already knew. And even though I was totally convinced that neither Elizabeth nor I were guiding the indicator, information like this was not acceptable under Hyslop's conditions. I was impressed, however.

"Can you clarify?"

CAPTAIN NEVER CHECKED PSA SECOND LANDING PESTOELSPUAL TO WHEEL

This was also garbled, as if a radio signal were breaking up. Perhaps we were missing some letters, or perhaps we misread some. Whatever the situation was, the message was only partially articulate.

"Were you clearly seen by crew members and passengers when you reappeared on the L-1011s?"

SOME DID SOME DID NOT

"Did you appear before crew members who knew you before the accident?"

USUALLY

The words were clear now, without an apparent breakup of the signal, whatever this strange energy force was. I tried to think of some questions that neither Elizabeth nor I knew the answer to, and yet we could check fairly quickly.

"Can you give us your wife's first name?"

SASSY

That was a strange name: Sassy. "Is that really it?" I asked. Maybe it was a nickname.

NO

"What is the correct name?"

ANICE

"Spell that again, please."

ALICE

Somewhere in my research material, I felt sure I had information on Don Repo's family that I had not yet checked

over. I spent nearly half an hour digging through it, and finally found a newspaper clipping with this information on it. The name was Alice, and I brought it back to Elizabeth.

"That's pretty good evidence," she said.

"I know I never knew this before," I said, "but good old Professor Hyslop would probably say I had noticed it before and forgotten it."

"Yes," Elizabeth said, "but you weren't guiding the indicator, were you?"

I wasn't, and I told her that.

"Whether it's strong evidence or not," she said, "it indicates that we may be in touch with Don Repo. Let's go on."

The news clipping had the names of other relatives of Repo on it, and we decided to check some of those, even though it could not count as heavy evidence in view of the fact that we now consciously could see what the names were.

"Can you give us the name of one of your daughters?"
DONNA

This was correct. Donna was herself a flight attendant on Eastern, the clipping noted.

"Can you give us the first name of one of your sisters?" There were four listed. The board spelled out correctly the names of two of them:
MARY        ANN

There were two others, and I wanted to get more verification. "Can you name the two others?" I asked. Without hesitation, the indicator spelled out quickly and firmly:
SEE NEWS CLIP IN YOUR HAND

This was startling and unexpected. It began to appear that whatever this energy or intelligence force was, it was alert and perceptive—and also with a sense of humor.

"Have you any general message for us?" Elizabeth asked.
TO GO PHONE DONNA

This message brought up a point that had been bothering me all through the research for the story. I had been feeling that, regardless of whether the story turned out to be legend or fact, that it should be written as an impersonal allegory. I wanted to avoid personalities as much as possible, and dig into the larger question of the fragility of life—as evidenced

by the plane crash—and the question of whether we lived after death. It seemed to be shaping up that the book should be a serious philosophic or metaphysical inquiry into these questions, as illustrated by a jet-age story that provoked questions that had not yet been scientifically answered.

But the incidents on the L-1011s were to serve only as an illustrative springboard. It actually did not matter what airline or airplane or crew was involved. Eastern or Repo or Loft or the others were not involved as personalities. The point to me was that in this modern age there could be a legend, based on fact, that might affect our outlook and our thinking, to make it less confined and bound up in a straitjacket.

If the material of the story appeared to turn out to be real, that would be all the better. It would provoke thought and interest in the big question as to whether we lived on after death. Now, with the response that was alleged to be coming from Don Repo, I could not avoid getting into a personal story if I were to follow the very clear words:

TO GO PHONE DONNA.

I was hesitant in doing this for other reasons. There was no way of telling how the accident had affected her outlook. The same was true of Mrs. Repo. I wanted to disturb them as little as possible. Under ordinary circumstances of journalism, the first thing I would have done was to contact both of them and approach the story from that angle. But it became apparent from the start that this was not ordinary journalism. The nature of the story demanded that it reach out far beyond that, while at the same time maintaining a rational perspective.

For the first time, I was beginning to get a little awed by the strange messages coming out on the Ouija board. There was a cryptic sense of command in the words. There was no telling what the next letter to come up was. When we expected it to go one way, it would go in another. Most of the time, we would have to wait until we listened to the letters we had called off on the tape recorder to find out what the sequence of words was. Many questions were in our minds: Why had the first half hour on the board turned up nothing but gibberish? Why had some coherent sentences broken up in the middle? If this actually was a discarnate Don Repo, how did he know

when to show up? What method of propulsion moved the indicator, whether it was coherent or incoherent? How did it turn out that he seemed to know our names?

We decided to go on. "Do you have any message for Donna, if we should call her?" Elizabeth asked.

FORGET DAD    JOHN TO PHONE HER    TELL HER I AM FINE WORKING HARD

"Any other messages for her?" Elizabeth asked again.

BE GOOD GIRL    PS I LOVE HER VERY MUCH

We felt, both of us, a strong sense of poignancy. This increased after we asked the next question: "Are there any messages for your wife Alice, Don?" Elizabeth said. She continued to call out the questions vocally.

I LOVE HER    FORGET DON    TEARS DONT HELP ME TO COME BACK

It was hard to concentrate on questions at this point. I was still trying to avoid getting into a personal situation. I felt what was needed most was factual confirmation. I said: "For confirmation, Don, name three things you check on a preflight walk-around." I was surprised to find myself calling out the name "Don." I caught myself up short on this, because there was still not enough clinical evidence that actual contact was being made. Elizabeth was inclined to accept that idea more than I was. In answer to the preflight check questions, the answer came:

WHEELS    VISUAL NOSE GEAR    TIRES

"Any other information?" I asked.

CAPTAIN HAND PANEL LIGHTS NEAR FLIGHT ENGINEER

I couldn't quite understand this, but his "walk-around" answer was in line with fact. I pressed for further technical details.

"What did pilot do before the crash?" I asked.

RELEASED CONTROLS ACCIDENTALLY

This was also in line. I followed up with a series of questions. "Who is here on the board?"

DON REPO

"Can you confirm the name of the pilot at the time?"

STOCKSTILL

This was correct, because the controls had been turned over to him. "Anything else you can tell us?"

THE PILOT EVERGLADES FRIEND HAD MORE
HURT FOR US PILOTS IN EASTERN CREW IN
THERE HOUSE THE GIRLS SEE ME IN GALLEY
OVEN DID MICE LEAVE THAT FAMILY CLOSET

This message was incoherent, but there were certain statements clearly evident. The most important was the message about being seen in the galley ovens. The reference to "pilot Everglades friend" may have concerned the Coast Guard rescuer. The most puzzling and seemingly ridiculous part was the question, "Did mice leave that family closet?" This meant nothing whatever to either Elizabeth or me, and we discarded the idea of trying to make any sense out of it. It was not until later when we found out that we were quite wrong in doing so.

Nor did the next sequence make any sense to us at the time. It involved a penny that was to be looked for, but we couldn't make any sense out of it. The sequence ended up with: TO GO INTO WASTE BASKET PENNIES SIT THERE BOYS ROOM

Again we were perplexed and baffled. Some of the information seemed so tantalizingly near to giving sound evidence. And yet it still didn't meet the yardstick Hyslop had indicated. We even got a message about Don's fondness for beer. But quite suddenly, the tone changed, and several answers came out on the board that had nothing to do with the questions we asked:

TO GO TO WORK ON STORY
TELEPHONE DONNA TODAY
GO BACK TO WORK STORY MUST BE WRITTEN
YOU ARE WASTING THE WHOLE STORY TO GO
TO WORK
SO GO TO TYPEWRITER TO SEE
CALL DONNA
DO NOT USE WIJI BOARD ANY MORE TODAY

Elizabeth and I had been at the board for over an hour. We were exhausted. I was interested in the way he had spelled "wiji" board. Neither Elizabeth nor I would spell it in that way. This seemed to me to be a fairly strong clue for a cross-check on validity. But what troubled me most was the apparent insistence on getting in touch with Donna. It would create a marked shift in the direction of the story, from the impersonal to the personal. I had no idea whether she would be receptive in sharing her information. It would be totally ridiculous for me to say we thought we had been in touch with her father.

And yet the more I thought about it, the more I began to feel that it was necessary to get in touch with both Donna and Mrs. Repo, regardless of the messages that had come across the board. On impulse, I sat down and wrote a letter to Donna, after phoning a friend in Miami to find her address in the phone book. It was a sensitive situation, and I didn't quite know how to approach the subject. I finally wrote:

Dear Donna Repo:
I'm in the process of writing a story on the L-1011 tragedy, which in no way will reflect badly on the flight crew or Eastern Air Lines. The underlying theme of the story is very simple: the fragility of life, and the importance of life after death.

In the background research I've done, I've of course come across a tremendous amount of material regarding the reappearances of the flight crew of Flight 401 in the galleys and elsewhere on Plane 318, and several others. This material, in turn, bears heavily on the theme. Some of it may be of interest to you.

I'd very much like to share with you some of the material I've come across in many months of research, much of it turned up by Elizabeth Manzione, my re-

search assistant, who has been a cabin attendant for Northwest Orient Air Lines for the past seven years.

Both of us would like to meet you, and have you as our guest for dinner when we come to Miami within the next few weeks . . .

Elizabeth and I have run across several friends of yours during the research, so we feel almost as if we know you.

Thanks in advance for your interest, and very best regards.

Cordially,
John G. Fuller

I sent the letter off. Elizabeth and I tried several more sessions with the Ouija board. The messages were similar to our first attempts and were basically correct and consistent as far as the technical facts of the plane were concerned. The messages also demonstrated Don Repo's reported sense of humor. Everyone I had talked to who knew him emphasized this quality in his personality; it seemed to have been his dominant characteristic.

I was still after more direct information that could be checked out. In one session on the board, I asked, "What state were you from before you came to Florida?"

The letters moved swiftly again:

NEW YORK TEXAS KANSAS ISLAND MAINE CALIFORNIA BOSTON ATLANTA GEORGIA HARD TO VERIFY

"Please be serious, Don," Elizabeth said. The indicator kept moving:

SEE ST LOUIS INSTEAD SOUTH CAROLINA WAS LOUISIANA SOMETIMES

"Why do you do this, Don?" Elizabeth asked. "You're not serious."

FUN TO GAG WITH YOU

He must have been referring to the inordinate number of

places he had been stationed while in the service. "What are the main sections of the plane you appeared in?" I asked.

COACH CLASS GALLEY OVEN

"What are your reasons for coming back, Don?" Elizabeth asked the board.

TO PLAY GAMES TODAY

"Be serious, Don," Elizabeth continued. "What are your reasons for coming back?"

DON LIKES TO CLOWN AROUND AND GAG HERE IN SPIRIT YOU SEE I LIKE TO JOKE AROUND

Whatever was happening, a personality was emerging from the letters on the board. Elizabeth and I both began to feel a real affection for him, confusing as it was. We waited patiently to hear from Donna Repo, but no letter came for over a week. Finally, in one day's mail, my letter came back, stamped: RETURN TO SENDER NO SUCH NUMBER.

I finally was able to locate Mrs. Repo's address, and sent the letter to Donna in care of Mrs. Repo. Again there was a wait, but four days after the letter was sent, I received a phone call. It was from Donna Repo, calling from Miami.

I was relieved to find that she was cordial and receptive. "I've got to tell you something strange," she said. "Your letter arrived at my mother's house, and she brought it over to me. She mentioned that your name seemed familiar, but couldn't recall where she had heard it. I opened the letter and read it later, after she had left. Frankly, I didn't want to talk about the story. I had heard about the reports many times, but the flight crews didn't want to talk to me directly about it. I guess they felt embarrassed. I neither believed nor disbelieved the stories. I guess I couldn't believe them unless it happened to me.

"Anyway, I was about to throw your letter away when I got a phone call from my mother. She had gone home, trying to think of where she had seen your name before. Then she remembered. Just a few days before your letter arrived, a friend of hers brought her a copy of a book. The friend said that the book was very interesting and inspiring. It turned out to be one of your books. *Arigo: Surgeon of the Rusty Knife*. My mother read it and found it to be just what her friend said it was.

"It was only when she got home after delivering your letter to me, that she looked at the book cover and she realized that the name on the outside of the envelope was yours. She called me and said that she was very interested in talking with you. She also said that she would like to share with you some of the experiences she has had since the time of the accident. They are very strange. So we'd be glad to take you up on your invitation."

I was pleased and relieved, even though it would move the story from the impersonal to the personal. Elizabeth was in the process of tracking down more interviews, but when I saw her later, she was delighted.

"Do you see some kind of cosmic signal there?" she asked me. Her tone was mischievous.

"How do you mean?" I said.

"If your letter arrived the first time, it would have been thrown away."

"That's ridiculous," I said.

"Isn't that what Donna Repo told you?"

"Well, perhaps."

"You are *impossible*," Elizabeth said. "If the letter had arrived *before* Mrs. Repo had read the book, Donna would have thrown the letter away. What does it take to convince you? Don't you think this is an important story?"

"I do if it checks out," I said. "Very important."

"But it *is* checking out. How much evidence do you need? You seem to be resisting everything that falls into your lap."

"Maybe that's why I resist it," I said. "As I said before, it seems too fortuitous."

"You've got to have more faith," she said.

"All right," she said. "Let's try the board right now. If it's running true to form, Don must know about this. Let's see what he has to say."

We got the board out. Elizabeth asked the usual question: "Are you here, Don?"

YES

"So you know what happened today?"

CALL FROM DONNA

"How did you feel about it?"

261

ELATED HER FATHER BE NICE TO BABY GIRL
FOR THE VISIT MRS KNOW I LOVE THEM

"What are we planning to do when we meet them?" I
asked. My skepticism, which was benevolent, but still present, was beginning to fade. The answer came:

TAKE TO DINNER

"How did you know that, Don?" I asked the board.

SEE DON IS SMART

"I see you still have your sense of humor," I said.

YES MRS MAKE HER JUST HAPPY SAY HI FROM
DON

The dinner was set up for Sunday, March 7, 1976, at the
Marriott Hotel near the Miami International Airport. I looked
forward to it with some apprehension. The shift from the
theoretical to the deeply personal was a major one. I felt very
reluctant to tell Alice Repo and Donna about the strange
messages we had received on the board, which had started
out as almost a clinical experiment. Now we were going to be
dealing with very real human beings and an unknown human
equation.

And yet the subject went beyond individual personalities.
It dealt with a question that all of mankind had to face whether
it wanted to or not. Don Repo was emerging from a shadow to
a reality. He was also becoming a very real symbol. Whatever was to come of our meeting, I knew that I would respect
the feelings of the Repos, and would follow their wishes in
every way.


Donna Repo was tall, slim, attractive to the point of being
beautiful. Her mother was gracious, affable, and youthful.
From almost the moment they came into the hotel room, there
was none of the strain I had anticipated. Alice Repo was calm
and assured. She seemed admirably able to cope with her
grief. Her immediate reaction to the long series of reports
about her husband appearing on the L-1011s was that she
would by no means rule them out. She spoke of Don with
deep and simple affection. They had obviously been very
close. It was also obvious that Donna adored her father.
Neither was morbidly sentimental about him. Their
memories were fresh and ventilated, sifted by the three years

262

that had gone by since the crash which had lifted the veil of mourning without destroying the sharpness of recollection.

Alice Repo shaped the personality of Don vividly. He truly enjoyed every day he lived, she said. He loved the outdoors, and had a deep attachment for birds. His life was marked by action. He never wished to do things; he did them. When an impulse would strike him, and he had several days of spare time, he would whisk Alice and the children off to Canada for a camping trip. When he was flying military charters to Germany, he insisted that Alice and the children come back there on vacation with him. When this was impossible, he would bring back generous gifts from abroad to both his family and friends. He was outgoing and generous to a fault. At one time, he brought back a full set of Michelin tires for his son John, hauling them personally through various airport changes.

His most marked characteristic was his outgoing sense of humor. He was never without a joke or a gag. They were his trademark. He was well liked, popular, handsome. But he never hung his fiddle at the door; his ebullience and love of life carried over within the home.

Donna Repo revealed that she was perplexed and baffled by the constant reports of his reappearance. Her initial reaction was one of skepticism, but the persistence of the reports made her wonder. She knew that other crew members made it a point not to talk to her about the incidents, out of consideration for her. In one way, this was bothersome. She would rather talk about it freely, to try to get at the bottom of the story. She still did not know what to make of it. She stated that she neither believed nor disbelieved, and she was keeping a full open mind. She felt her colleagues were being overprotective.

There were other things that had been happening as far as Alice Repo was concerned that were puzzling. She had mentioned them only to close friends or family. The first incident happened just about one year before the crash of Flight 401. She received a phone call from Don, who had just arrived back from a trip. He always made it a point to call Alice on his return, and this was no exception. He asked if he could bring anything home from the store, but Alice told him

there was nothing at the time. They hung up. But within seconds, the phone rang again. It was a strange male voice. It announced one thing: her husband Don had just been killed in an air crash. Alice was shocked at first, and then realized that Don could not even have reached his car from the airport phone. She dismissed it as a macabre joke of the most tasteless sort, and could not understand how anyone could be so depraved as to do anything like that.

When Don arrived within the next half hour, she told him about it. Neither of them could figure out why anyone would tell such an outrageous story. They shrugged it off and forgot about it.

Just about a month before the Flight 401 tragedy, Don came home from a trip in a reflective mood. He told her that he just couldn't wait to get home from the trip, that he wanted to tell her how much she meant to him and how much he loved her. "He was so much more intense than usual," Alice recalled. "I thought about it quite awhile. I finally said to my best friend, 'I'm scared, Elsie. The things Don told me. It almost was like he was trying to tell me more than he should have.' "

As the holiday season of 1972 arrived, the thoughts and doubts left Alice's mind. But on the morning of Don's trip on Flight 401, the phone rang and Alice answered it. It was crew scheduling with the routine call for the assignment. Alice put the phone down, and went out to get Don, who was in the garage. As she walked toward the garage, a sudden impression struck her. It was the identical voice that had spoken to her with the macabre joke almost a year before. She shuddered, but she called Don to the phone and tried to put it out of her mind. Don finished his conversation on the phone. Alice said nothing about her reaction to the voice.

Don said, "What do you think? Should I go out on this trip. I don't have to, because it's not my regular one. But if I take it, I'll be back home for New Year's Eve. What do you think."

As usual, Alice left the decision up to Don. They had no special plans for the holiday, so it would not matter either way. Don decided to take it. It was a turnaround, so he would be home that same night.

After he left for the trip, Alice could not get the voice out of her mind. Don left about noon that day for the trip up to New York, and at about 8:00 P.M., December 29, 1972, he called Alice from Kennedy in New York. He was cheerful and buoyant. It looked as if Flight 401 would depart on time, and he'd be home shortly after midnight. He was glad he had taken the trip because they would be free for the holidays.

This was the last Alice talked to Don before the tragedy took place. She retired early that evening and was asleep until 4:00 the next morning. As she was sleeping, their son John was watching the late news on television, home from the University of Florida in Gainesville on vacation. The moment the news came over, he rushed to the phone and called Donna at her apartment. She came over immediately. They called the hospital, and the information given was that Don was alive and that it looked as if the only injury was a broken leg. They woke Alice to tell her about it and rushed to the hospital.

It was clear when they got there that the injuries were considerably worse than just a broken leg. But Don was a fighter. After long surgery, he was still conscious. When Alice entered the room, he recognized her immediately and squeezed her hand. A priest arrived and Don called him by name. Characteristically, he rebelled against the treatment, the hospital routine. He was annoyed by the tubes in his nose and wanted Alice to remove them.

"Don loved birds," Alice Repo told Elizabeth and me as we sat in the hotel room. "We had a bird feeder in our yard. He'd have coffee and watch the birds feed. The day Don died, we came home from the hospital at about eight-thirty in the morning. My mother was in the kitchen. She called to me and said, 'Alice, come here and see this.'

"I went out to the kitchen and looked out on the screened patio. There were at least thirty birds there, flying back and forth. Usually I keep the screen door slightly open for our dogs to come in and out. And once in a great while, a single bird or maybe two will fly in there. When they do, I keep a broom there so I can guide them out. I might have seen one or two birds there before, but this was strange. I wondered what to do because they never before had found their way out

without the help of the broom. But on this day, they suddenly swept out through the small crack in the door the way they came in, all thirty or so of them. No one had to guide them out. I said to myself, well, they all just came to say good-bye to Don. I just knew it because he loved birds so. I know that when grief strikes you, you can make all kinds of interpretations about things that could just be your imagination. But even today, I'm convinced this was a kind of sign that Don was going to leave us.''

As we talked at length that afternoon in Miami, it became obvious that neither Donna nor Alice Repo were prone to exaggeration or instability. Their devotion to Don was intense, but calm. They recalled that they were not allowed to see him in the last hours before he died. Just 31 hours after the crash, he succumbed. At the funeral, the casket was closed. The grief and the shock were almost unbearable for Alice. The family was close-knit, comforted her, surrounded her with love.

There were several things that followed during the long period of bereavement, both puzzling and vividly real. Alice recalled that one night, she woke up with an overpowering odor of Vitalis on the pillow next to her. Don had always used Vitalis, but there had been none in the house for over a year when this happened. The pillows were new and clean. But the odor was so strong that it woke her up. She turned the pillow over in the hope it would go away; the memory was too poignant. But it did not disappear until well into the next day.

On another night, some time after that, she woke up and felt Don beside her in the bed. It was not a dream. She reached over, and distinctly felt his hand. For a long time, his wedding ring had a clearly discernible dent in it. Carefully, her hand slipped to the ring finger. The ring was there. She slid her fingers around the surface. The dent was there.

The incident did not startle her. She felt nothing but peace and love. There were other signs, later, that she took to be indications that Don was somehow trying to communicate with her. A bird would appear at the window during some of her moments of grief, as if it were trying to soothe her sorrow. A nun brought her a little gift; when she opened it, it turned out to be a ceramic white dove—one of Don's favorite birds.

The nun mentioned that she had no idea as to why she had picked it out; she had no idea of Don's fondness for the bird.

It was getting near dinner time. Outside the windows of the hotel room, the lights were turned out in the courtyard. Elizabeth and I were afraid of tiring Alice and Donna with our questions, but she assured us that there was no strain. She and Donna both had learned to cope with their grief. We shared with them some of the reports that we had learned. They were interested, and told of Don's interest in and love for the airplanes he flew. They were convinced that if the reports were true, Don would be very likely to be around just to make sure the planes were running right.

I didn't quite know how to bring up some of the information we had come across in our clinical experiments on the Ouija board. If anyone had told me he had been in touch with a deceased friend or relative of mine via this device, I should have been convinced that he had departed from his senses. Yet we did have some puzzling information that, if it turned out to be verified, would create some extremely strong evidence of validity.

I cautiously brought up one of the messages that had been so puzzling when it was spelled out on the board, without revealing the bizarre way Elizabeth and I had picked it up. "Tell me," I said to Alice Repo, "this might seem like a crazy question to you. But did you ever have any trouble with mice in what you call your 'family closet'?"

Both Donna and Alice Repo looked startled. "How did you know about *that*?" Alice asked.

"I know it seems a silly question," I said.

"It's not all that silly," Alice said. "Just a couple of months ago, some mice built a nest in the attic above what we call our family room. We couldn't get rid of them for quite some time. Finally my son John set a bunch of traps. Actually, it wasn't the family closet, it was the family room; and the only way you could get through to the attic was through the family-room closet. But how did you ever hear about that?"

I think Elizabeth and I were as startled as the Repos. A weird piece of nonsense was suddenly making sense. I told Alice that I'd tell her after I asked her another crazy question. She laughed and said she'd be glad to answer it.

"Can you tell me anything about this," I said. I still felt foolish, but I was encouraged by the results of the first question. "Did Don have anything to do with some pennies in a wastebasket in your boy's room?"

"This is amazing," Alice said. "You've got to tell me where you learned these things. Don used to collect Indian head pennies. There is a small barrel full of them in my son's room. But who told you about this? I'm curious."

I finally confessed that Elizabeth and I had been experimenting very cautiously with the Ouija board, and that we had received these two cryptic messages, among others.

"I haven't played with one of those since I was a child," Alice said. "Did you actually get that information that way?"

We assured her that we did, among many other things. I finally showed her a transcript of the material we had collected during our weeks of experimentation. Both Alice and Donna were fascinated. They agreed that the answers, the quips, the gags were just like Don. I asked her about the name "Sassy." But Alice could not associate that with anything. They asked if we had brought the board with us. We had, but it was down in the car. I was hesitant. I was afraid that it might not work in front of them, and that some of the interference and gibberish might come through which would make the process senseless.

However, I went down to the car and brought the board back up. Both Donna and Alice were in a calm and experimental frame of mind, and I assured myself of that before we started. We jointly decided to make an objective, evidential test. Alice suggested that Elizabeth and I ask the board the name of a beer that Don liked. We would also ask the board to identify who was alleged to be communicating, by name, and also to spell out Alice's name as a confirmation.

We were all a little tense as Elizabeth and I sat down at the board. We were all a little tired, and hungry, too.

Elizabeth asked: "Don, are you there? If you are, will you spell your name, please."

The indicator moved swiftly to spell out DON.

I was relieved. At least we seemed to be getting results at the start.

"Don, who is here with us now?"

Without hesitation, the letters spelled out ALICE.

"What's your favorite beer, Don?" Elizabeth asked.

BUDWEISER COORS GO TO DINNER SHE KNOWS

Alice and Donna laughed. "It sounds just like Don," Alice said. "But it's not the right brand."

We asked if there was any special message, and the letters spelled:

ALICE IS HERE LOVE HER JUST YOU ALICE-FOR WIFE LOVE

To try to eliminate error, I asked Alice if she would try the board with Elizabeth. She did so, and the indicator still moved swiftly. We asked her to look away from the board so that she wouldn't influence the movement, and ask questions where Elizabeth would not know the answers. She agreed, and the board spelled out the answer to several personal questions correctly. Donna was now stunned with the response. "I can't stay skeptical after this," she said. "I'm really convinced." Then she asked the board: "Dad, did you know I was recently married?"

YES I KNOW WORK HARD LOVE ALICE TO JUST YOU WIFE LOVE YOU

Donna asked if she could work the board with her mother, and she replaced Elizabeth. The indicator moved slowly at first, gaining speed as Donna got used to the feel of it. The first letters were gibberish again, then:

I LOVE YOU I LOVE YOU MORE ALICE I LOVE DONALYN TOO EU MARRIED

"Donalyn" was Donna's formal name, which she rarely used. "Have you any message for my sister?" Donna asked.

HOW ARE YOU MY SPECIAL DAUGHTER KISS ALISON FOR ME DEAR ALICE I LOVE YOU

"Funny how it spelled 'Alison,' " Donna said. "That's the way we spelled it."

Alice was interested in further evidential checks. "Don, is there any other message?"

ALICE NORKO REPO I LOVE YOU NEVER FORGET PLEASE I LOVE YOU GOOD NIGHT

There were tears in Alice's eyes, but she was calm. "Nor-

ko. That's my maiden name," she said. "It's a Czechoslova-
kian name. There's no question in my mind now."

"Do you feel uneasy about the communication?" I asked
her.

"Not in the least," Alice said. "In fact, I feel comfort."

We went to dinner at the restaurant at the top of the hotel.
Miami International Airport could be seen off in the distance.
We were all in a reflective state. Donna, particularly, was
awed and shocked. She said she had completely lost her
reservations about the validity of the communications. We
emphasized that it was not always dependable; that false
messages and interference would often come through; that
only material that could be verified could be considered
valid. I told them about my doubts and reservations, but that I
was losing a lot of them as a result.

After dinner, we said good-bye to the Repos. We felt that
we had come to know them intimately in a very short time.
We also felt that we knew Don Repo, with his puckish sense
of humor and deep affection for his wife and family. As we
said good-bye, Alice Repo said, "There's one thing, though,
that never came through. He never told you the beer he likes
to drink!"

When we got back to the hotel room, we couldn't resist
trying to pick up that information. Don was there, ready to
talk, as he always seemed to be. We asked him to identify the
brand, and the indicator spelled: MEISTER BRAU. Neither
of us had ever heard of such a brand. Later we phoned Alice
Repo. At first she said no, that wasn't the particular brand she
had in mind. Then she asked us to hold on a minute. When
she came back to the phone, she said she was checking some
souvenir beer mugs Don had brought back from Germany.
His favorite beer there, she now recalled, was spelled out on
the mugs: MARTIN'S BRAU. We all laughed and agreed
that might be close enough.

Elizabeth and I went down in the courtyard for a nightcap.
The day had been so full, so strange. The whole story was still
so incredible, so hard to assimilate. I still found myself
alternating between believing and not believing. I wasn't

even sure whether we had met Professor Hyslop's demands for rigid confirmation that we had been in touch with Don Repo, wherever he was. I was sure of one thing: we had come very close to meeting the demands. Elizabeth felt more confident that we had met them than I did. Later, I asked her to sum up her feelings resulting from all the interviews and research briefly. She did so:

1. The pilots involved are down-to-earth, solid citizens. I've been flying with different pilots on Northwest for seven years, and practically all of them run true to form. They are excellent observers, and not the least inclined to exaggerate.

2. There are too many people involved in this story. They all check out.

3. The descriptions given us from widely separated sources are all similar, and in many cases identical. Most of the parties involved did not know each other, so there was no chance of collusion.

4. Why did three flight crew members at two separate times, unknown to each other, go to all the trouble to exorcise the plane?

5. Why have there been no more reports of the apparitions since these exorcisms?

6. Groups of people, including passengers, claim to have seen the reappearances. They could not all have been hallucinating.

7. Why do some flight crews try to avoid flying Plane #318, while many others try to put in a line bid on the L-1011s because they think Repo is there to help?

8. Why does the same situation exist as far as the flight attendants are concerned in regard to the lower galley?

9. What about the Mexico City incident?

10. Why would all the crew members we interviewed make this story up—IT'S NOT THAT GOOD A JOKE!

Elizabeth was right. It wasn't that good a joke. And something seemingly trivial happened a few weeks after we had seen Donna and Alice Repo that was more startling than a

joke, because it seemed to put a punctuation mark to the end of the strange telegramlike messages we had been receiving on the Ouija board.

Alice Repo phoned one night to say she had finally recalled what the word "Sassy" meant. It had completely slipped her mind when we had been talking with her in Miami. It seems that Don at one time had been joking with her about putting on a little weight. He had made a big point about affectionately calling her his "fat and sassy love." He particularly had emphasized the "sassy" part of it. Why it had slipped her mind when I had first mentioned it to her, she didn't know.

It was strange how a bit of minutiae like this could affect my thinking, but it did. Trivial as the word and the incident were, it seemed to reflect without question that the message carrying the word "sassy" could never have been a part of either Elizabeth's or my unconscious mind. It was too unique a word to be coincidence. The pennies in the wastebasket and the mice in the closet were of the same nature. Together, these three pieces of evidence, meaningless when we first received them, finally convinced me that we had met the rigid demands set down by Professor Hyslop. It was as if "we received the same incidents over a telegraph wire or through a telephone."

But whatever the story was, whatever anyone wanted to believe or disbelieve, it was deeply absorbing to me, with definite intimations of immortality hidden in it. And actually a heartening story. Don Repo seems to be at rest and at ease. The Eastern L-1011 Whisperliners continue to be technically among the best in the air. In spite of corporate fears of Eastern about its public relations image, the fears are groundless. Don Repo and Bob Loft, if they have reappeared so many times as reported, are benevolent ghosts, as helpful as extra crew members.

I can't help feeling that somewhere Don Repo, with his delightful sense of humor is laughing with us, not at us. That he may even be showing us that there is a lot more to our existence than materialistic science would like us to believe. And that he will turn into a gentle and benign legend that will benevolently haunt the airways for a long time to come.

# MORE BESTSELLERS FROM BERKLEY

NICOLETTE                        (03588-3—$1.50)
  by Herbert M. Katz

THE FIRST DEADLY SIN             (03424-0—$2.25)
  by Lawrence Sanders

ESTABLISHMENT OF
INNOCENCE                        (03288-4—$1.95)
  by Harvey Aronson &
  Mike McGrady

THE TANGENT OBJECTIVE            (03441-0 –$1.95)
  by Lawrence Sanders

WHEN THE BOUGH BREAKS            (03388-0—$1.95)
  by Stuart Rosenberg

Send for a *free* list of all our books in print

These books are available at your local bookstore, or send
price indicated plus 30¢ per copy to cover mailing costs to
Berkley Publishing Corporation
390 Murray Hill Parkway
East Rutherford, New Jersey 07073

W9-ALX-731